the RANSOMED HEART

OTHER BOOKS BY JOHN ELDREDGE

Captivating
(with Stasi Eldredge)

Epic

Waking the Dead

Wild at Heart

The Journey of Desire

The Sacred Romance
(with Brent Curtis)

the RANSOMED HEART

A COLLECTION *of* DEVOTIONAL READINGS

JOHN ELDREDGE

NELSON BOOKS
A Division of Thomas Nelson Publishers
Since 1798

Published in Nashville, Tennessee, by Thomas Nelson, Inc.

Yates & Yates—Published in association with Yates & Yates, LLP, Attorneys and Counselors, Orange, California.

Nelson Books titles may be purchased in bulk for educational, business, fundraising, or sales promotional use. For information, please e-mail SpecialMarkets@ThomasNelson.com.

Unless otherwise noted, Scripture quotations are from the HOLY BIBLE: NEW INTERNATIONAL VERSION®. Copyright © 1973, 1978, 1984 by International Bible Society. Used by permission of Zondervan Publishing House. All rights reserved.

Scripture quotations noted NLT are from the *Holy Bible*, New Living Translation, copyright © 1996. Used by permission of Tyndale House Publishers, Inc., Wheaton, Illinois 60189. All rights reserved.

Scripture quotations noted NKJV are from THE NEW KING JAMES VERSION of the Bible. Copyright © 1979, 1980, 1982 by Thomas Nelson, Inc., Publishers.

Scripture quotations noted *The Message* are from *The Message*, copyright ©1993, 1994, 1995, 1996, 2000, 2001, 2002. Used by permission of NavPress Publishing Group.

Scripture quotations noted NASB are from the NEW AMERICAN STANDARD BIBLE®, copyright © The Lockman Foundation 1960, 1962, 1963, 1968, 1971, 1972, 1973, 1975, 1977, 1995. Used by permission. (www.Lockman.org)

Scripture quotations noted KJV are from the KING JAMES VERSION.

Scripture quotations noted NRSV are from the NEW REVISED STANDARD VERSION of the Bible © 1989 by the Division of Christian Education of the National Council of the Churches of Christ in the U.S.A. All rights reserved.

Scripture quotations noted *Alter* are from *Genesis: Translation and Commentary*. Copyright © 1996 by Robert Alter.

ISBN 0-7852-0706-6

Printed in the United States of America
05 06 07 08 09 QW 5 4 3 2 1

To George, Jack, Dallas, Larry, and Dan,
whose own writings have shaped mine
more deeply than I know.

Only be careful, and watch yourselves closely so that you do not forget the things your eyes have seen or let them slip from your heart as long as you live.

—DEUTERONOMY 4:9

I will always remind you of these things, even though you know them and are firmly established in the truth you now have. I think it is right to refresh your memory . . .

—2 PETER 2:12–13

Life, you'll notice, is a story.

Life doesn't come to us like a math problem. It comes to us the way that a story does, scene by scene. You wake up. What will happen next? You don't get to know—you have to enter in, take the journey as it comes. The sun might be shining. There might be a tornado outside. Your friends might call and invite you to go sailing. You might lose your job.

Life unfolds like a drama. Doesn't it? Each day has a beginning and an end. There are all sorts of characters, all sorts of settings. A year goes by like a chapter from a novel. Sometimes it seems like a tragedy. Sometimes like a comedy. Most of it feels like a soap opera. Whatever happens, it's a story through and through.

"All of life is a story," Madeleine L'Engle reminds us.

This is helpful to know. When it comes to figuring out this life you're living, you'd do well to know the rest of the story.

You come home one night to find that your car has been totaled. Now, all you know is that you loaned it for a couple of hours to your teenage daughter, and now here it is, all smashed up. Isn't the first thing out of your mouth, "What *happened?*"

In other words, "Tell me the story."

Somebody has some explaining to do, and that can be done only in hearing the tale *they* have to tell. Careful now—you might jump to the wrong conclusion. Doesn't it make a difference to know that she wasn't speeding, that in fact the other car ran a red light? It changes the way you feel about the whole thing. Thank God, she's all right.

Truth be told, you need to know the rest of the story if you want to understand just about anything in life. Love affairs, lay-offs, the collapse of empires, your child's day at school—none of it makes sense without a story.

(Epic, 2–4)

2 | OUR LIVES ARE STORIES

If you want to get to know someone, you need to know *their* story. Their life is a story. It, too, has a past and a future. It, too, unfolds in a series of scenes over the course of time. Why is Grandfather so silent? Why does he drink too much? Well, let me tell you. There was a terrible battle in World War II, in the South Pacific, on an island called Okinawa. Tens of thousands of American men died or were wounded there; some of them were your grandfather's best friends. He was there, too, and saw things he has never been able to forget.

"But in order to make you understand," explained novelist Virginia Woolf, "to give you my life, I must tell you a story."

I expect all of us, at one time or another, in an attempt to understand our lives or discover what we ought to do, have gone to someone else with our stories. This is not merely the province of psychotherapists and priests, but of any good friend. "Tell me what happened. Tell me your story, and I'll try to help you make some sense of it."

We humans share these lingering questions: "Who am I really? Why am I here? Where will I find life? What does God want of me?" The answers to these questions seem to come only when we know the rest of the story.

As Neo said in *The Matrix Reloaded*, "I just wish I knew what I am supposed to do." If life is a story, what is the plot? What is your role to play? It would be good to know that, wouldn't it? What is this all about?

(*Epic*, 6–7)

Picture yourself in an ancient European city—Florence perhaps or Madrid. You find yourself at dusk, wandering through the older parts of town. Narrow streets are lined with dimly lit shops—pawnbrokers, no doubt, alongside various dealers in antiquities, booksellers, curious haunts harboring mysteries from far-off lands. Partly out of curiosity, partly out of a wish to avoid the jostling crowds, you turn into a musty parlor. As your eyes adjust to the twilight inside, you discover aisles crammed with Babylonian trinkets, Persian rugs, suits of armor, Colombian pottery. You browse indifferently among everything old and intriguing.

Then, something catches your eye. Sitting in a pile of forgotten silver urns and incense burners, it might have escaped your notice altogether. But it seemed to call to you, whisper your name. In fact, it is already in your hands. *This is ridiculous*, you think. You turn the lamp over and over most carefully, looking for . . . you're not quite sure what. Obviously it is from the Middle East, Arabia most likely. *What am I thinking? These things happen only in fairy tales.*

Something you read long ago—was it in Chesterton?—crosses your mind. "An adventure is, by its nature, a thing that comes to us. It is a thing that chooses us, not a thing that we choose." *He's right about that*, you admit. *Alice wasn't looking for Wonderland when she fell through the looking glass. Come to think of it, the four children just stumbled into Narnia through the back of the wardrobe. Anodos simply woke to find fairyland had taken over his bedroom.*

But another voice rises within you, urging caution. *You've got places to go, for heaven's sake. Don't let yourself get carried away.* The voice is full of common sense, of course. But the voice also seems old and tired. From how many adventures has it swayed you in your life? How many dreams left in the closet? "Closing time," calls the curator of the shop. He begins to blow out the lamps. Your heart is racing. Somewhere back in your mind you hear the voice urging you on to your duties. But it is too late. You've already rubbed the lamp.

(*The Sacred Romance Workbook & Journal*, v–vi)

4 | A Passionate Voice Within

S ome years into our spiritual journey, after the waves of anticipation that mark the beginning of any pilgrimage have begun
to ebb into life's middle years of service and busyness, a voice
speaks to us in the midst of all we are doing. *There is something
missing in all of this*, it suggests. *There is something more.*

The voice often comes in the middle of the night or the early
hours of morning, when our hearts are most unedited and vulnerable. At first, we mistake the source of this voice and assume it is just
our imagination. We fluff up our pillow, roll over, and go back to
sleep. Days, weeks, even months go by and the voice speaks to us
again: *Aren't you thirsty? Listen to your heart. There is something missing.*

We listen and we are aware of . . . a sigh. And under the sigh is
something dangerous, something that feels adulterous and disloyal
to the religion we are serving. We sense a passion deep within; it
feels reckless, wild.

We tell ourselves that this small, passionate voice is an intruder
who has gained entry because we have not been diligent enough in
practicing our religion. Our pastor seems to agree with this assess-
ment and exhorts us from the pulpit to be more faithful. We try to
silence the voice with outward activity, redoubling our efforts at
Christian service. We join a small group and read a book on estab-
lishing a more effective prayer life. We train to be part of a church
evangelism team. We tell ourselves that the malaise of spirit we feel
even as we step up our religious activity is a sign of spiritual imma-
turity, and we scold our heart for its lack of fervor.

Sometime later, the voice in our heart dares to speak to us again,
more insistently this time. *Listen to me—there is something missing
in all this. You long to be in a love affair, an adventure. You were made
for something more. You know it.*

(*The Sacred Romance*, 1–2)

When the young prophet Samuel heard the voice of God calling to him in the night, he had the counsel from his priestly mentor, Eli, to tell him how to respond. Even so, it took them three times to realize it was God calling. Rather than ignoring the voice, or rebuking it, Samuel finally listened.

In our modern, pragmatic world we often have no such mentor, so we do not understand it is God speaking to us in our heart. Having so long been out of touch with our deepest longing, we fail to recognize the voice and the One who is calling to us through it. Frustrated by our heart's continuing sabotage of a dutiful Christian life, some of us silence the voice by locking our heart away in the attic, feeding it only the bread and water of duty and obligation until it is almost dead, the voice now small and weak. But sometimes in the night, when our defenses are down, we still hear it call to us, oh so faintly—a distant whisper. Come morning, the new day's activities scream for our attention, the sound of the cry is gone, and we congratulate ourselves on finally overcoming the flesh.

Others of us agree to give our heart a life on the side if it will only leave us alone and not rock the boat. We try to lose ourselves in our work, or "get a hobby" (either of which soon begins to feel like an addiction); we have an affair, or develop a colorful fantasy life fed by dime-store romances or pornography. We learn to enjoy the juicy intrigues and secrets of gossip. We make sure to maintain enough distance between ourselves and others, and even between ourselves and our own heart, to keep hidden the practical agnosticism we are living now that our inner life has been divorced from our outer life. Having thus appeased our heart, we nonetheless are forced to give up our spiritual journey because our heart will no longer come with us. It is bound up in the little indulgences we feed it to keep it at bay.

(*The Sacred Romance*, 2–3)

6 | WE HAVE LOST OUR STORY

And here's where we run into a problem.

For most of us, life feels like a movie we've arrived at forty-five minutes late.

Something important seems to be going on . . . maybe. I mean, good things do happen, sometimes beautiful things. You meet someone, fall in love. You find that work that is yours alone to fulfill. But tragic things happen too. You fall out of love, or perhaps the other person falls out of love with you. Work begins to feel like a punishment. Everything starts to feel like an endless routine.

If there is meaning to this life, then why do our days seem so *random*? What is this drama we've been dropped into the middle of? If there is a God, what sort of story is he telling here? At some point we begin to wonder if Macbeth wasn't right after all: Is life a tale "told by an idiot, full of sound and fury, signifying nothing"?

No wonder we keep losing heart.

We find ourselves in the middle of a story that is sometimes wonderful, sometimes awful, often a confusing mixture of both, and we haven't a clue how to make sense of it all. It's like we're holding in our hands some pages torn out of a book. These pages are the days of our lives. Fragments of a story. They seem important, or at least we long to know they are, but what does it all mean? If only we could find the book that contains the rest of the story.

Chesterton had it right when he said, "With every step of our lives we enter into the middle of some story which we are certain to misunderstand."

(Epic, 7–9)

Walk into any large mall, museum, amusement park, university, or hospital, and you will typically meet at once a very large map with the famous red star and the encouraging words *You are here*. These maps are offered to visitors as ways to orient themselves to their situation, get some perspective on things. This is the Big Picture. This is where you are in that picture. Hopefully you now know where to go. You have your bearings.

Oh, that we had something like this for our lives.

"This is the Story in which you have found yourself. Here is how it got started. Here is where it went wrong. Here is what will happen next. Now this—this is the role you've been given. If you want to fulfill your destiny, this is what you must do. These are your cues. And here is how things are going to turn out in the end."

We can.

We can discover *the* Story. Maybe not with perfect clarity, maybe not in the detail that you would like, but in greater clarity than most of us now have, and that would be worth the price of admission. I mean, to have some clarity would be gold right now. Wouldn't it?

(*Epic*, 10–11)

8 | THE HEART IS CENTRAL

The heart is central. That I would even need to remind you of this only shows how far we have fallen from the life we were meant to live—or how powerful the spell has been. The subject of the heart is addressed in the Bible more than any other topic—more than "works" or "serve," more than "believe" or "obey," more than money and even more than worship. Maybe God knows something we've forgotten. But of course—all those other things are matters of the heart. Consider but a few passages:

> Love the LORD your God with all your heart and with all your soul and with all your strength. (Deut. 6:5) [Jesus called this the greatest of all the commandments—and notice that the heart comes first.]

> Man looks at the outward appearance, but the LORD looks at the heart. (1 Sam. 16:7)

> Where your treasure is, there your heart will be also. (Luke 12:34)

> Trust in the LORD with all your heart, and lean not on your own understanding. (Prov. 3:5)

> Your word I have treasured in my heart, that I may not sin against You. (Ps. 119:11 NASB)

> These people honor me with their lips, but their hearts are far from me. (Matt 15:8)

> For the eyes of the LORD range throughout the earth to strengthen those whose hearts are fully committed to him. (2 Chron. 16:9)

(Waking the Dead, 39–40)

According to the Scriptures, the heart can be troubled, wounded, pierced, grieved, even broken. How well we all know that. Thankfully, it can also be cheerful, glad, merry, joyful, rejoicing. The heart can be whole or divided—as in that phrase we often use, "Well, part of me wants to, but the other part of me doesn't." It can be wise or foolish. It can be steadfast, true, upright, stout, valiant. (All of these descriptions can be found by perusing the listings for the word *heart* in any concordance.) It can also be frightened, faint, cowardly, melt like wax. The heart can be wandering, forgetful, dull, stubborn, proud, hardened. Wicked and perverse. I think we know that as well.

Much to our surprise, according to Jesus, a heart can also be pure, as in, "Blessed are the pure in heart, for they will see God" (Matt. 5:8). And even noble, as in his story about the sower: "But the seed on good soil stands for those with a noble and good heart, who hear the word, retain it, and by persevering produce a crop" (Luke 8:15). The Bible sees the heart as the source of all creativity, courage, and conviction. It is the source of our faith, our hope, and of course, our love. It is the "wellspring of life" within us (Prov. 4:23), the very essence of our existence, the center of our being, the fount of our life.

There is no escaping the centrality of the heart. God knows that; it's why he made it the central theme of the Bible, just as he placed the physical heart in the center of the human body. The heart is central; to find our lives, we must make it central again.

(*Waking the Dead*, 40–41)

10 | A SUBTLE EROSION

There are few things more crucial to us than our own lives. And there are few things we are less clear about.

This journey we are taking is hardly down the yellow brick road. Then again, that's not a bad analogy at all. We may set out in the light, with hope and joy, but eventually, our path always seems to lead us through dark woods, shrouded with a low-lying mist. Where is this abundant life that Christ supposedly promised? Where is God when we need him most? What is to become of us?

The cumulative effect of days upon years that we do not really understand is a subtle *erosion*. We come to doubt our place, we come to question God's intentions toward us, and we lose track of the most important things in life.

We're not fully convinced that God's offer to us *is* life. We have forgotten that the heart is central. And we had no idea that we were born into a world at war.

(Waking the Dead, 1–2)

What exactly are you perfectly clear on these days? How about your life—why have things gone the way they have? Where was God in all that? And do you know what you ought to do next, with a deep, settled confidence that it will work out? Neither do I. Oh, I'd *love* to wake each morning knowing exactly who I am and where God is taking me. Zeroed in on all my relationships, undaunted in my calling. It's awesome when I do see. But for most of us, life seems more like driving along with a dirty windshield and then turning into the sun. I can sort of make out the shapes ahead, and I think the light is green.

Wouldn't a little bit of clarity go a long way right now?

Let's start with why life is so dang *hard*. You try to lose a little weight, but it never seems to happen. You think of making a shift in your career, maybe even serving God, but you never actually get to it. Perhaps a few of you do make the jump, but it rarely pans out the way you thought. You try to recover something in your marriage, and your spouse looks at you with a glance that says, "Nice try," or "Isn't it a little late for that?" and the thing actually blows up into an argument in front of the kids. Yes, we have our faith. But even there—maybe *especially* there—it all seems to fall rather short of the promise. There's talk of freedom and abundant life, of peace like a river and joy unspeakable, but we see precious little of it, to be honest.

(*Waking the Dead,* 5)

I n the end, it doesn't matter how well we have performed or what we have accomplished—a life without heart is not worth living. For out of this wellspring of our soul flow all true caring and all meaningful work, all real worship and all sacrifice. Our faith, hope, and love issue from this fount, as well. Because it is in our heart that we first hear the voice of God and it is in the heart that we come to know him and learn to live in his love.

So you can see that to lose heart is to lose everything. And a "loss of heart" best describes most men and women in our day. It isn't just the addictions and affairs and depression and heartaches, though, God knows, there are enough of these to cause even the best of us to lose heart. But there is the busyness, the drivenness, the fact that most of us are living merely to survive. Beneath it we feel restless, weary, and vulnerable.

Indeed, the many forces driving modern life have not only assaulted the life of our heart, they have also dismantled the heart's habitat—that geography of mystery and transcendence we knew so well as children.

All of us have had that experience at one time or another, whether it be as we walked away from our teachers, our parents, a church service, or sexual intimacy; the sense that something important, perhaps the only thing important, had been explained away or tarnished and lost to us forever. Sometimes little by little, sometimes in large chunks, life has appropriated the terrain meant to sustain and nourish the wilder life of the heart, forcing it to retreat as an endangered species into smaller, more secluded, and often darker geographies for its survival. As this has happened, something has been lost, something vital.

(*The Sacred Romance*, 3—5)

Notice that all the great stories pretty much follow the same story line. Things were once good, then something awful happened, and now a great battle must be fought or a journey taken. At just the right moment (which feels like the last possible moment), a hero comes and sets things right, and life is found again.

It's true of every fairy tale, every myth, every Western, every epic—just about every story you can think of, one way or another. *Braveheart, Titanic,* the *Star Wars* series, *Gladiator, The Lord of the Rings* trilogy. They pretty much all follow the same story line.

Have you ever wondered why?

Every story, great and small, shares the same essential structure because every story we tell borrows its power from a Larger Story, a Story woven into the fabric of our being—what pioneer psychologist Carl Jung tried to explain as archetype, or what his more recent popularizer Joseph Campbell called myth.

All of these stories borrow from *the* Story. From Reality. We hear echoes of it through our lives. Some secret written on our hearts. A great battle to fight, and someone to fight for us. An adventure, something that requires everything we have, something to be shared with those we love and need.

There is a Story that we just can't seem to escape. There *is* a Story written on the human heart.

(*Epic,* 12–13)

A Story. An Epic.
Something hidden in the ancient past.
Something dangerous now unfolding.
Something waiting in the future for us to discover.
Some crucial role for us to play.

Christianity, in its true form, tells us that there is an Author and that he is good, the essence of all that is good and beautiful and true, for he is the source of all these things. It tells us that he has set our hearts' longings within us, for he has made us to live in an Epic. It warns that the truth is always in danger of being twisted and corrupted and stolen from us because there is a Villain in the Story who hates our hearts and wants to destroy us. It calls us up into a Story that is truer and deeper than any other, and assures us that there we will find the meaning of our lives.

What if?

What if all the great stories that have ever moved you, brought you joy or tears—what if they are telling you something about the *true* Story into which you were born, the Epic into which you have been cast?

We won't begin to understand our lives, or what this so-called gospel is that Christianity speaks of, until we understand the Story in which we have found ourselves. For when you were born, you were born into an Epic that has already been under way for quite some time. It is a Story of beauty and intimacy and adventure, a Story of danger and loss and heroism and betrayal.

(*Epic*, 14–15)

I f you learned about Eden in Sunday school, with poster board and flannel graphs, you missed something. Imagine the most beautiful scenes you have ever known on this earth—rain forests, the prairie in full bloom, storm clouds over the African savanna, the Alps under a winter snow. Then imagine it all on the day it was born.

It's Tolkien's Shire in its innocence, Iguazu Falls in the garden of *The Mission*, the opening scene of *The Lion King*.

And it doesn't stop there.

Into this world God opens his hand, and the animals spring forth. Myriads of birds, in every shape and size and song, take wing—hawks, herons, warblers. All the creatures of the sea leap into it—whales, dolphins, fish of a thousand colors and designs. Thundering across the plains race immense herds of horses, gazelles, buffalo, running like the wind. It is more astonishing than we could possibly imagine. No wonder "the morning stars sang together and all the angels shouted for joy" (Job 38:7). A great hurrah goes up from the heavens!

We have grown dull toward this world in which we live; we have forgotten that it is not *normal* or *scientific* in any sense of the word. It is fantastic. It is fairy tale through and through. Really now. Elephants? Caterpillars? Snow? At what point did you lose your wonder at it all?

Even so, once in a while something will come along and shock us right out of our dullness and resignation.

We come round a corner, and there before us is a cricket, a peacock, a stag with horns as big as he. Perhaps we come upon a waterfall, the clouds have made a rainbow in a circle round the sun, or a mouse scampers across the counter, pauses for a moment to twitch its whiskers, and disappears into the cupboard. And for a moment we realize that we were born into a world as astonishing as any fairy tale.

A world made for romance.

(*Epic*, 44–45)

16 | THE GREATEST DIGNITY OF ALL

He enables us to love.

He gives us the greatest treasure in all creation: a heart. For he intends that we should be his intimate allies, to borrow Dan Allender's phrase, who join in the Sacred Circle of intimacy that is the core of the universe, to share in this great Romance.

Just as we have lost our wonder at the world around us, we have forgotten what a treasure the human heart is. All of the happiness we have ever known and all of the happiness we hope to find is unreachable without a heart. You could not live or love or laugh or cry had God not given you a heart.

And with that heart comes something that just staggers me.

God gives us the freedom to reject him.

He gives to each of us a will of our own.

Good grief, *why?* He knows what free-willed creatures can do. He has already suffered one massive betrayal in the rebellion of the angels. He knows how we will use our freedom, what misery and suffering, what hell will be unleashed on earth because of our choices. *Why?* Is he out of his mind?

The answer is as simple and staggering as this: if you want a world where love is real, you must allow each person the freedom to choose.

(*Epic*, 50–51)

It was to the most religious people of his time that Jesus spoke his strongest warnings about a loss of heart.

It is tragic for any person to lose touch with the life of their heart but especially so for those of us who once heard the call in our heart and recognized it as the voice of Jesus of Nazareth. We may remember him inviting us to a life of beauty, intimacy, and adventure that we thought was lost. For others of us, when he called, it felt for the first time in our lives as if our heart had finally found a home. We responded in faith, in hope, and in love and began the journey we call the Christian life. Each day seemed a new adventure as we rediscovered the world with God by our side.

But for many of us, the waves of first love ebbed away in the whirlwind of Christian service and activity, and we began to lose the Romance. Our faith began to feel more like a series of problems that needed to be solved or principles that had to be mastered before we could finally enter into the abundant life promised us by Christ. We moved our spiritual life into the outer world of activity, and internally we drifted. We sensed that something was wrong, and we perhaps tried to fix it—by tinkering with our outer life. We tried the latest spiritual fad, or a new church, or simply redoubled our commitment to make faith work. Still, we found ourselves weary, jaded, or simply bored. Others of us immersed ourselves in busyness without really asking where all the activity was headed. At one point in my own spiritual pilgrimage, I stopped to ask myself this question: "What is it that I am supposed to be *doing* to live the spiritual life in any way that is both truthful and passionately alive?"

(*The Sacred Romance*, 7–8)

We all share the same dilemma—we long for life and we're not sure where to find it. We wonder if we ever do find it, can we make it last? The longing for life within us seems incongruent with the life we find around us. What is available seems at times close to what we want, but never quite a fit. Our days come to us as a riddle, and the answers aren't handed out with our birth certificates. We must journey to find the life we prize. And the guide we have been given is the desire set deep within, the desire we often overlook or mistake for something else or even choose to ignore.

The greatest human tragedy is simply to give up the search. There is nothing of greater importance than the life of our deep heart. To lose heart is to lose everything. And if we are to bring our hearts along in our life's journey, we simply must not, we cannot, abandon this desire. Gerald May writes in *The Awakened Heart,*

> There is a desire within each of us, in the deep center
> of ourselves that we call our heart. We were born with
> it, it is never completely satisfied, and it never dies.
> We are often unaware of it, but it is always awake . . .
> Our true identity, our reason for being, is to be found
> in this desire.

The clue as to who we really are and why we are here comes to us through our heart's desire.

(The Journey of Desire, 2)

W e all—men and women—were created in the image of
God. Fearfully and wonderfully made, fashioned as living icons of the bravest, wisest, most stunning Person who ever
lived. Those who have ever seen him fell to their knees without
even thinking about it, as you find yourself breathless before the
Grand Canyon or the Alps or the sea at dawn. That glory was
shared with us; we were, in Chesterton's phrase, "statues of God
walking about in a Garden," endowed with a strength and beauty
all our own. All that we ever wished we could be, we were—and
more. We were fully alive.

> So God created man in his own image, in the image
> of God he created him; male and female he created
> them. (Gen. 1:27)

> When I look at the night sky and see the work of
>   your fingers—
>   the moon and the stars you have set in place—
> what are mortals that you should think of us,
>   mere humans that you should care for us?
> For you made us only a little lower than God,
>   and you crowned us with glory and honor.
>   (Ps. 8:3–5 NLT)

I daresay we've heard a bit about original sin, but not nearly
enough about original glory, which comes *before* sin and is deeper to
our nature. We were crowned with glory and honor. Why does a
woman long to be beautiful? Why does a man hope to be found
brave? Because we remember, if only faintly, that we were once more
than we are now. The reason you doubt there could be a glory to your
life is because that glory has been the object of a long and brutal war.

(*Waking the Dead*, 13–14)

On the day Adam and Eve fell from grace, they ran off and hid in the bushes. And God came looking for them. He called to Adam, "Where are you?" (Gen. 3:9). Thus began the long and painful story of God's pursuit of mankind. Though we betrayed him and fell into the hands of the Evil One, God did not abandon us. Even a quick read of the Old Testament would be enough to convince you that *rescue* is God's plan. First with Noah, then with Abraham, and then with the nation Israel, you see God looking for a people who will turn to him from the heart, be his intimate allies once more.

The dramatic archetype is the Exodus, where God goes to war against the Egyptian taskmasters to set his captive people free.

Four hundred years they have languished in a life of despair. Suddenly—blood. Hail. Locusts. Darkness. Death. Plague after plague descends on Egypt like the blows of some unrelenting ax. Pharaoh releases his grip, but only for a moment. The fleeing slaves are pinned against the Red Sea when Egypt makes a last charge, hurtling down on them in chariots. God drowns those soldiers in the sea, every last one of them. Standing in shock and joy on the opposite shore, the Hebrews proclaim, "The LORD is a warrior" (Ex. 15:3). God is a warrior. He has come to rescue us.

(Epic, 61–62)

For above all else, the Christian life is a love affair of the heart. It cannot be lived primarily as a set of principles or ethics. It cannot be managed with steps and programs. It cannot be lived exclusively as a moral code leading to righteousness. In response to a religious expert who asked him what he must do to obtain real life, Jesus asked a question in return:

> "What is written in the Law? . . . How do you read it?"
>
> He answered: "'Love the Lord your God with *all your heart* and with all your soul and with all your strength and with all your mind'; and, 'Love your neighbor as yourself.'"
>
> "You have answered correctly," Jesus replied. "Do this and you will live." (Luke 10:26–28, emphasis added)

The truth of the gospel is intended to free us to love God and others with our whole heart. When we ignore this heart aspect of our faith and try to live out our religion solely as correct doctrine or ethics, our passion is crippled, or perverted, and the divorce of our soul from the heart purposes of God toward us is deepened.

(*The Sacred Romance,* 8)

It seems to me we can never give up longing and wishing while we are alive. There are certain things we feel to be beautiful and good, and we must hunger for them. (George Eliot)

And I still haven't found what I'm looking for. (U2)

There is a secret set within each of our hearts. It often goes unnoticed, we rarely can put words to it, and yet it guides us throughout the days of our lives. This secret remains hidden for the most part in our deepest selves. It is simply the desire for life as it was meant to be. Isn't there a life you have been searching for all your days? You may not always be aware of your search, and there are times when you seem to have abandoned looking altogether. But again and again it returns to us, this yearning that cries out for the life we prize. It is elusive, to be sure. It seems to come and go at will. Seasons may pass until it surfaces again. And though it seems to taunt us, and may at times cause us great pain, we know when it returns that it is priceless. For if we could recover this desire, unearth it from beneath all other distractions, and embrace it as our deepest treasure, we would discover the secret of our existence.

(*The Journey of Desire*, 1–2)

In all of our hearts lies a longing for a Sacred Romance.

It will not go away in spite of our efforts over the years to anesthetize or ignore its song, or attach it to a single person or endeavor. It is a Romance couched in mystery and set deeply within us. It cannot be categorized into propositional truths or fully known any more than studying the anatomy of a corpse would help us know the person who once inhabited it.

Philosophers call this Romance, this heart yearning set within us, the longing for transcendence; the desire to be part of something larger than ourselves, to be part of something out of the ordinary that is good. Transcendence is what we experience in a small but powerful way when our city's football team wins the big game against tremendous odds. The deepest part of our heart longs to be bound together in some heroic purpose with others of like mind and spirit.

Indeed, if we reflect back on the journey of our heart, the Romance has most often come to us in the form of two deep desires: the longing for adventure that *requires* something of us, and the desire for intimacy—to have someone truly know us for ourselves, while at the same time inviting us to *know* them in the naked and discovering way lovers come to know each other on the marriage bed. The emphasis is, perhaps, more on adventure for men and slightly more on intimacy for women. Yet, both desires are strong in us as men and women. In the words of friends, these two desires come together in us all as a longing to be in a relationship of heroic proportions.

(*The Sacred Romance*, 19)

The sense of being part of some bigger story, a purposeful adventure that is the Christian life, begins to drain away again after those first-love years in spite of everything we can do to stop it. Instead of a love affair with God, your life begins to feel more like a series of repetitive behaviors, like reading the same chapter of a book or writing the same novel over and over. The orthodoxy we try to live out, defined as "Believe and Behave Accordingly," is not a sufficient story line to satisfy whatever turmoil and longing our heart is trying to tell us about. Somehow our head and heart are on separate journeys and neither feels like life.

Eventually this division of head and heart culminates in one of two directions. We can either deaden our heart or divide our life into two parts, where our outer story becomes the theater of the should and our inner story the theater of needs, the place where we quench the thirst of our heart with whatever water is available. I chose the second route, living what I thought of as my religious life with increasing dryness and cynicism while I found "water" where I could: in sexual fantasies, alcohol, the next dinner out, late-night violence videos, gaining more knowledge through religious seminars—whatever would slake the thirsty restlessness inside. Whichever path we choose—heart deadness or heart and head separation—the wounds, the Arrows win, and we lose heart.

This is the story of all our lives, in one way or another. The haunting of the Romance and the Message of the Arrows are so radically different and they seem so mutually exclusive they split our hearts in two. In every way that the Romance is full of beauty and wonder, the Arrows are equally powerful in their ugliness and devastation.

(The Sacred Romance, 30–31)

What makes the Day of Judgment so unnerving is that all our posing and all our charades will be pulled back, all secrets will be made known, and our Lord will "expose the motives of men's *hearts*" (1 Cor. 4:5, emphasis added).

This is the point of the famous Sermon on the Mount. Jesus first says we haven't a hope of heaven unless our righteousness "surpasses that of the Pharisees" (Matt. 5:20). How can that be? They were fastidious rule keepers, pillars of the church, model citizens. Yes, Jesus says, and most of it was hypocrisy. The Pharisees prayed to impress men with their spirituality. They gave to impress men with their generosity. Their actions looked good, but their motives were not. Their hearts, as the saying goes, weren't in the right place. A person's character is determined by his motives, and motive is always a matter of the heart. This is what Scripture means when it says that man looks at the outward appearance, but God looks at the heart. God doesn't judge us by our looks or our intelligence; he judges us by our hearts.

It makes sense, then, that Scripture also locates our conscience in our hearts. Paul says that even those who do not know God's law "show that the requirements of the law are written on their hearts, their consciences also bearing witness" (Rom. 2:15), such as when your child looks guilty for having told a lie. This is why it is so dangerous to harden our hearts by silencing our consciences, and why the offer of forgiveness is such good news, to have our "hearts sprinkled clean from an evil conscience" (Heb. 10:22 NRSV). Oh, the joy of living from right motives, from a clean heart. I doubt that those who want to dismiss the heart want to dismiss our consciences, set aside the importance of character.

(*Waking the Dead*, 43–44)

God created us in freedom to be his intimate allies, and he will not give up on us. He seeks his allies still. Not religion. Not good church people. Lovers. Allies. Friends of the deepest sort.

> I will give them a heart to know me, that I am the LORD.
> They will be my people, and I will be their God, for
> they will return to me with all their heart. (Jer. 24:7)

It is the most beautiful of all love stories. On the other hand, Kierkegaard's tale *The King and the Maiden* doesn't capture the cost the King will have to pay to ransom his Beloved. He'll have to die.

Have you noticed that in the great stories the hero must often die to win the freedom of his beloved?

William Wallace is slowly and brutally tortured for daring to oppose the wicked king. He is executed (upon a cross), and yet his death breaks the grip that darkness has held over Scotland. Neo is the Chosen One, faster and more daring than any other before him. Even so, he is killed—shot in the chest at point-blank range. His death and resurrection shatter the power of the Matrix, set the captives free.

Aslan dies upon the stone table for the traitor Edmund and for all Narnia. Maximus dies in the arena to win the freedom of his friends and all Rome. They are all pictures of an even greater sacrifice.

> The Son of Man . . . [came] to give his life as a ransom
> for many. (Matt. 20:28)

Remember, God warned us back in the Garden that the price of our mistrust and disobedience would be death. Not just a physical death, but a *spiritual* death—to be separated from God and life and all the beauty, intimacy, and adventure forever. Through an act of our own free will, we became the hostages of the Kingdom of Darkness and death. The only way out is ransom.

(*Epic*, 66–67)

The coming of Jesus of Nazareth was like the opening scenes of *Saving Private Ryan*. A dangerous mission, a great invasion, a daring raid into enemy territory, to save the free world, but also to save one man.

Jesus told a story like that in order to shed light on his own coming: "If a man owns a hundred sheep, and one of them wanders away, will he not leave the ninety-nine on the hills and go to look for the one?" (Matt. 18:12). In the midst of the great invasion, like the storming of the beaches at Normandy, God yet sets his eye on one lost soul. On you.

Historically speaking, Jesus of Nazareth was betrayed by one of his followers, handed over to the Romans by the Jewish religious leaders, and crucified. But there was a Larger Story unfolding in that death. He gave his life willingly to ransom us from the Evil One, to pay the price for our betrayal, and to prove for all time and beyond any shadow of a doubt that the heart of God is good. And that your heart matters to him, matters more than tongue can tell.

> He has rescued us from the dominion of darkness and brought us into the kingdom of the Son he loves, in whom we have redemption, the forgiveness of sins. (Col. 1:13–14)

(Epic, 67–68)

This is not to say the heart is only swirling emotion, mixed motives, and dark desire, without thought or reason. Far from it. According to Scripture, the heart is also where we do our deepest thinking. "Jesus, knowing what they were thinking in their hearts," is a common phrase in the Gospels. This might be most surprising for those who have accepted the Great Modern Mistake that "the mind equals reason and the heart equals emotion." Most people believe that. I heard it again, just last night, from a very astute and devoted young man. "The mind is our reason; the heart is emotion," he said. What popular nonsense. Solomon is remembered as the wisest man ever, and it was not because of the size of his brain. Rather, when God invited him to ask for anything in all the world, Solomon asked for a wise and discerning *heart* (1 Kings 3:9).

Our deepest thoughts are held in our hearts. Scripture itself claims to be "sharper than any double-edged sword, it penetrates even to dividing soul and spirit, joints and marrow; it judges the thoughts and attitudes of the heart" (Heb. 4:12). Not the feelings of the heart, the *thoughts* of the heart. Remember, when the shepherds reported the news that a company of angels had brought them out in the field, Mary "pondered them in her heart" (Luke 2:19), as you do when some news of great import keeps you up in the middle of the night. If you have a fear of heights, no amount of reasoning will get you to go bungee jumping. And if you are asked why you're paralyzed at the thought of it, you won't be able to explain. It is not rational, but it is your conviction nonetheless. Thus, the writer of Proverbs preempts Freud by about two thousand years when he says, "As [a man] thinketh in his heart, so is he" (Prov. 23:7 KJV). It is the thoughts and intents of the *heart* that shape a person's life.

(*Waking the Dead*, 44–45)

I love watching a herd of horses grazing in an open pasture, or running free across the wide, sage-covered plateaus in Montana. I love hiking in the high country when the wildflowers are blooming—the purple lupine and the Indian paintbrush when it's turning magenta. I love thunder clouds, massive ones. My family loves to sit outside on summer nights and watch the lightning, hear the thunder as a storm rolls in across Colorado. I love water, too—the ocean, streams, lakes, rivers, waterfalls, rain. I love jumping off high rocks into lakes with my boys. I love old barns, windmills, the West. I love vineyards. I love it when Stasi is loving something, love watching her delight. I love my boys. I love God.

Everything you love is what makes a life worth living. Take a moment, set down the book, and make a list of all the things you love. Don't edit yourself; don't worry about prioritizing or anything of that sort. Simply think of all the things you love. Whether it's the people in your life or the things that bring you joy or the places that are dear to you or your God, you could not love them if you did not have a heart. Loving requires a heart alive and awake and free. A life filled with loving is a life most like the one that God lives, which is life as it was meant to be (Eph. 5:1–2).

Of all the things that are required of us in this life, which is the most important? What is the real point of our existence? Jesus was confronted with the question point-blank one day, and he boiled it all down to two things: loving God and loving others. Do this, he said, and you will find the purpose of your life. Everything else will fall into place. Somewhere down inside we know it's true; we know love is the point. We know if we could truly love, and be loved, and never lose love, we would finally be happy. And is it even possible to love *without* your heart?

(*Waking the Dead,* 47–48)

Everyone has been betrayed by someone, some more profoundly than others. Betrayal is a violation that strikes at the core of our being; to make ourselves vulnerable and entrust our well-being to another, only to be harmed by those on whom our hopes were set, is among the worst pain of human experience.

Sometimes the way God treats us feels like betrayal. We find ourselves in a dangerous world, unable to arrange for the water our thirsty souls so desperately need. Our rope won't take the bucket to the bottom of the well. We know God has the ability to draw water for us, but oftentimes he won't. We feel wronged. After all, doesn't Scripture say that if we have the power to do someone good, we should do it (Prov. 3:27)? So why doesn't God?

As I spoke with a friend about her painful life, how reckless and unpredictable God seems, she turned and with pleading eyes asked the question we are all asking somewhere deep within: "How can I trust a lover who is so wild?" Indeed, how do we not only trust him, but love him in return? There's only one possible answer: You could love him if you *knew* his heart was good.

(*The Sacred Romance,* 70)

Does God have a good heart? When we think of God as Author, the Grand Chess Player, the Mind Behind It All, we doubt his heart. As Melville said, "The reason the mass of men fear God and at bottom dislike him is because they rather distrust his heart, and fancy him all brain, like a watch." Do you relate to the author when reading a novel or watching a film? Caught up in the action, do you even think about the author? We identify with the characters in the story precisely because they are *in* the story. They face life as we do, on the ground, and their struggles win our sympathy because they are our struggles also. We love the hero because he is one of us, and yet somehow rises above the fray to be better and wiser and more loving as we hope one day we might prove to be.

The Author lies behind, beyond. His omniscience and omnipotence may be what creates the drama, but they are also what separates us from him. Power and knowledge don't qualify for heart. Indeed, the worst sort of villain is the kind who executes his plans with cold and calculated precision. He is detached; he has no heart. If we picture God as the mastermind behind the story—calling the shots while we, like Job, endure the calamities—we can't help but feel at times what C. S. Lewis was bold enough to put words to: "We're the rats in the cosmic laboratory." Sure, he may have our good in mind, but that still makes him the "vivisectionist"—the experimenter.

We root for the hero and heroine, even come to love them, because they are living *in* the drama. They feel the heartache, they suffer loss and summon courage and shed their own blood in their struggles against evil. What if? Just what if we saw God not as Author, the cosmic mastermind behind all human experience, but as the central character *in* the larger story? What could we learn about his heart?

(The Sacred Romance, 71–72)

The story that is the Sacred Romance begins not with God alone, the Author at his desk, but God in relationship, intimacy beyond our wildest imagination, heroic intimacy. The Trinity is at the center of the universe; perfect relationship is the heart of all reality. Think of your best moments of love or friendship or creative partnership, the best times with family or friends around the dinner table, your richest conversations, the acts of simple kindness that sometimes seem like the only things that make life worth living. Like the shimmer of sunlight on a lake, these are reflections of the love that flows among the Trinity. We long for intimacy because we are made in the image of perfect intimacy. Still, what we don't have and may never have known is often a more powerful reminder of what *ought* to be.

Our story begins with the hero in love. As Frederick Buechner reminds us, "God does not need the Creation in order to have something to love because within himself love happens."

And yet, what kind of love? There are selfish forms of love, relationships that create closed systems, impenetrable to outsiders. Real love creates a generous openness. Have you ever been so caught up in something that you just had to share it? When you are walking alone in the woods, something takes your breath away—a sunset, a waterfall, the simple song of a bird—and you think, *If only my beloved were here.* The best things in life were meant to be shared. That is why married lovers want to increase their joy by having children. And so it is with God. "Father," Jesus says, "I want those you gave me to be with me, right where I am. I want them to be one heart and mind with us" (John 17). Overflowing with the generosity that comes from the abundance of real love, he creates us to share in the joy of this heroic intimacy.

(*The Sacred Romance,* 73–74)

The heart is the connecting point, the meeting place between any two persons. The kind of deep soul intimacy we crave with God and with others can be experienced only from the heart. I know a man who took his daughter to dinner; she was surprised, delighted. For years she had been hoping he would pursue her. When they had been seated, he pulled out his Day Timer and began to review the goals he had set for her that year. "I wanted to burst into tears and run out of the restaurant," she said. We don't want to be someone's project; we want to be the desire of their heart. Gerald May laments, "By worshiping efficiency, the human race has achieved the highest level of efficiency in history, but how much have we grown in love?"

We've done the same to our relationship with God. Christians have spent their whole lives mastering all sorts of principles, done their duty, carried on the programs of their church . . . and never known God intimately, heart to heart. The point is not an efficient life of activity—the point is intimacy with God. "You will find me," God says, "when you seek me with all your heart" (Jer. 29:13). As Oswald Chambers said, "So that is what faith is—God perceived by the heart."

What more can be said, what greater case could be made than this: to find God, you must look with all your heart. To remain present to God, you must remain present to your heart. To hear his voice, you must listen with your heart. To love him, you must love with all your heart. You cannot be the person God meant you to be, and you cannot live the life he meant you to live, unless you live from the heart.

(*Waking the Dead,* 48–49)

Look at the life of Jesus. Notice what he did.

When Jesus touched the blind, they could *see*; all the beauty of the world opened before them. When he touched the deaf, they were able to *hear*; for the first time in their lives they heard laughter and music and their children's voices. He touched the lame, and they *jumped* to their feet and began to dance. And he called the dead back to *life* and gave them to their families.

Do you see? Wherever humanity was broken, Jesus restored it. He is giving us an illustration here, and there, and there again. The coming of the kingdom of God *restores* the world he made.

God has been whispering this secret to us through creation itself, every year, at springtime, ever since we left the Garden. Sure, winter has its certain set of joys. The wonder of snowfall at midnight, the rush of a sled down a hill, the magic of the holidays. But if winter ever came for good and never left, we would be desolate. Every tree leafless, every flower gone, the grasses on the hillsides dry and brittle. The world forever cold, silent, bleak.

After months and months of winter, I long for the return of summer. Sunshine, warmth, color, and the long days of adventure together. The garden blossoms in all its beauty. The meadows soft and green. Vacation. Holiday. Isn't this what we most deeply long for? To leave the winter of the world behind, what Shakespeare called "the winter of our discontent," and find ourselves suddenly in the open meadows of summer?

If we listen, we will discover something of tremendous joy and wonder. The restoration of the world played out before us each spring and summer is *precisely* what God is promising us about our lives. Every miracle Jesus ever did was pointing to this Restoration, the day he makes all things new.

(*Epic*, 82–83)

Can you imagine if on your honeymoon one of you sneaked off for a rendezvous with a perfect stranger? Adam and Eve kicked off the honeymoon by sleeping with the Enemy. Then comes one of the most poignant verses in all Scripture: "What is this you have done?" (Gen. 3:13). You can almost hear the shock, the pain of betrayal in God's voice. The fall of Adam and Eve mustn't be pictured as a crime like theft, but as a betrayal of love. In love God creates us for love, and we give him the back of our hand. Why? Satan gets us to side with him by sowing the seed of doubt in our first parents' minds: "God's heart really isn't good. He's holding out on you. You've got to take things into your own hands." And Paradise was lost.

Yet there was something about the heart of God that the angels and our first parents had not yet seen. Here, at the lowest point in our relationship, God announces his intention never to abandon us but to seek us out and win us back. "I will come for you." *Grace* introduces a new element of God's heart. Up till this point we knew he was rich, famous, influential, even generous. Behind all that can still hide a heart that is less than good. Grace removes all doubt.

(*The Sacred Romance,* 78–79)

Christ did not die for an idea. He died for a person, and that person is you. But there again, we have been led astray. Ask any number of people why Christ came, and you'll receive any number of answers, but rarely the real one. "He came to bring world peace." "He came to teach us the way of love." "He came to die so that we might go to heaven." "He came to bring economic justice." On and on it goes, much of it based in a partial truth. But wouldn't it be better to let him speak for himself?

Jesus steps into the scene. He reaches back to a four-hundred-year-old prophecy to tell us why he's come. He quotes from Isaiah 61:1, which goes like this:

> The Spirit of the Sovereign LORD is upon me,
>   because the LORD has anointed me
>   to preach good news to the poor.
> He has sent me to bind up the brokenhearted,
>   to proclaim freedom for the captives
>   and release from darkness for the prisoners.

The meaning of this quotation has been clouded by years of religious language and ceremonial draping. What is he saying? It has something to do with good news, with healing hearts, with setting someone free.

Christ could have chosen any one of a thousand other passages to explain his life purpose. But he did not. He chose this one; this is the heart of his mission. Everything else he says and does finds its place under this banner: "I am here to give you back your heart and set you free." *That* is why the glory of God is man fully alive: it's what he said he came to do. But of course. The opposite can't be true. "The glory of God is man barely making it, a person hardly alive." How can it bring God glory for his very image, his own children, to remain so badly marred, broken, captive?

(*Waking the Dead*, 50–51)

I t is simply diabolical, despicable, downright *evil* that the heart should be so misunderstood, maligned, feared, and dismissed. But there is our clue again. The war we are in would explain so great a loss. This is the *last* thing the Enemy wants you to know. His plan from the beginning was to assault the heart, just as the Wicked Witch did to the Tin Woodman. Make them so busy, they ignore the heart. Wound them so deeply, they don't want a heart. Twist their theology, so they despise the heart. Take away their courage. Destroy their creativity. Make intimacy with God impossible for them.

Of course your heart would be the object of a great and fierce battle. It is your most precious possession. Without your heart you cannot have God. Without your heart you cannot have love. Without your heart you cannot have faith. Without your heart you cannot find the work you were meant to do. In other words, without your heart you cannot have *life.* The question is, Did Jesus keep his promise? What has he done for our hearts?

The answer will astound you.

(*Waking the Dead,* 51–52)

38 | THE KING WHO LOVED A HUMBLE MAIDEN

Here is Soren Kierkegaard's version of the story:

> Suppose there was a king who loved a humble maiden. The king was like no other king. No one dared breathe a word against him, for he had the strength to crush all opponents. And yet this mighty king was melted by love for a humble maiden. How could he declare his love for her? In an odd sort of way, his kingliness tied his hands. If he brought her to the palace and crowned her head with jewels and clothed her body in royal robes, she would surely not resist—no one dared resist him. But would she love him?
>
> She would say she loved him, of course, but would she truly? Or would she live with him in fear, nursing a private grief for the life she had left behind? Would she be happy at his side? How could he know? If he rode to her forest cottage in his royal carriage, with an armed escort waving bright banners, that too would overwhelm her. He did not want a cringing subject. He wanted a lover, an equal. He wanted her to forget that he was a king and she a humble maiden and to let shared love cross the gulf between them. For it is only in love that the unequal can be made equal. (as quoted in *Disappointment with God*)

The king clothes himself as a beggar and renounces his throne in order to win her hand. The Incarnation, the life and the death of Jesus, answers once and for all the question, "What is God's heart toward me?" This is why Paul says in Romans 5, "Look here, at the Cross. Here is the demonstration of God's heart. At the point of our deepest betrayal, when we had run our farthest from him and gotten so lost in the woods we could never find our way home, God came and died to rescue us."

(*The Sacred Romance*, 80–81)

W hat is God like? Is his heart good? We know he is the initiator from first to last. As Simon Tugwell reminds, God is the one pursuing us:

> So long as we imagine that it is we who have to look for God, we must often lose heart. But it is the other way about; He is looking for us. And so we can afford to recognize that very often we are not looking for God; far from it, we are in full flight from him, in high rebellion against him. And He knows that and has taken it into account. He has followed us into our own darkness; there where we thought finally to escape him, we run straight into his arms. So we do not have to erect a false piety for ourselves, to give us the hope of salvation. Our hope is in his determination to save us, and he will not give in. (*Prayer*)

When we feel that life is finally up to us, it becomes suffocating. When we are the main character, the world is so small there's barely room to move. It frees our souls to have something going on before us that involves us, had us in mind, yet doesn't depend on us or culminate in us, but invites us up into something larger. And what about the Romance and the Arrows? It wasn't supposed to be like this. Once upon a time we lived in a garden; we lived in the place for which we were made. There were no Arrows, only beauty. Our relationships weren't tainted with fear, guardedness, manipulation, quid pro quo. Our work was rewarding; we received more than we gave. There is beauty, and we so long for it to last; we were made for the Garden. But now there is affliction also, and that is because we live East of Eden. The Arrows seem like the truest part of life, but they are not. The heart of the universe is still perfect love.

(*The Sacred Romance*, 81–82)

AND THEY LIVED HAPPILY EVER AFTER

And they lived happily ever after. Stop for just a moment, and let it be true. *They lived happily ever after.*

These may be the most beautiful and haunting words in the entire library of mankind. Why does the end of a great story leave us with a lump in our throats and an ache in our hearts? If we haven't become entirely cynical, some of the best endings can even bring us to tears.

Because God has set eternity in our hearts. Every story we tell is our attempt to put into words and images what God has written there, on our hearts. Think of the stories that you love. Remember how they end.

This is written on the human heart, this longing for happily ever after.

You see, every story has an ending. Every story. Including yours. Have you ever faced this? Even if you do manage to find a little taste of Eden in this life, even if you are one of the fortunate souls who find some love and happiness in the world, you cannot hang on to it. You know this. Your health cannot hold out forever. Age will conquer you. One by one your friends and loved ones will slip from your hand. Your work will remain unfinished. Your time on this stage will come to an end. Like every other person gone before you, you will breathe your last breath.

And then what? Is that the end of the Story?

If that is the end, this Story is a tragedy. Macbeth was right. Life is a tale told by an idiot, full of sound and fury, signifying nothing. Sooner or later, life will break your heart. Or rather, death will break your heart. Perhaps you have to lose someone you love to be shaken from denial. The final enemy is death. It will come. Is there no way out? Do we have a future?

(Epic, 73, 78–79)

I will give you a new heart and put a new spirit in you;
I will remove from you your heart of stone and give
you a heart of flesh. And I will put my Spirit in you
and move you to follow my decrees and be careful to
keep my laws. (Ezek. 36:26–27)

This we now know: the heart is central. It matters—deeply.
When we see with the eyes of the heart, which is to say,
when we see mythically, we begin to awaken, and what we discover is that things are not what they seem. We *are* at war. We
must fight for the life God intends for us, which is to say, we must
fight for our heart, for it is the wellspring of that life within us.

Standing in the way of the path to life—the way of the heart—
is a monstrous barrier. It has stopped far too many pilgrims dead
in their tracks for far too long. There is a widespread belief among
Christians today that the heart is desperately wicked—even after a
person comes to Christ.

It is a crippling belief.

And it is untrue.

(*Waking the Dead*, 53–54)

Few have ever felt so pursued. Sometimes we wonder if we've even been *noticed.* Father was too busy to come to our games, or perhaps he jumped ship altogether. Mother was lost in a never-ending pile of laundry or, more recently, in her own career. We come into the world longing to be special to someone and from the start we are disappointed. It is a rare soul indeed who has been sought after for who she is—not because of what she can do, or what others can gain from her, but simply for herself. Can you recall a time when a significant someone in your life sat you down with the sole purpose of wanting to know your heart more deeply, fully expecting to enjoy what he found there? More people have climbed Mt. Everest than have experienced real pursuit, and so what are we left to conclude? There is nothing in our hearts worth knowing. Whoever and what-ever this mystery called *I* must be, it cannot be much.

"In fact," we continue, "if I am not pursued, it must be because there is something wrong with me, something dark and twisted inside." We long to be known, and we fear it like nothing else. Most people live with a subtle dread that one day they will be dis-covered for who they really are and the world will be appalled.

(*The Sacred Romance,* 83–84)

Now—is Jesus more like Mother Teresa or William Wallace? The answer is . . . it depends. If you're a leper, an outcast, a pariah of society whom no one has *ever* touched, if all you have ever longed for is just one kind word, then Christ is the incarnation of tender mercy. On the other hand, if you're a Pharisee, one of those self-appointed doctrine police . . . watch out. On more than one occasion Jesus "picks a fight" with those notorious hypocrites.

> One Sabbath day as Jesus was teaching in a synagogue, he saw a woman who had been crippled by an evil spirit. She had been bent double for eighteen years and was unable to stand up straight. When Jesus saw her, he called her over and said, "Woman, you are healed of your sickness!" Then he touched her, and instantly she could stand straight. How she praised and thanked God! But the leader in charge of the synagogue was indignant that Jesus had healed her on the Sabbath day. "There are six days of the week for working," he said to the crowd. "Come on those days to be healed, not on the Sabbath."
>
> But the Lord replied, "You hypocrite! You work on the Sabbath day! Don't you untie your ox or your donkey from their stalls on the Sabbath and lead them out for water? Wasn't it necessary for me, even on the Sabbath day, to free this dear woman from the bondage in which Satan has held her for eighteen years?" This shamed his enemies. And all the people rejoiced at the wonderful things he did. (Luke 13:10–17 NLT)

Does Jesus tiptoe around the issue, so as not to "rock the boat"? Does he drop the subject in order to "preserve church unity"? Nope. He walks right into it, he baits them, he picks a fight. Christ draws the enemy out, exposes him for what he is, and shames him in front of everyone. The Lord is a *gentleman*???

(*Wild at Heart*, 24–25)

44 | Is That the God You Find in the Bible?

God has a battle to fight, and the battle is for our freedom. As Tremper Longman says, "Virtually every book of the Bible—Old and New Testaments—and almost every page tells us about God's warring activity." I wonder if the Egyptians who kept Israel under the whip would describe Yahweh as a Really Nice Guy? Plagues, pestilence, the death of every firstborn—that doesn't seem very gentlemanly, now, does it?

You remember that wild man, Samson? He's got a pretty impressive masculine résumé: killed a lion with his bare hands, pummeled and stripped thirty Philistines when they used his wife against him, and finally, after they burned her to death, he killed a thousand men with the jawbone of a donkey. Not a guy to mess with. But did you notice? All those events happened when "*the Spirit of the LORD came upon him*" (Judg. 15:14, emphasis added). Now, let me make one thing clear: I am not advocating a sort of "macho man" image. I'm not suggesting we all head off to the gym and then to the beach to kick sand in the faces of wimpy Pharisees. I am attempting to rescue us from a very, very mistaken image we have of God—especially of Jesus—and therefore of men as his image-bearers. Dorothy Sayers wrote that the church has "very efficiently pared the claws of the Lion of Judah," making him "a fitting household pet for pale curates and pious old ladies." Is that the God you find in the Bible?

You can tell what kind of man you've got simply by noting the impact he has on you. Does he make you bored? Does he scare you with his doctrinal nazism? Does he make you want to scream because he's just so very nice? In the Garden of Gethsemane, in the dead of night, a mob of thugs "carrying torches, lanterns and weapons" comes to take Christ away. Note the cowardice of it—why didn't they take him during the light of day, down in the town? Does Jesus shrink back in fear? No, he goes to face them head-on.

(*Wild at Heart*, 25–27)

I f you have any doubts as to whether or not God loves wildness, spend a night in the woods . . . alone. Take a walk out in a thunderstorm. Go for a swim with a pod of killer whales. Get a bull moose mad at you. Whose idea was this, anyway? The Great Barrier Reef with its great white sharks, the jungles of India with their tigers, the deserts of the Southwest with all those rattlesnakes—would you describe them as "nice" places? Most of the earth is not safe; but it's good. That struck me a little too late when hiking in to find the upper Kenai River in Alaska. My buddy Craig and I were after the salmon and giant rainbow trout that live in those icy waters. We were warned about bears, but didn't really take it seriously until we were deep into the woods. Grizzly signs were everywhere—salmon strewn about the trail, their heads bitten off. Piles of droppings the size of small dogs. Huge claw marks on the trees, about head-level. *We're dead*, I thought. *What are we doing out here?*

It then occurred to me that after God made all this, he pronounced it *good*, for heaven's sake. It's his way of letting us know he rather prefers adventure, danger, risk, the element of surprise. This whole creation is unapologetically *wild*. God loves it that way.

(*Wild at Heart*, 29–30)

The resurrection of Jesus was the first of many, the forerunner of our own. He paved the way, as the saying goes.

> The fact is that Christ has been raised from the dead. He has become the first of a great harvest of those who will be raised to life again. (1 Cor. 15:20 NLT)

> God knew what he was doing from the very beginning. He decided from the outset to shape the lives of those who love him along the same lines as the life of his Son. The Son stands first in the line of humanity he restored. (Rom. 8:29 *The Message*)

So we, too, shall live and never die. Creation will be restored, and *we* will be restored. And we shall share it together. "Today," Jesus said to the thief on the cross, "you will be with me in paradise" (Luke 23:43). Imagine that. Imagine being reunited with the ones you love, and with all the great and noble hearts of this Story, in paradise.

We will walk with God in the Garden in the cool of the day. We will see our Jesus face-to-face. We will hear him laugh. All that has ever stood between us will be swept away, and our hearts will be released to real loving. It begins with a great party, just as in *Titanic*, what the Scriptures call the "wedding feast of the Lamb" (Rev. 19:9 NLT). You'll raise a glass with Adam and Eve, with Paul and St. Patrick, with your grandmother and your grandson.

Imagine the stories that you'll hear. And all the questions that shall finally have answers. And the answers won't be one-word answers, but story after story, a feast of wonder and laughter and glad tears.

(*Epic*, 87–88)

I n an attempt to secure the sovereignty of God, theologians have overstated their case and left us with a chess-player God playing both sides of the board, making all his moves and all ours too. But clearly, this is not so. God is a person who takes immense risks. No doubt the biggest risk of all was when he gave angels and men free will, including the freedom to reject him—not just once, but every single day. Does God cause a person to sin? "Absolutely not!" says Paul (Gal. 2:17). Then he can't be moving all the pieces on the board, because people sin all the time. Fallen angels and men use their powers to commit horrendous daily evil. Does God stop every bullet fired at an innocent victim? Does he prevent teenage liaisons from producing teenage pregnancies? There is something much more risky going on here than we're often willing to admit.

Most of us do everything we can to *reduce* the element of risk in our lives. We wear our seat belts, watch our cholesterol, and practice birth control. I know some couples who have decided against having children altogether; they simply aren't willing to chance the heartache children often bring. What if they are born with a crippling disease? What if they turn their backs on us, and God? What if . . . ? God seems to fly in the face of all caution. Even though he *knew* what would happen, what heartbreak and suffering and devastation would follow upon our disobedience, God chose to have children. And unlike some hyper-controlling parents, who take away every element of choice they can from their children, God gave us a remarkable choice. He did not *make* Adam and Eve obey him. He took a risk. A staggering risk, with staggering consequences. He let others into his story, and he lets their choices shape it profoundly.

(*Wild at Heart,* 30–31)

The shriveled figure lay in the sun like a pile of rags dumped there by accident. It hardly appeared to be human. But those who used the gate to go in and out of Jerusalem recognized him. He was disabled, dropped off there every morning by someone in his family, and picked up again at the end of the day. A rumor was going around that sometimes (no one really knew when) an angel would stir the waters, and the first one in would be healed. Sort of a lottery, if you will. And as with every lottery, the desperate gathered round, hoping for a miracle.

It had been so long since anyone had actually *spoken* to him, he thought the question was meant for someone else. Squinting upward into the sun, he didn't recognize the figure standing above him. The misshapen man asked the fellow to repeat himself; perhaps he had misheard. Although the voice was kind, the question felt harsh, even cruel.

"Do you want to get well?"

He sat speechless, blinking into the sun. Slowly, the words seeped into his consciousness, like a voice calling him out of a dream. *Do I want to get well?* Slowly, like a wheel long rusted, his mind began to turn over. *What kind of question is that? Why else would I be lying here? Why else would I have spent every day for the past thirty-eight seasons lying here? He is mocking me.* But now that his vision had adjusted to the glare, he could see the inquisitor's face, his eyes. The face was as kind as the voice he heard. Apparently, the man meant what he said, and he was waiting for an answer. "Do you want to get well? What is it that you want?"

It was Jesus who posed the question, so there must be something we're missing here. He is love incarnate. Why did he ask the paraplegic such an embarrassing question?

(*The Journey of Desire*, 33–34)

L ife *is* the offer, friends. Let us not forget that.

> For God so loved the world that he gave his one and only Son, that whoever believes in him shall not perish but have eternal life. (John 3:16)

> The thief comes only to steal and kill and destroy; I have come that they may have life, and have it to the full. (John 10:10)

> This is the way to have eternal life—to know you, the only true God, and Jesus Christ, the one you sent to earth. (John 17:3 NLT)

There is no simpler or more beautiful way to say it than this: Act Four is the restoration of life as it was always meant to be.

It is the return of the beauty, the intimacy, and the adventure we were created to enjoy and have longed for every day of our lives. And yet, *better*, for it is immortal. We can never lose it again. It cannot be taken away. Sunrise and sunset tell the tale every day, remembering Eden's glory, foretelling Eden's return.

And what adventures shall unfold when we are given the kingdom that was always meant to be ours? Listen to this:

> Then the King will say to those on his right, "Come, you who are blessed by my Father; take your inheritance, *the kingdom prepared for you since the creation of the world.*" (Matt. 25:34, emphasis added)

Adam and Eve, and all their sons and daughters after them, were created to reign over the earth—to explore and discover and create and do all those things you see people do when they are at their very best.

That is our destiny.

(*Epic,* 92–94)

At some point we all face the same decision—what will we do with the Arrows we've known? Maybe a better way to say it is, what have they tempted us to do? However they come to us, whether through a loss we experience as abandonment or some deep violation we feel as abuse, their message is always the same: Kill your heart. Divorce it, neglect it, run from it, or indulge it with some anesthetic (our various addictions). Think of how you've handled the affliction that has pierced your own heart. How did the Arrows come to you? Where did they land? Are they still there? What have you done as a result?

To say we all face a decision when we're pierced by an Arrow is misleading. It makes the process sound so rational, as though we have the option of coolly assessing the situation and choosing a logical response. Life isn't like that—the heart cannot be managed in a detached sort of way (certainly not when we are young, when some of the most defining Arrows strike). It feels more like an ambush, and our response is at a gut level. We may never put words to it. Our deepest convictions are formed without conscious effort, but the effect is a shift deep in our soul. Commitments form never to be in that position again, never to know that sort of pain again. The result is an approach to life that we often call our personality. If you'll listen carefully to your life, you may begin to see how it has been shaped by the unique Arrows you've known and the particular convictions you've embraced as a result. The Arrows also taint and partially direct even our spiritual life.

(*The Sacred Romance*, 27–28)

This may come as a surprise to you: Christianity is not an invitation to become a moral person. It is not a program for getting us in line or for reforming society. It has a powerful effect upon our lives, but when transformation comes, it is always the *aftereffect* of something else, something at the level of our hearts. And so at its core, Christianity begins with an invitation to *desire*.

Look again at the way Jesus relates to people. There is the Samaritan woman Jesus meets at the well. She has come alone in the heat of the day to draw water, and they both know why. By coming when the sun is high, she is less likely to run into anyone. You see, her sexual lifestyle has earned her a "reputation." Back in those days, having one partner after another wasn't looked so highly upon. She's on her sixth lover, and so she'd rather bear the scorching rays of the sun than face the searing words of the "decent" women of the town who come at evening to draw water. She succeeds in avoiding the women, but runs into God instead. What does he choose to talk to her about—her immorality? No, he speaks to her about her *thirst*: "If you knew the generosity of God and who I am, you would be asking *me* for a drink, and I would give you fresh, living water" (John 4:10 *The Message*). Remarkable. He doesn't give a little sermon about purity; he doesn't even mention it, except to say that he knows what her life has been like: "You've had five husbands, and the man you're living with now isn't even your husband" (John 4:18 *The Message*). In other words, now that we both know it, let's talk about your heart's real thirst, since the life you've chosen obviously isn't working. "The water I give will be an artesian spring within, gushing fountains of endless life" (John 4:14 *The Message*).

(*The Journey of Desire*, 35–36)

This is the world [God] has made. This is the world that is still going on. And he doesn't walk away from the mess we've made of it. Now he lives, almost cheerfully, certainly heroically, in a dynamic relationship with us and with our world. "Then the Lord intervened" is perhaps the single most common phrase about him in Scripture, in one form or another. Look at the stories he writes. There's the one where the children of Israel are pinned against the Red Sea, no way out, with Pharaoh and his army barreling down on them in murderous fury. Then God shows up. There's Shadrach, Meshach, and Abednego, who get rescued only *after* they're thrown into the fiery furnace. Then God shows up. He lets the mob kill Jesus, bury him . . . then he shows up. Do you know why God loves writing such incredible stories? Because *he loves to come through.* He loves to show us that he has what it takes.

It's not the nature of God to limit his risks and cover his bases. Far from it. Most of the time, he actually lets the odds stack up against him. Against Goliath, a seasoned soldier and a trained killer, he sends . . . a freckle-faced little shepherd kid with a slingshot. Most commanders going into battle want as many infantry as they can get. God cuts Gideon's army from thirty-two thousand to three hundred. Then he equips the ragtag little band that's left with torches and watering pots. It's not just a battle or two that God takes his chances with, either. Have you thought about his handling of the gospel? God needs to get a message out to the human race, without which they will perish . . . forever. What's the plan? First, he starts with the most unlikely group ever: a couple of prostitutes, a few fishermen with no better than a second-grade education, a tax collector. Then, he passes the ball to us. Unbelievable.

(*Wild at Heart,* 31–32)

God's relationship with us and with our world is just that: a *relationship*. As with every relationship, there's a certain amount of unpredictability, and the ever-present likelihood that you'll get hurt. The ultimate risk anyone ever takes is to love, for as C. S. Lewis says, "Love anything and your heart will be wrung and possibly broken. If you want to make sure of keeping it intact you must give it to no one, not even an animal." But God does give it, again and again and again, until he is literally bleeding from it all. God's willingness to risk is just astounding—far beyond what any of us would do were we in his position.

Trying to reconcile God's sovereignty and man's free will has stumped the church for ages. We must humbly acknowledge that there's a great deal of mystery involved, but for those aware of the discussion, I am not advocating open theism. Nevertheless, there is definitely something wild in the heart of God.

(*Wild at Heart,* 32)

Dare we forget King David? Yes, his passions got him in a heap of trouble—and gave us our book of *worship*, the Psalms. Sure, Peter was a hotheaded disciple always quick with a reply. Remember in the Garden of Gethsemane—he's the one who lopped off the ear of the high priest's servant. But he was also the first to acknowledge that Jesus was the Messiah, and despite his Good Friday betrayals he became a key apostle, contributed important pieces to the Scripture, and followed Jesus all the way to his own crucifixion, asking to be nailed to the cross upside down because he was not worthy to die in the manner of his Lord. Surely we remember that Paul was once Saul, the fiery young Pharisee "advancing in Judaism beyond many Jews of my own age and . . . extremely zealous for the traditions of my fathers" (Gal. 1:14). His zeal made him the foremost persecutor of the church. When Christ knocked him off his donkey on the Damascus road, Paul was hunting down the church, "uttering threats with every breath" (Acts 9:1 NLT). Christ captured his zeal, and after Damascus it led him to "work harder than all the other apostles" (1 Cor. 15:10 NLT).

Augustine was also a passionate young man, sexually licentious, enamored with the pleasures of Rome, "scratching the sore of lust," as he would call it after Christ got hold of him. He went on to become one of the great pillars of the church, laying the foundation for the rise of Christendom after the fall of Rome. Desire, a burning passion for more, is at the heart of both saints and sinners. Those who would kill the passion altogether would murder the very essence that makes heroes of the faith.

(The Journey of Desire, 52–53)

I thought of the last story we have from the life of the prophet Elisha. Jehoash was king of Israel at the time, and he went to visit Elisha on his sickbed. He knew that without the help of this great prophet, the future of Israel was looking dim. Enemies were closing in on every side, waiting for the kill. Elisha told the king to take in hand some arrows.

> And the king took them. Elisha told him, "Strike the ground." He struck it three times and stopped. The man of God was angry with him and said, "You should have struck the ground five or six times; then you would have defeated [your enemies] completely . . . But now you will defeat [them] only three times." Elisha died and was buried. (2 Kings 13:18–20)

That's it? What a strange story! Why was the old prophet so angry? Because the king was nonchalant; he was passionless, indifferent. He gave the ground a whack or two. His heart wasn't in it. God says, in effect, "If that is how little you care about the future of your people, that is all the help you will get." In other words, if your heart's not in it, well then, neither is mine. You can't lead a country, let alone flourish in a marriage, with an attitude like that. To abandon desire is to say, "I don't really need you; I don't really want you. But I will live with you because, well, I'm supposed to." It is a grotesque corruption of what was meant to be a beautiful dance between desire and devotion.

(*The Journey of Desire,* 56–57)

You may recall the story Jesus told of the man who entrusted three of his servants with thousands of dollars (literally, "talents"), urging them to handle his affairs well while he was away. When he returned, he listened eagerly to their reports. The first two fellows went out into the marketplace and doubled their investment. As a result, they were handsomely rewarded. The third servant was not so fortunate. His gold was taken from him, and he was thrown into "outer darkness, where there will be weeping and gnashing of teeth." My goodness. Why? All he did was bury the money under the porch until his master's return. Most of us would probably agree with the path he chose—at least the money was safe there. But listen to his reasoning. Speaking to his master, he said, "I know you are a hard man, harvesting crops you didn't plant and gathering crops you didn't cultivate. I was afraid I would lose your money, so I hid it" (see Matt. 25:14–30 NLT). He was afraid of the master, whom he saw as a hard man. He didn't trust his master's heart.

The issue isn't capital gains—it's what we think of God. When we bury our desires, we are saying the same thing: "God, I don't dare desire because I fear you; I think you are hard-hearted."

Even though we may profess at one level a genuine faith in him, at another level we are like the third servant. Our obedience is not so much out of love as it is out of carefulness. "Just tell me what to do, God, and I'll do it." Killing desire may look like sanctification, but it's really godlessness. Literally, our way of handling life without God. The deepest moral issue is always what we, in our heart of hearts, believe about God. And nothing reveals this belief as clearly as what we do with our desire.

(The Journey of Desire, 57–59)

Our false self demands a formula before he'll engage; he wants a guarantee of success; and mister, you aren't going to get one. So there comes a time in a man's life when he's got to break away from all that and head off into the unknown with God. This is a vital part of our journey and if we balk here, the journey ends.

Before the moment of Adam's greatest trial God provided no step-by-step plan, gave no formula for how he was to handle the whole mess. That was not abandonment; that was the way God *honored* Adam. *You are a man; you don't need me to hold you by the hand through this. You have what it takes.* What God *did* offer Adam was friendship. He wasn't left alone to face life; he walked with God in the cool of the day, and there they talked about love and marriage and creativity, what lessons he was learning and what adventures were to come. This is what God is offering to us as well. As Oswald Chambers says,

> There comes the baffling call of God in our lives also. The call of God can never be stated explicitly; it is implicit. The call of God is like the call of the sea, no one hears it but the one who has the nature of the sea in him. It cannot be stated definitely what the call of God is to, *because his call is to be in comradeship with himself* for his own purposes, and the test is to believe that God knows what he is after. (*My Utmost for His Highest*, emphasis added)

The only way to live in this adventure—with all its danger and unpredictability and immensely high stakes—is in an ongoing, intimate relationship with God. The control we so desperately crave is an illusion. Far better to give it up in exchange for God's offer of companionship, set aside stale formulas so that we might enter into an informal friendship.

(*Wild at Heart*, 213–14)

All his wildness and all his fierceness are inseparable from God's romantic heart. That theologians have missed this says more about theologians than it does about God. Music, wine, poetry, sunsets . . . those were *his* inventions, not ours. We simply discovered what he had already thought of. Lovers and honeymooners choose places like Hawaii, the Bahamas, or Tuscany as a backdrop for their love. But whose idea was Hawaii, the Bahamas, and Tuscany? Let's bring this a little closer to home. Whose idea was it to create the human form in such a way that a kiss could be so delicious? And he didn't stop there, as only lovers know. Starting with her eyes, King Solomon is feasting on his beloved through the course of their wedding night. He loves her hair, her smile; her lips "drop sweetness as the honeycomb," and "milk and honey are under her tongue." You'll notice he's working his way *down:*

> Your neck is like the tower of David,
>   built with elegance . . .
> Your two breasts are like two fawns . . .
> Until the day breaks
>   and the shadows flee,
> I will go to the mountain of myrrh
>   and to the hill of incense. (Song 4:4–6)

And his wife responds by saying, "Let my lover come into his garden and taste its choice fruits" (Song 4:16).

What kind of God would put the Song of Songs in the canon of Holy Scripture? Really now, is it conceivable that such an erotic and scandalous book would have been placed in the Bible by the Christians *you* know?

(*Wild at Heart,* 32–33)

I hope you're getting the picture by now. If a man does not find those things for which his heart is made, if he is never even invited to live for them from his deep heart, he will look for them in some other way. Why is pornography the number one snare for men? He longs for the beauty, but without his fierce and passionate heart he cannot find her or win her or keep her. Though he is powerfully drawn to the woman, he does not know how to fight for her or even that he *is* to fight for her. Rather, he finds her mostly a mystery that he knows he cannot solve and so at a soul level he keeps his distance. And privately, secretly, he turns to the imitation. What makes pornography so addictive is that more than anything else in a lost man's life, it makes him *feel* like a man without ever requiring a thing of him. The less a guy feels like a real man in the presence of a real woman, the more vulnerable he is to porn.

And so a man's heart, driven into the darker regions of the soul, denied the very things he most deeply desires, comes out in darker places. Now, a man's struggles, his wounds and addictions, are a bit more involved than that, but those are the core reasons. As the poet George Herbert warned, "He begins to die, that quits his desires." And you know what? We all know it. Every man knows that something's happened, something's gone wrong . . . we just don't know what it is.

(*Wild at Heart*, 44)

God gives Adam some instructions on the care of creation and his role in the unfolding story. It's pretty basic, and very generous (see Gen. 2:16–17). But notice what God *doesn't* tell Adam.

There is no warning or instruction over what is about to occur: the Temptation of Eve. This is just staggering. Notably missing from the dialogue between Adam and God is something like this: "Adam, one more thing. A week from Tuesday, about four in the afternoon, you and Eve are going to be down in the orchard and something dangerous is going to happen. Adam, are you listening? The eternal destiny of the human race hangs on this moment. Now, here's what I want you to do . . ." He doesn't tell him. He doesn't even mention it, so far as we know. Good grief—*why not?!* Because God *believes* in Adam. This is what he's designed to do— to come through in a pinch. Adam doesn't need play-by-play instructions because this is what Adam is *for*. It's already there, everything he needs, in his design, in his heart.

Needless to say, the story doesn't go well. Adam fails; he fails Eve and the rest of humanity. Let me ask you a question: Where is Adam, while the serpent is tempting Eve? He's standing right there: "She also gave some to her husband, who was with her. Then he ate it, too" (Gen. 3:6 NLT). The Hebrew for "with her" means right there, elbow to elbow. Adam isn't away in another part of the forest; he has no alibi. He is standing right there, watching the whole thing unravel. What does he do? Nothing. Absolutely nothing. He says not a word, doesn't lift a finger.* He won't risk, he won't fight, and he won't rescue Eve. Our first father—the first real man—gave in to paralysis. He denied his very nature and went passive. And every man after him, every son of Adam, carries in his heart now the same failure. Every man repeats the sin of Adam, every day. We won't risk, we won't fight, and we won't rescue Eve. We truly are a chip off the old block.

(*Wild at Heart,* 50–51)

---

* I'm indebted to Crabb, Hudson, and Andrews for pointing this out in *The Silence of Adam.*

Now Beauty feared that she had caused his death. She ran throughout the palace, sobbing loudly. After searching everywhere, she recalled her dream and ran into the garden toward the canal, where she had seen him in her sleep. There she found the poor Beast stretched out unconscious. She thought he was dead. Without concern for his horrifying looks, she threw herself on his body and felt his heart beating. So she fetched some water from the canal and threw it on his face.

Beast opened his eyes and said, "You forgot your promise, Beauty. The grief I felt upon having lost you made me decide to fast to death. But I shall die content since I have the pleasure of seeing you one more time."

"No, my dear Beast, you shall not die," said Beauty. "You will live to become my husband. I give you my hand, and I swear that I belong only to you from this moment on. Alas! I thought that I only felt friendship for you, but the torment I am feeling makes me realize that I cannot live without you."

Beauty had scarcely uttered these words when the castle radiated with light. Fireworks and music announced a feast. These attractions did not hold her attention, though. She returned her gaze to her dear Beast, whose dangerous condition made her tremble. How great was her surprise when she discovered that the Beast had disappeared, and at her feet was a prince more handsome than Eros himself, who thanked her for putting an end to his enchantment.

It is the deepest and most wonderful of all mythic truths, unveiled here in the original *Beauty and the Beast*, written by Jeanne-Marie Leprince de Beaumont. The Transformation. A creature that no one could bear to look upon is transformed into a handsome prince. That which was dark and ugly is now glorious and good. Is it not the most beautiful outcome of any story to be written? Perhaps that is because it is the deepest yearning of the human heart.

(*Waking the Dead*, 55–56)

THE UGLY DUCKLING BECOMES A BEAUTIFUL SWAN

The Phoenix rises from the ashes. Cinderella rises from the cinders to become a queen. The Ugly Duckling becomes a beautiful swan. Pinocchio becomes a real boy. The frog becomes a prince. The Cowardly Lion gets his courage, the Scarecrow his brains, and the Tin Woodman a new heart. They are all transformed into the very thing they never thought they could be.

Why are we enchanted by tales of transformation? I can't think of a movie or novel or fairy tale that doesn't somehow turn on this. Why is it an essential part of any great story? Because it is the secret to Christianity, and Christianity is the secret to the universe. "You must be born again" (John 3:7). You must be transformed. Keeping the Law, following the rules, polishing up your manners—none of that will do. "What counts is whether we really have been changed into new and different people" (Gal. 6:15). Is this not the message of the Gospel? Zacchaeus the trickster becomes Zacchaeus the Honest One. Mary the whore becomes Mary the Last of the Truly Faithful. Paul the self-righteous murderer becomes Paul the Humble Apostle.

And us? I doubt many of us would go so far as to say we're *transformed*. Perhaps we have changed a bit in what we believe and how we act. We confess the creeds now, and we've gotten our temper under control . . . for the most part. But "transformed" seems a bit too much to claim. How about "forgiven and on our way"? That's how most Christians would describe what's happened to them. It's partly true . . . and partly *untrue*, and the part that's untrue is what's killing us. We've been told that even though we have placed our hope in Christ, even though we have become his followers, our *hearts* are still desperately wicked. And of course, so long as we believe that our hearts remain untouched, unchanged, we will pretty much live untouched and unchanged. For our heart is the wellspring of life within us.

(*Waking the Dead*, 56–57)

S omething has gone wrong with the human race, and we know it. Better said, something has gone wrong *within* the human race. It doesn't take a theologian or a psychologist to tell you that. Read a newspaper. Spend a weekend with your relatives. Simply pay attention to the movements of your own heart in a single day. Most misery is the fruit of the human heart gone bad.

Scripture could not be more clear on this. Yes, God created us to reflect his glory, but barely three chapters into the drama we torpedoed the whole project. By the sixth chapter of Genesis, our downward spiral had reached the point where God himself couldn't bear it any longer: "The LORD saw how great man's wickedness on the earth had become, and that every inclination of the thoughts of his heart was only evil all the time. The LORD was grieved that he had made man on the earth, and his heart was filled with pain" (Gen. 6:5–6). This is the first mention of God's heart in the Bible, by the way, and it's a sad beginning, to be sure. His heart is broken because ours is fallen.

Any honest person knows this. We know we are not what we were meant to be. Most of the world religions concur on this point. Something needs to be done.

But the usual remedies involve some sort of shaping up on our part, some sort of face-lift whereby we clean up our act and start behaving as we should. Jews try to keep the Law. Buddhists follow the Eightfold Path. Muslims live by the Five Pillars. Christians try church attendance and moral living. It never works. It never will. For heaven's sake—we've given it several thousand years. You'd think we'd have gotten *somewhere*. Of course, the reason all those treatments ultimately fail is that we quite misdiagnosed the disease. The problem is not in our behavior; the problem is *in us*. As Jesus said, "For out of the heart come evil thoughts, murder, adultery, sexual immorality, theft, false testimony, slander" (Matt. 15:19). We don't need an upgrade. We need transformation. We need a miracle.

(*Waking the Dead*, 57–59)

We come into the world with a longing to be known and a deep-seated fear that we aren't what we should be. We are set up for a crisis of identity. And then, says Frederick Buechner, the world goes to work:

> Starting with the rather too pretty young woman and the charming but rather unstable young man, who together know no more about being parents than they do the far side of the moon, the world sets in to making us what the world would like us to be, and because we have to survive after all, we try to make ourselves into something that we hope the world will like better than it apparently did the selves we originally were. That is the story of all our lives, needless to say, and in the process of living out that story, the original, shimmering self gets buried so deep that most of us hardly end up living out of it at all. Instead, we live out all the other selves which we are constantly putting on and taking off like coats and hats against the world's weather. (*Telling Secrets*)

Think about the part you find yourself playing, the self you put on like a costume. Who cast you in this role? Most of us are living out a script that someone else has written for us. We've not been invited to live from our heart, to be who we truly are, so we put on these false selves hoping to offer something more acceptable to the world, something functional. We learn our roles starting very young and we learn them well.

(*The Sacred Romance,* 84–85)

According to the part of the story God has allowed us to see, the Haunting we sense is his calling us forth on a journey. The resurrection of our heart requires that the Sacred Romance be true and that is precisely what the Scriptures tell us. As Frederick Buechner reminds us in his wonderful book *Telling the Truth: The Gospel as Tragedy, Comedy and Fairy Tale*, the world of the gospel is the world of fairy tale, with one notable exception:

> It is a world of magic and mystery, of deep darkness and flickering starlight. It is a world where terrible things happen and wonderful things too. It is a world where goodness is pitted against evil, love against hate, order against chaos, in a great struggle where often it is hard to be sure who belongs to which side because appearances are endlessly deceptive. Yet for all its confusion and wildness, it is a world where the battle goes ultimately to the good, who live happily ever after, and where in the long run everybody, good and evil alike, becomes known by his true name . . . . That is the fairy tale of the Gospel with, of course, one crucial difference from all other fairy tales, which is that the claim made for it is that it is true, that it not only happened once upon a time but has kept on happening ever since and is happening still.

Let us explore together the drama that God has been weaving since before the beginning of time, which he has also placed in our hearts. Who are the main players in this Larger Story? What is the plot? How do we fit in? As we rediscover the oldest Story in the world, one that is forever young, we journey into the heart of God and toward the recovery of our own hearts. For perhaps God would be reason enough to stay open to the Romance if we knew he would keep us safe. And therein we experience a great fear and confusion.

(*The Sacred Romance*, 46)

> The thief comes only to steal and kill and destroy;
> I have come that they may have life, and have it to the
> full. (John 10:10)

Have you ever wondered why Jesus married those two statements? Did you even know he spoke them at the same time? I mean, he says them in one breath. And he has his reasons. By all means, God intends life for you. But right now that life is *opposed*. It doesn't just roll in on a tray. There is a thief. He comes to steal and kill and destroy. Why won't we face this? I know so few people who will face this. The offer is life, but you're going to have to fight for it, because there's an Enemy in your life with a different agenda.

There *is* something set against us.

We are at war.

I don't like that fact any more than you do, but the sooner we come to terms with it, the better hope we have of making it through to the life we do want. This is not Eden. You probably figured that out. This is not Mayberry, this is not *Seinfeld*'s world, this is not *Survivor*. The world in which we live is a combat zone, a violent clash of kingdoms, a bitter struggle unto the death. I am sorry if I'm the one to break this news to you: you were born into a world at war, and you will live all your days in the midst of a great battle, involving all the forces of heaven and hell and played out here on earth.

Where *did* you think all this opposition was coming from?

(*Waking the Dead*, 12–13)

Something awful has happened, something terrible. Something worse, even, than the fall of man. For in that greatest of all tragedies, we merely lost Paradise—and with it, everything that made life worth living. What has happened since is unthinkable: we've gotten used to it. We're broken in to the idea that this is just the way things are. The people who walk in great darkness have adjusted their eyes. Regardless of our religious or philosophical beliefs, most of us live as though this life is pretty much the way things are supposed to be. We dismiss the whispers of joy with a cynical "Been there, done that." That way we won't have to deal with the Haunting.

I was just talking with some friends about summer vacations, and I recommended that they visit the Tetons. "Oh, yeah, we've been there. Nice place." Dismissal. And we deaden our sorrows with cynicism as well, sporting a bumper sticker that says, "Life sucks. Then you die." Then we try to get on with life. We feed the cat, pay the bills, watch the news, and head off to bed, so we can do it all again tomorrow.

Standing before the open fridge, I'm struck by what I've just watched. Famine in Africa. Genocide . . . where? Someplace I can't even pronounce. Corruption in Washington. Life as usual. It always ends with the anchor folding his notes and offering a pleasant "Good night." Good night? That's it? You have nothing else to say? You've just regaled us with the horrors of the world we live in, and all you can say is "Good night"? Just once I wish he would pause at the close of his report, take a long, deep breath, and then say, "How far we are from home," or "If only we had listened," or "Thank God, our sojourn here is drawing to an end." It never happens. I doubt it ever will. And not one of us gives it a second thought. It's just the way things are.

(*The Journey of Desire*, 9–10)

By the grace of God, we cannot quite pull it off. In the quiet moments of the day we sense a nagging within, a discontentment, a hunger for something else. But because we have not solved the riddle of our existence, we assume that something is wrong—not with life, but with us. *Everyone else seems to be getting on with things. What's wrong with me?* We feel guilty about our chronic disappointment. *Why can't I just learn to be happier in my job, in my marriage, in my church, in my group of friends?* You see, even while we are doing other things, "getting on with life," we still have an eye out for the life we secretly want. When someone seems to have gotten it together, we wonder, *How did he do it?* Maybe if we read the same book, spent time with him, went to his church, things would come together for us as well. You see, we can never entirely give up our quest. Gerald May reminds us,

> When the desire is too much to bear, we often bury it beneath frenzied thoughts and activities or escape it by dulling our immediate consciousness of living. It is possible to run away from the desire for years, even decades, at a time, but we cannot eradicate it entirely. It keeps touching us in little glimpses and hints in our dreams, our hopes, our unguarded moments. (*The Awakened Heart*)

He says that even though we sleep, our desire does not. "It is who we are." We *are* desire. It is the essence of the human soul, the secret of our existence. Absolutely nothing of human greatness is ever accomplished without it. Desire fuels our search for the life we prize. The same old thing is not enough. It never will be.

(*The Journey of Desire,* 10–11)

M y gender seems to need little encouragement. It comes naturally, like our innate love of maps. In 1260 Marco Polo headed off to find China, and in 1967, when I was seven, I tried to dig a hole straight through from our backyard with my friend Danny Wilson. We gave up at about eight feet, but it made a great fort. Hannibal crosses his famous Alps, and there comes a day in a boy's life when he first crosses the street and enters the company of the great explorers. Scott and Amundsen race for the South Pole, Peary and Cook vie for the North, and when last summer I gave my boys some loose change and permission to ride their bikes down to the store to buy a soda, you'd have thought I'd given them a charter to go find the equator. Magellan sails due west, around the tip of South America—despite warnings that he and his crew will drop off the end of the earth—and Huck Finn heads off down the Mississippi ignoring similar threats. Powell follows the Colorado into the Grand Canyon, even though—no, *because*—no one has done it before and everyone is saying it can't be done.

(*Wild at Heart,* 4)

And then, alas, there is the church. Christianity, as it currently exists, has done some terrible things to men. When all is said and done, I think most men in the church believe that God put them on the earth to be a good boy. The problem with men, we are told, is that they don't know how to keep their promises, be spiritual leaders, talk to their wives, or raise their children. But, if they will try real hard they can reach the lofty summit of becoming . . . a nice guy. That's what we hold up as models of Christian maturity: Really Nice Guys. We don't smoke, drink, or swear; that's what makes us *men*. Now let me ask my male readers: In all your boyhood dreams growing up, did you ever dream of becoming a Nice Guy? (Ladies, was the Prince of your dreams dashing . . . or merely nice?)

Really now—do I overstate my case? Walk into most churches in America, have a look around, and ask yourself this question: What is a Christian man? Don't listen to what is said, look at what you find there. There is no doubt about it. You'd have to admit a Christian man is . . . bored. At a recent church retreat I was talking with a guy in his fifties, listening really, about his own journey as a man. "I've pretty much tried for the last twenty years to be a good man as the church defines it." Intrigued, I asked him to say what he thought that was. He paused for a long moment. "Dutiful," he said. "And separated from his heart." *A perfect description*, I thought. *Sadly right on the mark.*

(Wild at Heart, 7)

The desire to be beautiful is an ageless longing.

Beauty has been extolled and worshiped and kept just out of reach for most of us. (Do you like having your picture taken? Do you like *seeing* those pictures later? How do you feel when people ask you your age? This issue of beauty runs deep!) For others, beauty has been shamed, used, and abused. Some of you have learned that possessing beauty can be dangerous. And yet—and this is just astounding—*in spite* of all the pain and distress that beauty has caused us as women, the desire remains.

And it's *not* just the desire for an outward beauty, but more—a desire to be captivating in the depths of *who you are*. Cinderella is beautiful, yes, but she is also good. Her outward beauty would be hollow were it not for the beauty of her heart. That's why we love her. In *The Sound of Music*, the Countess has Maria beat in the looks department, and they both know it. But Maria has a rare and beautiful depth of spirit. She has the capacity to love whiskers on kittens and mean-spirited children. She sees the handiwork of God in music and laughter and climbing trees. Her soul is Alive. And we are drawn to her.

Ruth may have been a lovely, strong woman, but it is to her unrelenting courage and vulnerability and faith in God that Boaz is drawn. Esther is the most beautiful woman in the land, but it is her bravery and her cunning, good heart that moves the king to spare her people. This isn't about dresses and makeup . . . Don't you recognize that a woman yearns to be *seen* and to be thought of as captivating? We desire to possess a beauty that is worth pursuing, worth fighting for, a beauty that is core to who we *truly* are. We want beauty that can be seen; beauty that can be felt; beauty that affects others; a beauty all our own to unveil.

(*Captivating*, 16–17)

The things that have happened to us often suggest that the real script of the play we're all living in is "God is indifferent" rather than "God is love." Deep down in our hearts, in the place where the story is formed, this experience of God as indifferent drives us to write our own scripts. Job apparently lived with this anxiety about God even before his tribulations descended upon him, as evidenced by his exclamation from the ashes of his home and his life: "What I *feared* has come upon me; what I *dreaded* has happened to me" (Job 3:25, emphasis added).

Job was a God-fearing man and yet something in him suspected that faith in God did not necessarily translate into peace and safety. Of course, Job had no inkling of the discussion going on in heaven between God and Satan. It was a debate over whether the foundation of God's kingdom was based on genuine love or power. And astonishingly, God was placing the perception of his own integrity as well as the reputation of his whole kingdom on the genuineness of Job's heart. (See Job 1:6–12; 2:1–10.)

Indeed, when we consider how central a part Job was given in the drama God was directing, we are confronted with the reality that we, too, could be in the same position. It seems that the part God has written for us is much too big and certainly too dangerous. Paul confirms this thought in Ephesians when he tells us, "The church, you see, is not peripheral to the world; the world is peripheral to the church. The church is Christ's body, in which he speaks and acts, by which he fills everything with his presence" (1:22–23 *The Message*). Every human being is of great significance to God, but those whom God has drawn to believe in him are center stage in a drama of cosmic proportions.

(*The Sacred Romance,* 50, 53)

When God comes to call Jeremiah to be his prophet of hard sayings to Judah, Jeremiah protests, saying, "'Ah, Sovereign LORD . . . I do not know how to speak; I am only a child.' But the LORD said to me, 'Do not say, "I am only a child." You must go to everyone I send you to and say whatever I command you. Do not be afraid of them, for I am with you and will rescue you,' declares the LORD" (Jer. 1:6–8).

God is saying that these things will be done through Jeremiah's dependence on his strength and provision, and that he will rescue him. Yet there is something about God's rescues that make them a little less timely than dialing 911. He leaves Abraham with his knife raised and ready to plunge into Isaac's heart, and Isaac waiting for the knife to descend; he leaves Joseph languishing for years in an Egyptian prison; he allows the Israelites to suffer four hundred years of bondage under the Egyptians and leaves those same Israelites backed against the Red Sea with Pharaoh's chariots thundering down on them. He abandons Jesus to the cross and does not rescue him at all. And then there are those of us who, along with the saints under heaven's very altar, are groaning under the weight of things gone wrong, waiting for that same Jesus to return and sweep us up with him in power and glory. "How long, O Lord?" we whisper in our weariness and pain.

Indeed, God calls us to battles where the deck appears stacked in favor of those who are his enemies and ours, just to increase the drama of the play. And there is the clear picture, even from God himself, that he does so to enhance his own glory.

(*The Sacred Romance,* 55)

Until we come to terms with *war* as the context of our days, we will not understand life. We will misinterpret 90 percent of what is happening around us and to us. It will be very hard to believe that God's intentions toward us are life abundant; it will be even harder not to feel that somehow we are just blowing it. Worse, we will begin to accept some really awful things about God. That four-year-old little girl being molested by her daddy—that is "God's *will*"? That ugly divorce that tore your family apart—God wanted that to happen too? And that plane crash that took the lives of so many—that was ordained by God?

Most people get stuck at some point because God appears to have abandoned them. He is not coming through. Speaking about her life with a mixture of disappointment and cynicism, a young woman recently said to me, "God is rather silent right now." Yes, it's been awful. I don't discount that for a moment. She is unloved; she is unemployed; she is under a lot. But her attitude strikes me as deeply naive, on the level of someone caught in a cross fire who asks, rather shocked and with a sense of betrayal, "God, why won't you make them stop firing at me?" I'm sorry, but that's not where we are right now. It's not where we are in the Story. That day is coming, *later*, when the lion shall lie down with the lamb and we'll beat swords into plowshares. For now, it's bloody battle.

It sure explains a whole heckuva lot.

You won't understand your life, you won't see clearly what has happened to you or how to live forward from here, unless you see it as *battle*. A war against your heart.

(*Waking the Dead*, 17–18)

Therefore we do not lose heart. Though outwardly we are wasting away, yet inwardly we are being renewed day by day. For our light and momentary troubles are achieving for us an eternal glory that far outweighs them all. So we fix our eyes not on what is seen, but what is unseen. For what is seen is temporary, but what is unseen is eternal. (2 Cor. 4:16–18)

The first line grabs me by the throat. "Therefore we do not lose heart." Somebody knows how not to lose heart? I'm all ears. For we *are* losing heart. All of us. Daily. It is the single most unifying quality shared by the human race on the planet at this time. We are losing—or we have already lost—heart. That glorious, resilient image of God in us is fading, fading, fading away. And this man claims to know a way out.

So, how, Paul—*how?* How do we not lose heart?

So we fix our eyes not on what is seen, but on what is unseen. (2 Cor. 4:18)

What? I let out a sigh of disappointment. *Now that's helpful. "Look at what you cannot see."* That sounds like Eastern mysticism, that sort of wispy wisdom dripping in spirituality but completely inapplicable to our lives. Life is an illusion. Look at what you cannot see. *What can this mean?* Remembering that a little humility can take me a long way, I give it another go. This wise old seer is saying that there is a way of looking at life, and that those who discover it are able to live from the heart no matter what. How do we do this? By seeing with the eyes of the heart. Later in life, writing from prison to some friends he was deeply concerned about, Paul said, "I pray . . . that the eyes of your heart may be enlightened" (Eph. 1:18).

(*Waking the Dead*, 21–23)

What do all the great stories and myths tell us? What do they have in common? What are they trying to get across? Wherever they may come from, whatever their shape might be, they nearly always speak to us Three Eternal Truths. First, these stories are trying to remind us that *things are not what they seem*. There is a whole lot more going on here than meets the eye. Much more. After the tornado sets her down, Dorothy wakes and steps out of her old farmhouse to find herself in a strange new world, a land of Munchkins and fairies and wicked witches. The Land of Oz. How brilliant for the filmmakers to have waited for this moment to introduce color in the movie. Up till now the story has been told in black and white; when Dorothy steps out of the house, the screen explodes in color, and she whispers to her little friend, "Toto . . . I don't think we're in Kansas anymore."

Isn't this the very lesson of the Emmaus Road? You recall the story—two followers of Christ are headed out of town after the Crucifixion, as dejected as two people can be, with every reason in their minds to be so and more. Their hopes have been shattered. They staked it all on the Nazarene, and now he's dead. As they slump back toward their homes, Jesus sort of sneaks up alongside, very much alive but incognito, and joins their conversation, feigning ignorance—and they not seeing it is him.

We live in two worlds—or better, in one world with two parts, one part that we can see and one part that we cannot. We are urged, for our own welfare, to act as though the unseen world (the rest of reality) is, in fact, more weighty and more real and more dangerous than the part of reality we can see. The lesson from the story of the Emmaus Road—the lesson the whole Bible is trying to get across—begins with this simple truth: There is more going on here than meets the eye. Far more.

(Waking the Dead, 26–27, 29)

The Second Eternal Truth brought to us comes like a broken message over the radio or an urgent e-mail from a distant country telling us that some great struggle or quest or battle is well under way. May even be hanging in the balance. When the four children stumble into Narnia, the country and all its lovely creatures are imprisoned under the spell of the White Witch and have been for a hundred years. In another story, Jack and his mother are starving and must sell their only cow. Frodo barely makes it out of the Shire with his life and the ring of power. In the nick of time he learns that Bilbo's magic ring is the One Ring, that Sauron has discovered its whereabouts, and that the Nine Black Riders are already across the borders searching for the little hobbit with deadly intent. The future of Middle Earth hangs on a thread.

Again, this is *exactly* what the Scriptures have been trying to wake us up to for years. "Wake up, O sleeper . . . Be very careful, then, how you live . . . because the days are evil" (Eph. 5:14–16). Or as *The Message* has it: "So watch your step. Use your head. Make the most of every chance you get. These are desperate times!" Christianity isn't a religion about going to Sunday school, potluck suppers, being nice, holding car washes, sending our secondhand clothes off to Mexico. This is a world at war. Something large and immensely dangerous is unfolding all around us, we are caught up in it, and above all we doubt we have been given a key role to play. Do you think I'm being too dramatic?

(*Waking the Dead*, 29–30)

Honest communication in love is the only way to live and grow in friendships. There are ebbs and flows. There may be real hurt and disappointment. But with the grace of God firmly holding us, it is possible to nurture and sustain deep friendships. We are designed to live in relationship and share in the lives of other women. We need one another. God knows that. We have only to ask and surrender, to wait, to hope, and, in faith, to love. We must also repent.

For a woman to enjoy relationship, she must repent of her need to control and her insistence that people fill her. Fallen Eve demands that people "come through" for her. Redeemed Eve is being met in the depths of her soul by Christ and is free to offer to others, free to desire, and willing to be disappointed. Fallen Eve has been wounded by others and withdraws in order to protect herself from further harm. Redeemed Eve knows that she has something of value to offer; that she is made for relationship. Therefore, being safe and secure in her relationship with her Lord, she can risk being vulnerable with others and offer her true self.

> To love at all is to be vulnerable. Love anything, and your heart will certainly be wrung and possibly broken. If you want to make sure of keeping it intact, you must give your heart to no one, not even to an animal. Wrap it carefully round with hobbies and little luxuries; avoid all entanglements; lock it up safe in the casket or coffin of your selfishness. But in that casket—safe, dark, motionless, airless—it will change. It will not be broken; it will become unbreakable, impenetrable, irredeemable . . . The only place outside Heaven where you can be perfectly safe from all the dangers . . . of love is Hell. (C. S. Lewis, *The Four Loves*)

> (*Captivating*, 181–82)

Every mythic story *shouts* to us that in this desperate hour *we have a crucial role to play.* This is an Eternal Truth, and it happens to be the one we most desperately need if we are ever to understand our days. For most of his life, Neo sees himself only as Thomas Anderson, a computer programmer for a large software corporation. As the drama really begins to heat up and the enemy hunts him down, he says to himself, "This is insane. Why is this happening to me? What did I do? I'm nobody. I didn't do anything." A very dangerous conviction . . . though one shared by most of you, my readers. What he later comes to realize—and not a moment too soon—is that he is "the One" who will break the power of the Matrix.

Frodo, the little Halfling from the Shire, young and naive in so many ways, "the most unlikely person imaginable," is the Ring Bearer. He, too, must learn through dangerous paths and fierce battles that a task has been appointed to him, and if he does not find a way, no one will. Dorothy is just a farm girl from Kansas, who stumbled into Oz not because she was looking for adventure but because someone had hurt her feelings and she decided to run away from home. Yet she's the one to bring down the Wicked Witch of the West. Joan of Arc was also a farm girl, illiterate, the youngest in her family, when she received her first vision from God. Just about everyone doubted her; the commander of the French army said she should be taken home and given a good whipping. Yet she ends up leading the armies in war.

You see this throughout Scripture: a little boy will slay the giant; a loudmouthed fisherman who can't hold down a job will lead the church; and a whore with a golden heart is the one to perform the deed that Jesus asked us all to tell "wherever the gospel is preached throughout the world" (Mark 14:9). Things are not what they seem. *We* are not what we seem.

(Waking the Dead, 32–33)

*I*n this desperate hour we have a crucial role to play. Of all the Eternal Truths we don't believe, this is the one we doubt most of all. Our days are not extraordinary. They are filled with the mundane, with hassles mostly. And we? We are . . . a dime a dozen. Nothing special really. Probably a disappointment to God. But as C. S. Lewis wrote, "The value of . . . myth is that it takes all the things we know and restores to them the rich significance which has been hidden by 'the veil of familiarity.'" You are not what you think you are. There is a glory to your life that your Enemy fears, and he is hell-bent on destroying that glory before you act on it. This part of the answer will sound unbelievable at first; perhaps it will sound too good to be true; certainly, you will wonder if it is true for you. But once you begin to see with those eyes, once you have begun to know it is true from the bottom of your heart, it will change everything.

The story of your life is the story of the long and brutal assault on your heart by the one who knows what you could be and fears it.

(*Waking the Dead,* 33–34)

Y ou will not think clearly about your life until you think
mythically. Until you see with the eyes of your heart.

About halfway through their journey—following a great deal of
hardship and facing a good deal more—Frodo's devoted friend
and servant, Sam Gamgee, wonders out loud: "I wonder what sort
of tale we've fallen into?" Sam is at that moment thinking mythically. He is wondering in the right way. His question assumes that
there *is* a story; there is something larger going on. He also assumes
that they have somehow tumbled into it; been swept up into it.
This is exactly what we've lost. Things happen to you. The car
breaks down, you have a fight with your spouse, or you suddenly
figure out how to fix a problem at work. What is *really* happening?
David Whyte says that we live our lives under a pale sky, "the lost
sense that we play out our lives as part of a greater story."

What sort of tale have I fallen into? is a question that would help
us all a great deal if we wondered it for ourselves. After my friend
Julie saw *The Fellowship of the Ring*, she turned to the girl with her
and whispered, "We've just gotten a clearer view of reality than we
usually see." Yes—that's the kind of "seeing" we need; that *is* our
reality. What grabbed me was the theatrical trailer for the film. In
a brilliantly crafted three-minute summary, the preview captures
the essential mythic elements of the story. As scene after scene
races before the eyes of the viewer, and a narrator describes the
tale, these lines cross the screen:

> Fate has chosen him.
> A Fellowship will protect him.
> Evil will hunt him.

(*Waking the Dead*, 34–35)

I know I am not alone in this nagging sense of failing to measure up, a feeling of not being good enough *as a woman*. Every woman I've ever met feels it—something deeper than just the sense of failing at what she does. An underlying, gut feeling of failing at who she *is*. *I am not enough*, and *I am too much* at the same time. Not pretty enough, not thin enough, not kind enough, not gracious enough, not disciplined enough. But too emotional, too needy, too sensitive, too strong, too opinionated, too messy. The result is Shame, the universal companion of women. It haunts us, nipping at our heels, feeding on our deepest fear that we will end up abandoned and alone.

After all, if we were better women—whatever *that* means—life wouldn't be so hard. Right? We wouldn't have so many struggles; there would be less sorrow in our hearts. Why is it so hard to create meaningful friendships and sustain them? Why do our days seem so unimportant, filled not with romance and adventure but with duties and demands? We feel *unseen*, even by those who are closest to us. We feel *unsought*—that no one has the passion or the courage to pursue us, to get past our messiness to find the woman deep inside. And we feel *uncertain*—uncertain what it even means to be a woman; uncertain what it truly means to be feminine; uncertain if we are or ever will be.

Aware of our deep failings, we pour contempt on our own hearts for wanting more. Oh, we long for intimacy and for adventure; we long to be the Beauty of some great story. But the desires set deep in our hearts seem like a luxury, granted only to those women who get their acts together. The message to the rest of us—whether from a driven culture or a driven church—is: *Try harder.*

(*Captivating,* 6–7)

Every man wants a battle to fight. It's the whole thing with boys and weapons.

And look at the movies men love—*Braveheart, Gladiator, Top Gun, High Noon, Saving Private Ryan.* Men are made for battle. (And ladies, don't you love the heroes of those movies? You might not want to fight in a war, but don't you long for a man who will fight for *you*? To have Daniel Day Lewis look you in the eyes and say, "No matter how long it takes, no matter how far, I will find you"? Women don't fear a man's strength if he is a good man.)

Men also long for adventure. Adventure is a deeply spiritual longing in the heart of every man. Adventure requires something of us, puts us to the test. Though we may fear the test, at the same time we yearn to be tested, to discover that we have what it takes.

Finally, every man longs for a Beauty to rescue. He really does. Where would Robin Hood be without Marian, or King Arthur without Guinevere? Lonely men fighting lonely battles. You see, it's not just that a man needs a battle to fight. He needs someone to fight *for*. There is nothing that inspires a man to courage so much as the woman he loves. Most of the daring (and okay, sometimes ridiculous) things young men do are to impress the girls. Men go to war carrying photos of their sweethearts in their wallets—that is a metaphor of this deeper longing to fight for the Beauty. This is not to say that a woman is a "helpless creature" who can't live her life without a man. I'm saying that men long to offer their strength on behalf of a woman.

Now—can you see how the desires of a man's heart and the desires of a woman's heart were at least *meant* to fit beautifully together? A woman in the presence of a good man, a real man, loves being a woman. His strength allows her feminine heart to flourish. His pursuit draws out her beauty. And a man in the presence of a real woman loves being a man. Her beauty arouses him to play the man; it draws out his strength. She inspires him to be a hero.

(*Captivating,* 17–18)

The new covenant has two parts to it: "I will give you a new heart and put a new spirit in you; I will remove from you your heart of stone and give you a heart of flesh" (Ezek. 36:26). God removed your old heart when he circumcised your heart; he gives you a new heart when he joins you to the life of Christ. That's why Paul can say "count yourselves dead to sin" *and* "alive to God in Christ Jesus" (Rom. 6:11).

> The story of the Incarnation is the story of a descent and resurrection . . . one has the picture of a diver, stripping off garment after garment, making himself naked, then flashing for a moment in the air, and then down through the green, and warm, and sunlit water into the pitch black, cold, freezing water, down into the mud and slime, then up again, his lungs almost bursting, back again to the green and warm and sunlit water, and then at last out into the sunshine, holding in his hand the dripping thing he went down to get. This thing is human nature. (C. S. Lewis, "The Grand Miracle")

The Resurrection affirms the promise Christ made. For it was *life* he offered to give us: "I have come that they may have life, and have it to the full" (John 10:10). We are saved by his life when we find that *we are able to live* the way we've always known we should live. We are free to be what he meant when he made us. You have a new life—the life of Christ. And you have a new heart. Do you know what this means? Your heart is good.

(*Waking the Dead*, 66–67)

"Do You Not Know That
Your Body Is a Temple
of the Holy Spirit?"

85

E ach person knows that now his *body* is the temple of God: "Do you not know that your body is a temple of the Holy Spirit, who is in you, whom you have received from God?" (1 Cor. 6:19). Indeed it is. "Don't you know that you yourselves are God's temple and that God's Spirit lives in you?" (1 Cor. 3:16). Okay—each of us is now the temple of God. So where, then, is the Holy of Holies?

Your heart.

That's right—your heart. Paul teaches us in Ephesians that "Christ may dwell in your hearts by faith" (3:17). God comes down to dwell in us, *in our hearts*. Now, we know this: God cannot dwell where there is evil. "You are not a God who takes pleasure in evil; with you the wicked cannot dwell" (Ps. 5:4). Something pretty dramatic must have happened in our hearts, then, to make them fit to be the dwelling place of a holy God.

Of course, none of this can happen for us until we give our lives back to God. We cannot know the joy or the life or the freedom of heart I've described here until we surrender our lives to Jesus and surrender them totally. Renouncing all the ways we have turned from God in our hearts, we forsake the idols we have worshiped and given our hearts over to. We turn, and give ourselves body, soul, and spirit back to God, asking him to cleanse our hearts and make them new.

(*Waking the Dead,* 68)

It's undeniable: the new covenant, accomplished through the work of Christ, means that we have new hearts. Our hearts *are* good. Or God's a liar.

Until we embrace that stunning truth, we will find it really hard to make decisions, because we can't trust what our hearts are saying. We'll have to be motivated by external pressure since we can't be motivated by our hearts. In fact, we won't find our calling, our place in God's kingdom, because that is written on our hearts' desires. We'll have a really hard time hearing God's voice in a deeply intimate way, because God speaks to us in our hearts. We'll live under guilt and shame for all sorts of evil thoughts and desires that the Enemy has convinced us were ours. God will seem aloof. Worship and prayer will feel like chores.

Of course, I just described the life most Christians feel doomed to live.

Now listen to Jesus:

> Each tree is recognized by its own fruit. People do not pick figs from thornbushes, or grapes from briers. *The good man brings good things out of the good stored up in his heart,* and the evil man brings evil things out of the evil stored up in his heart. (Luke 6:44–45, emphasis added)

Later, explaining the parable of the sower and the seed, Jesus says,

> The seed on good soil stands for those *with a noble and good heart,* who hear the word, retain it, and by persevering produce a crop. (Luke 8:15, emphasis added)

Jesus himself teaches that the heart can be good and even noble. That somebody is you, if you are his. God kept his promise. Our hearts have been circumcised to God. We have new hearts. Do you know what this means? Your heart is good. Let that sink in for a moment. Your heart is *good.*

What would happen if you believed it, if you came to the place where you *knew* it was true? Your life would never be the same. My friend Lynn got it, and that's when she exclaimed, "If we believed that . . . we could do *anything.* We would follow him *anywhere!*"

(*Waking the Dead,* 69–70)

God sets his own image on the earth. He creates a being like himself. He creates a son.

> The LORD God formed the man from the dust of the ground and breathed into his nostrils the breath of life, and the man became a living being. (Gen. 2:7)

It is nearing the end of the sixth day, the end of the Creator's great labor, as Adam steps forth, the image of God, the triumph of his work. He alone is pronounced the son of God. Nothing in creation even comes close. Picture Michelangelo's *David*. He is . . . magnificent. Truly, the masterpiece seems complete. And yet, the Master says that something is not good, not right. Something is missing . . . and that something is Eve.

> The Lord God cast a deep slumber on the human, and he slept, and He took one of his ribs and closed over the flesh where it had been, and the Lord God built the rib He had taken from the human into a woman and He brought her to the human. (Gen. 2:21–23 *Alter*)

She is the crescendo, the final, astonishing work of God. Woman. In one last flourish creation comes to a finish not with Adam, but with *Eve*. She is the Master's finishing touch. How we wish this were an illustrated book, and we could show you now some painting or sculpture that captures this, like the stunning Greek sculpture of the goddess Nike of Samothrace, the winged beauty, just alighting on the prow of a great ship, her beautiful form revealed through the thin veils that sweep around her. Eve is . . . breathtaking.

Given the way creation unfolds, how it builds to ever higher and higher works of art, can there be any doubt that Eve is the crown of creation? Not an afterthought. Not a nice addition like an ornament on a tree. She is God's final touch, his pièce de résistance. She fills a place in the world nothing and no one else can fill.

(*Captivating*, 24–25)

The vast desire and capacity a woman has for intimate relationships tells us of God's vast desire and capacity for intimate relationships. In fact, this may be *the* most important thing we ever learn about God—that he yearns for relationship with us. "Now this is eternal life: that they may know you, the only true God" (John 17:3). The whole story of the Bible is a love story between God and his people. He yearns for us. He *cares.* He has a tender heart.

> Zion said, "The LORD has forsaken me, the Lord has forgotten me." Can a mother forget the baby at her breast and have no compassion on the child she has borne? Though she may forget, I will not forget you! (Isa. 49:14–15)

> I will give them a heart to know me, that I am the LORD. They will be my people, and I will be their God, for they will return to me with all their heart. (Jer. 24:7)

> O Jerusalem, Jerusalem . . . how often I have longed to gather your children together, as a hen gathers her chicks under her wings, but you were not willing. (Matt. 23:37)

What a comfort to know that this universe we live in is relational at its core, that our God is a tenderhearted God who yearns for relationship with us. If you have any doubt about that, simply look at the message he sent us in Woman. Amazing. Not only does God long *for* us, but he longs to be loved *by* us. Oh, how we've missed this. How many of you see God as longing to be loved by you? We see him as strong and powerful, but not as needing us, vulnerable to us, yearning to be desired.

(Captivating, 28–29)

Every woman is in some way searching for or running from her beauty and every man is looking for or avoiding his strength. Why? In some deep place within, we remember what we were made to be, we carry with us the memory of gods, image-bearers walking in the Garden. So why do we flee our essence? As hard as it may be for us to see our sin, it is far harder still for us to remember our glory. The pain of the memory of our former glory is so excruciating, we would rather stay in the pigsty than return to our true home. We are like Gomer, wife of the prophet Hosea, who preferred to live in an adulterous affair rather than be restored to her true love.

We are the ones to be Fought Over, Captured and Rescued, Pursued. It seems remarkable, incredible, too good to be true. There really is something desirable within me, something the King of the universe has moved heaven and earth to get. George Herbert reached for words to express his wonder:

> My God, what is a heart
> That thou shouldst it so eye and woo
> Powering upon it with all thy art
> As if thou hadst nothing else to do? (*Mattens*)

King David used a similar refrain:

> What is man that you are mindful of him,
> the son of man that you care for him?
> You made him a little lower than the heavenly beings
> and crowned him with glory and honor. (Ps. 8:4–5)

(*The Sacred Romance,* 95–96)

O Living Flame of Love . . .
How gently and how lovingly
Thou wakest in my bosom,
Where alone thou secretly dwellest;
And in Thy sweet breathing
Full of grace and glory,
How tenderly Thou fillest me with Thy love.

These words, penned by St. John of the Cross in his book *Living Flame of Love*, capture the heart-cry of every soul for intimacy with God. For this we were created and for this we were rescued from sin and death. In Ephesians, Paul lets us in on a little secret: We've been more than noticed. God has pursued us from farther than space and longer ago than time. God has had us in mind since before the Foundations of the World. He loved us before the beginning of time, has come for us, and now calls us to journey toward him, with him, for the consummation of our love.

Who am I, really? The answer to that question is found in the answer to another: What is God's heart toward me, or, how do I affect him? If God is the Pursuer, the Ageless Romancer, the Lover, then there has to be a Beloved, one who is the Pursued. This is our role in the story.

In the end, all we've ever really wanted is to be loved. "Love comes from God," writes St. John. We don't have to get God to love us by doing something right—even loving him. "This is love: not that we loved God but that he loved us and sent his Son as an atoning sacrifice for our sins." Someone has noticed; someone has taken the initiative. There is nothing we need to do to keep it up, because his love for us is not based on what we've done, but who we are: His Beloved. "I belong to my lover, and his desire is for me" (Song 7:10).

(*The Sacred Romance*, 97–98)

Being unable to defeat God through raw power, Satan's legions decide to wound God as deeply as possible by stealing the love of his Beloved through seduction. And having "seduced them to his party," to ravish them body and soul; and having ravished them, to mock them even as they are hurled to the depths of hell with God himself unable to save them because of their rejection of him. This is Satan's motivation and goal for every man, woman, and child into whom God ever breathed the breath of life. Like a roaring lion, he "hungers" for us.

> Be self-controlled and alert. Your enemy the devil prowls around like a roaring lion looking for someone to devour. Resist him, standing firm in the faith, because you know that your brothers throughout the world are undergoing the same kind of sufferings. (1 Peter 5:8–9)

God could have given up on the love affair with mankind. He could have resorted to power and demanded our loyalty, or given us a kind of spiritual lobotomy that would take away our choice to love him. Even now, he could easily obliterate our Enemy and demand the allegiance of our hearts, but the love affair that began in the laughter of the Trinity would be over, at least for us. And Satan's accusation that the kingdom of God is established only through raw power would be vindicated.

(The Sacred Romance, 104–5)

Have you ever had to literally turn a lover over to a mortal enemy to allow her to find out for herself what his intentions toward her really were? Have you ever had to lie in bed knowing she was believing his lies and was having sex with him every night? Have you ever sat helplessly by in a parking lot, while your enemy and his friends took turns raping your lover even as you sat nearby, unable to win her heart enough so she would trust you to rescue her? Have you ever called this one you had loved for so long, even the day after her rape, and asked her if she was ready to come back to you only to have her say her heart was still captured by your enemy? Have you ever watched your lover's beauty slowly diminish and fade in a haze of alcohol, drugs, occult practices, and infant sacrifice until she is no longer recognizable in body or soul? Have you ever loved one so much that you even send your only son to talk with her about your love for her, knowing that he will be killed by her? (And in spite of knowing all of this, he was willing to do it because he loved her, too, and believed you were meant for each other.)

All this and more God has endured because of his refusal to stop loving us. Indeed, the very depth and faithfulness of his love for us, along with his desire for our freely given love in return, are what give Satan the ammunition to wound God so deeply as he carries out his unceasing campaign to make us into God's enemy.

(*The Sacred Romance*, 106)

A curious warning is given to us in Peter's first epistle. There he tells us to be ready to give the reason for the hope that lies within us to everyone who asks (3:15). Now, what's strange about that passage is this: no one ever asks. When was the last time someone stopped you to inquire about the reason for the hope that lies within you? You're at the market, say, in the frozen food section. A friend you haven't seen for some time comes up to you, grasps you by both shoulders and pleads, "Please, you've got to tell me. Be honest now. How can you live with such hope? Where does it come from? I must know the reason." In talking with hundreds of Christians, I've met only one or two who have experienced something like this.

Yet God tells us to be ready, so what's wrong? To be blunt, nothing about our lives is worth asking about. There's nothing intriguing about our hopes, nothing to make anyone curious. Not that we don't have hopes; we do. We hope we'll have enough after taxes this year to take a summer vacation. We hope our kids don't wreck the car. We hope our favorite team goes to the World Series. We hope our health doesn't give out, and so on. Nothing wrong with any of those hopes; nothing unusual, either. Everyone has hopes like that, so why bother asking us? It's life as usual. Sanctified resignation has become the new abiding place of contemporary Christians. No wonder nobody asks. Do *you* want the life of any Christian you know?

(*The Journey of Desire,* 64)

E ve is given to Adam as his *ezer kenegdo*—or as many trans-
lations have it, his "help meet" or "helper." Doesn't sound
like much, does it? It makes me think of Hamburger Helper. But
Robert Alter says this is "a notoriously difficult word to translate."
It means something far more powerful than just "helper"; it means
"lifesaver." The phrase is only used elsewhere of God, when you
need him to come through for you desperately. "There is no one
like the God of Jeshurun, who rides on the heavens to help you"
(Deut. 33:26). Eve is a life giver; she is Adam's ally. It is to *both* of
them that the charter for adventure is given. It will take both of
them to sustain life. And they will both need to fight together.

Eve is deceived . . . and rather easily, as my friend Jan Meyers
points out. In *The Allure of Hope,* Jan says, "Eve was convinced
that God was withholding something from her." Not even the
extravagance of Eden could convince her that God's heart is good.
"When Eve was [deceived], the artistry of being a woman took a
fateful dive into the barren places of control and loneliness." Now
every daughter of Eve wants to "control her surroundings, her relationships, her God." No longer is she vulnerable; now she will be
grasping. No longer does she want simply to share in the adventure; now she wants to control it. And as for her beauty, she either
hides it in fear and anger, or she uses it to secure her place in the
world. "In our fear that no one will speak on our behalf or protect
us or fight for us, we start to recreate both ourselves and our role
in the story. We manipulate our surroundings so we don't feel so
defenseless." Fallen Eve either becomes rigid or clingy. Put simply,
Eve is no longer simply *inviting.* She is either hiding in busyness
or demanding that Adam come through for her; usually, an odd
combination of both.

(*Wild at Heart,* 51–52)

I am here to tell you that you *can* get your heart back. But I need to warn you—if you want your heart back, if you want the wound healed and your strength restored and to find your true name, you're going to have to fight for it. Notice your reaction to my words. Does not something in you stir a little, a yearning to live? And doesn't another voice rush in, urging caution, maybe wanting to dismiss me altogether? *He's being melodramatic. What arrogance.* Or, *maybe some guys could, but not me.* Or, *I don't know . . . is this really worth it?* That's part of the battle, right there. See? I'm not making this up.

First and foremost, we still need to know what we never heard, or heard so badly, from our fathers. We *need to know* who we are and if we have what it takes. What do we do now with that ultimate question? Where do we go to find an answer? In order to help you find the answer to The Question, let me ask you another: What *have* you done with your question? Where have you taken it? You see, a man's core question does not go away. He may try for years to shove it out of his awareness, and just "get on with life." But it does not go away. It is a hunger so essential to our souls that it will compel us to find a resolution. In truth, it drives everything we do.

(*Wild at Heart,* 87–88)

YOUR DESPERATE HUNGER FOR VALIDATION

Why is pornography the most addictive thing in the universe for men? Certainly there's the fact that a man is visually wired, that pictures and images arouse men much more than they do women. But the deeper reason is because that seductive beauty reaches down inside and touches your desperate hunger for validation as a man you didn't even know you had, touches it like nothing else most men have ever experienced. You must understand—this is deeper than legs and breasts and good sex. It is mythological. Look at the lengths men will go to find the golden-haired woman. They have fought duels over her beauty; they have fought wars. You see, every man remembers Eve. We are haunted by her. And somehow we believe that if we could find her, get her back, then we'd also recover with her our own lost masculinity.

When a man takes his question to the woman, what happens is either addiction or emasculation. Usually both.

(*Wild at Heart*, 91−93)

If you'll recall, Moses put a veil over his face, first to hide his glory, then to hide the fact that it was fading away. That, too, was a picture of a deeper reality. We all do that. We all have veiled our glory, or someone has veiled it for us. Usually some combination of both. But the time has come to set all veils aside:

> Now if the ministry that brought death, which was engraved in letters on stone, came with glory, so that the Israelites could not look steadily at the face of Moses because of its glory, fading though it was, will not the ministry of the Spirit be even more glorious? . . . Therefore, since we have such a hope, we are very bold. We are not like Moses, who would put a veil over his face to keep the Israelites from gazing at it while the radiance was fading away . . . And we, who with unveiled faces all reflect the Lord's glory, are being transformed into his likeness with ever-increasing glory, which comes from the Lord, who is the Spirit. (2 Cor. 3:7–8, 12–13, 18)

We are in the process of being unveiled. Created to reflect God's glory, born to bear his image, he ransomed us back to reflect that glory again. Every heart was given a mythic glory, and that glory is being *restored*. Remember the mission of Christ: "I have come to give you back your heart and set you free." For as Saint Irenaeus said, "The glory of God is man fully alive." Certainly, you don't think the opposite is true. How do we bring God glory when we are sulking around in the cellar, weighed down by shame and guilt, hiding our light under a bushel? Our destiny is to come fully alive. To live with ever-*increasing* glory. This is the Third Eternal Truth every good myth has been trying to get across to us: *your heart bears a glory, and your glory is needed* . . . now. This is our desperate hour.

(*Waking the Dead*, 74–75)

Can there be any doubt that God wants to be sought after? The first and greatest of all commands is to love him (Mark 12:29–30; Matt. 22:36–38). He *wants* us to love him. To seek him with all our heart. A woman longs to be sought after, too, with the whole heart of her pursuer. God longs to be *desired*. Just as a woman longs to be desired. This is not some weakness or insecurity on the part of a woman, that deep yearning to be desired. God feels the same way. Remember the story of Martha and Mary? Mary chose God, and Jesus said *that* was what he wanted. "Mary has chosen what is better" (Luke 10:42). She chose me.

Life changes dramatically when romance comes into our lives. Christianity changes dramatically when we discover that it, too, is a great romance. That God yearns to share a life of beauty, intimacy, and adventure with us. "I have loved you with an everlasting love" (Jer. 31:3). This whole world was made for romance—the rivers and the glens, the meadows and the beaches. Flowers, music, a kiss. But we have a way of forgetting all that, losing ourselves in work and worry. Eve—God's message to the world in feminine form—invites us to romance. Through her, God makes romance a priority of the universe.

So God endows Woman with certain qualities that are essential to relationship, qualities that speak of God. She is inviting. She is vulnerable. She is tender. She embodies mercy. She is also fierce and fiercely devoted. As the old saying goes, "Hell hath no fury like a woman scorned." That's just how God acts when he isn't chosen. "I, the LORD your God, am a jealous God who will not share your affection with any other god!" (Ex. 20:5 NLT). A woman's righteous jealousy speaks of the jealousy of God for us.

Tender and inviting, intimate and alluring, fiercely devoted. Oh yes, our God has a passionate, romantic heart. Just look at Eve.

(Captivating, 29–30)

Beauty is powerful. It may be the most powerful thing on earth. It is dangerous. Because it *matters*. Let us try to explain why.

First, beauty *speaks*. Oxford bishop Richard Harries wrote, "It is the beauty of the created order which gives an answer to our questionings about God." And we do have questions, don't we? Questions born out of our disappointments, our sufferings, our fears. Augustine said he found answers to his questions in the beauty of the world:

> I said to all these things, "Tell me of my God who you are not, tell me something about him." And with a great voice they cried out: "He made us" (Ps. 99:3). My question was the attention I gave to them, and their response was their beauty.

And what does beauty say to us? Think of what it's like to be caught in traffic for more than an hour. Horns blaring, people shouting obscenities. Exhaust pouring in your windows, suffocating you. Then remember what it's like to come into a beautiful place, a garden or a meadow or a quiet beach. There is room for your soul. It expands. You can breathe again. You can rest. It is good. All is well. I sit outside on a summer evening and just listen and behold and drink it all in, and my heart begins to quiet and peace begins to come into my soul. My heart tells me that "all will be well," as Julian of Norwich concluded. "And all manner of things will be well."

That is what beauty says: *All shall be well.*

(*Captivating,* 37–38)

Beauty is *transcendent*. It is our most immediate experience of the eternal. Think of what it's like to behold a gorgeous sunset or the ocean at dawn. Remember the ending of a great story. We yearn to linger, to experience it all our days. Sometimes the beauty is so deep it pierces us with longing. For what? For life as it was meant to be. Beauty reminds us of an Eden we have never known, but somehow know our hearts were created for. Beauty speaks of heaven to come, when all shall be beautiful. It haunts us with eternity. Beauty says, *There is a glory calling to you.* And if there is a glory, there is a source of glory. What great goodness could have possibly created this? Beauty draws us to God.

All these things are true for any experience of Beauty. But they are *especially* true when we experience the beauty of a woman—her eyes, her form, her voice, her heart, her spirit, her life. She speaks all of this far more profoundly than anything else in all creation, because she is *incarnate*; she is personal. It flows to us from an immortal being. She is Beauty through and through.

Beauty is, without question, the most *essential* and the most *misunderstood* of all God's qualities—of all feminine qualities, too. We know it has caused untold pain in the lives of women. But even there something is speaking. Why so much heartache over beauty? We don't ache over being geniuses, or fabulous hockey players. Women ache over the issue of beauty—they ache to be beautiful, to believe they are beautiful, and they worry over keeping it if ever they can find it.

A woman knows, down in her soul, that she longs to bring beauty to the world. She might be mistaken on how (something every woman struggles with), but she longs for a beauty to unveil. This is not just culture, or the need to "get a man." This is in her heart, part of her design.

(Captivating, 40–41)

Indeed, part of God's victory over the enemy of our souls, which we will be invited to take part in, will be an open mocking of Satan and his forces in view of all the peoples of the earth along with the angelic hosts. We are given a picture of the enemy's defeat, which is the culmination of Act III of the Sacred Romance, by Isaiah:

> Those who see you stare at you [Satan], they ponder
>   your fate:
> "Is this the man who shook the earth
> and made kingdoms tremble,
> the man who made the world a desert,
> who overthrew its cities and would not let his captives
>   go home?" (14:16–17)

"You're the one we've been scared of all this time? You're the one we've been believing?" we will ask incredulously. And we will turn and walk away in the embrace of the Prince, never to speak Satan's name again. But in the meantime, our adversary will continue to use our Message of the Arrows, along with doubts about the goodness of the Prince, to lure us to spend our lives with less-wild lovers than God.

(*The Sacred Romance*, 121)

In the time of our innocence, we trusted in good because we had not yet known evil. On this side of Eden and our own experience of the Fall—whatever our own Arrows have been and however the adversary has woven them together into our particular Message of the Arrows—it appears that we are left to find our way to trust in good, having stared evil in the face.

Most of us remember the time of our innocence as a Haunting. I (Brent) mean innocence not as being sinless but as that time before our experience with the Arrows crystallized into a way of handling life which is the false self. The Haunting calls to us unexpectedly in the melody and words of certain songs that have become our "life music": the crooked smile of a friend; the laughter of our children (or their tears); the calling to mind of a mischievous face that still believed in joy; the smell of a perfume; the reading of a poem; or the hearing of a story. However the Haunting comes, it often brings with it a bittersweet poignancy of ache, the sense that we stood at a crossroads somewhere in the past and chose a turning that left some shining part of ourselves—perhaps the best part—behind, left it behind with the passion of youthful love, or the calling of a heart vocation, or simply in the sigh of coming to terms with the mundane requirements of life.

(*The Sacred Romance,* 123–25)

T he story of Eden is not over." Every day we reenact the Fall as we turn in our desire to the very things that will destroy us. As Gerald May reminds us,

> Addiction exists wherever persons are internally compelled to give energy to things that are not their true desires. To define it directly, addiction is a state of compulsion, obsession, or preoccupation that enslaves a person's will and desire. Addiction sidetracks and eclipses the energy of our deepest, truest desire for love and goodness. (*Addiction and Grace*)

Addiction may seem too strong a term to some of you. The woman who is serving so faithfully at church—surely, there's nothing wrong with that. And who can blame the man who stays long at the office to provide for his family? Sure, you may look forward to the next meal more than most people do, and your hobbies can be a nuisance sometimes, but to call any of this an addiction seems to stretch the word a bit too far.

I have one simple response: give it up. Let go of the things that provide you with a sense of security, or comfort, or excitement, or relief. You will soon discover the tentacles of attachment deep in your soul. There will be an anxiousness; you'll begin to think about work or food or golf even more. Withdrawal will set in. If you can make it a week or two out of sheer willpower, you will find a sadness growing in your soul, a deep sense of loss. Lethargy and a lack of motivation follow.

Remember, we will make an idol of anything, especially a good thing. So distant now from Eden, we are *desperate* for life, and we come to believe that we must arrange for it as best we can, or no one will. God must thwart us to save us.

(*The Journey of Desire,* 92–93)

God *promises* every man futility and failure; he *guarantees* every woman relational heartache and loneliness. We spend most of our waking hours attempting to end-run the curse. We will fight this truth with all we've got. Sure, other people suffer defeat. Other people face loneliness. But not me. I can beat the odds. We see the neighbor's kids go off the deep end, and we make a mental note: *They didn't pray for their kids every day.* And we make praying for our kids every day part of our plan. It doesn't have to happen to us. We watch a colleague suffer a financial setback, and we make another note: *He was always a little lax with his money.* We set up a rigid budget and stick to it.

Isn't there something defensive that rises up in you at the idea that you cannot make life work out? Isn't there something just a little bit stubborn, an inner voice that says, *I can do it?* Thus Pascal writes,

> All men seek happiness. This is without exception. Whatever different means they employ, they all tend to this end . . . This is the motive of every action of every man. *But example teaches us little.* No resemblance is ever so perfect that there is not some slight difference, and hence we expect that our hope will not be deceived on this occasion as before. And thus, while the present never satisfies us, experience dupes us and from misfortune to misfortune leads us to death. (*Pensées*)

It can't be done. No matter how hard we try, no matter how clever our plan, we cannot arrange for the life we desire. Set the book down for a moment and ask yourself this question: Will life ever be what I so deeply want it to be, in a way that cannot be lost? This is the second lesson we must learn, and in many ways the hardest to accept. We must have life; we cannot arrange for it.

(*The Journey of Desire,* 96–97)

I n this world you will have trouble." No kidding. Jesus, the master of understatement, captures in one sentence the story of our lives. He adds, "But take heart! I have overcome the world" (John 16:33). Why aren't we more encouraged? (Sometimes we'll try to *feel* encouraged when we hear a "religious" passage like this, but it never really lasts.) The reason is that we are still committed to arranging for life now. Be honest. Isn't there a disappointment when you realize that I'm not going to offer you the seven secrets of a really great life today? If I wanted to make millions, that's the book I would write. The only thing is, I would have to lie. It can't be done. Not *yet*. And that *yet* makes all the difference in the world, because desire cannot live without hope. But hope in what? *For* what?

> Set your hope *fully* on the grace to be given you when
> Jesus Christ is revealed. (1 Peter 1:13, emphasis added)

I read passages like this, and I don't know whether to laugh or to cry. Fully? We don't even set our hope *partially* on the life to come. Not really, not in the desires of our hearts. Heaven may be coming. Great. But it's a long way off and who really knows, so I'm getting what I can now. For most Christians, heaven is a backup plan. Our primary work is finding a life we can at least get a little pleasure from here. Heaven is an investment we've made, like Treasury bonds or a retirement account, which we're hoping will take care of us in the future sometime, but which we do not give much thought to at present.

(The Journey of Desire, 98–99)

| # There Comes a Time When You Have to Leave All That Is Familiar

The history of a man's relationship with God is the story of how God calls him out, takes him on a journey, and gives him his true name. Most of us have thought it was the story of how God sits on his throne waiting to whack a man broadside when he steps out of line. Not so. He created Adam for adventure, battle, and beauty; he created us for a unique place in his story and he is committed to bringing us back to the original design. So God calls Abram out from Ur of the Chaldeas to a land he has never seen, to the frontier, and along the way Abram gets a new name. He becomes Abraham. God takes Jacob off into Mesopotamia somewhere to learn things he has to learn and cannot learn at his mother's side. When he rides back into town, he has a limp and a new name as well.

Even if your father did his job, he can only take you partway. There comes a time when you have to leave all that is familiar and go on into the unknown with God.

Saul was a guy who really thought he understood the story and very much liked the part he had written for himself. He was the hero of his own little miniseries, *Saul the Avenger*. After that little matter on the Damascus road he becomes *Paul*; and rather than heading back into all of the old and familiar ways, he is led out into Arabia for three years to learn directly from God. Jesus shows us that initiation can happen even when we've lost our father or grandfather. He's the carpenter's son, which means Joseph was able to help him in the early days of his journey. But when we meet the young man Jesus, Joseph is out of the picture. Jesus has a new teacher—his true Father—and it is from him he must learn who he really is and what he's really made of.

(*Wild at Heart*, 103–4)

Most of us have been misinterpreting life and what God is doing for a long time. "I think I'm just trying to get God to make my life work easier," a client of mine confessed, but he could have been speaking for most of us. We're asking the wrong questions. Most of us are asking, "God, why did you let this happen to me?" Or, "God, why won't you just _____" (fill in the blank—help me succeed, get my kids to straighten out, fix my marriage—you know what you've been whining about). But to enter into a journey of initiation with God requires a new set of questions: What are you trying to teach me here? What issues in my heart are you trying to raise through this? What is it you want me to see? What are you asking me to let go of? In truth, God has been trying to initiate you for a long time. What is in the way is how you've mishandled your wound and the life you've constructed as a result.

"Men are taught over and over when they are boys that a wound that hurts is shameful," notes Robert Bly in *Iron John*. Like a man who's broken his leg in a marathon, he finishes the race even if he has to crawl and he doesn't say a word about it. A man's not supposed to get hurt; he's certainly not supposed to let it really matter. We've seen too many movies where the good guy takes an arrow, just breaks it off, and keeps on fighting; or maybe he gets shot but is still able to leap across a canyon and get the bad guys. And so most men minimize their wound. King David (a guy who's hardly a pushover) didn't act like that at all. "I am poor and needy," he confessed openly, "and my heart is wounded within me" (Ps. 109:22).

Or perhaps they'll admit it happened, but deny it was a wound because they deserved it. Suck it up, as the saying goes. The only thing more tragic than the tragedy that happens to us is the way we handle it.

(*Wild at Heart*, 104–6)

108 | WE HAVE NO IDEA WHO WE REALLY ARE

We have no idea who we really are. Whatever glory was bestowed, whatever glory is being restored, we thought this whole Christian thing was about . . . something else. Trying not to sin. Going to church. Being nice. Jesus says it is about healing your heart, setting it free, restoring your glory. A religious fog has tried to veil all that, put us under some sort of spell or amnesia, to keep us from coming alive. As Blaise Pascal said, "It is a monstrous thing . . . an incomprehensible enchantment, and a supernatural slumber." And, Paul said, it is time to take that veil away.

> When anyone turns to the Lord, the veil is taken away. Now the Lord is the Spirit, and where the Spirit of the Lord is, there is freedom. And we, who with unveiled faces all reflect the Lord's glory, are being transformed into his likeness with ever-increasing glory, which comes from the Lord, who is the Spirit. (2 Cor. 3:16–18)

A veil removed, bringing freedom, transformation, glory. Do you see it? I am not making this up—though I have been accused of making the gospel better than it is. The charge is laughable. Could anyone be more generous than God? Could any of us come up with a story that beats the one God has come up with?

(Waking the Dead, 80–81)

Then from on high—somewhere in the distance
There's a voice that calls—remember who you are.
If you lose yourself—your courage soon will follow.
(Gavin Greenaway and Trevor Horn, *Sound the Bugle*)

You are going to need your whole heart in all its glory for this Story you've fallen into. So, who did God mean when he meant you? We at least know this: we know that we are not what we were meant to be. Most of us spend our energy trying to hide that fact, through all the veils we put on and the false selves we create. Far better to spend our energy trying to recover the image of God and unveil it for his glory. One means that will help us is any story that helps us see with the eyes of the heart.

To live with an unmasked, unveiled glory that reflects the glory of the Lord? That's worth fighting for.

The disciples of Jesus were all characters. Take James and John, for instance, "the sons of Zebedee." You might remember them as the ones who cornered Jesus to angle for the choice seats at his right and left hands in the kingdom. Or the time they wanted to call down fire from heaven to destroy a village that wouldn't offer Jesus a place for the night. Their buddies called them idiots; Jesus called them the Sons of Thunder (Mark 3:17). He saw who they *really* were. It's their mythic name, their true identity. They looked like fishermen out of work; they were actually the Sons of Thunder.

(*Waking the Dead*, 82–83)

Our deepest fear is not that we are inadequate. Our deepest fear is that we are powerful beyond measure. It is our light, not our darkness, that most frightens us. We ask ourselves, "Who am I to be brilliant, gorgeous, talented and fabulous?" Actually, who are you not to be? You are a child of God. Your playing small doesn't serve the world. There's nothing enlightened about shrinking so that other people won't feel insecure around you. We were born to manifest the glory of God that is within us . . . And as we let our own light shine, we unconsciously give other people permission to do the same. As we are liberated from our own fear, our presence automatically liberates others. (Nelson Mandela)

When I first read this quote, I thought, *No, that's not true. We don't fear our glory.* We fear we are not glorious at all. We fear that at bottom, we are going to be revealed as . . . disappointments. Mandela is just trying to make a nice speech, like a sermon, to buoy us up for a day or two. But as I thought about it more, I realized we *do* fear our glory. We fear even heading this direction because, for one thing, it seems prideful. Now pride is a bad thing, to be sure, but it's not prideful to embrace the truth that you bear the image of God. Paul says it brings glory to God. We walk in humility because we know it is a glory *bestowed*. It reflects something of the Lord's glory.

(*Waking the Dead*, 87)

What have we come to accept as "discipleship"? A friend of mine recently handed me a program from a large and successful church somewhere in the Midwest. It's a rather exemplary model of what the idea has fallen to. Their plan for discipleship involves, first, becoming a member of this particular church. Then they encourage you to take a course on doctrine. Be "faithful" in attending the Sunday morning service and a small group fellowship. Complete a special course on Christian growth. Live a life that demonstrates clear evidence of spiritual growth. Complete a class on evangelism. Consistently look for opportunities to evangelize. Complete a course on finances, one on marriage, and another on parenting (provided that you are married or a parent). Complete a leadership training course, a hermeneutics course, a course on spiritual gifts, and another on biblical counseling. Participate in missions. Carry a significant local church ministry "load."

You're probably surprised that I would question this sort of program; most churches are trying to get their folks to complete something like this, one way or another. No doubt a great deal of helpful information is passed on. My goodness, you could earn an MBA with less effort. But let me ask you: A program like this—does it teach a person how to apply principles, or how to walk with God? They are not the same thing.

(*Waking the Dead*, 95–96)

We take folks through a discipleship program whereby they master any number of Christian precepts and miss the most important thing of all, the very thing for which we were created: intimacy with God. There are, after all, those troubling words Jesus spoke to those who were doing all the "right" things: "Then I will tell them plainly, 'I never knew you'" (Matt. 7:23). Knowing God. That's the point.

You might recall the old proverb: "Give a man a fish and you feed him for a day; teach a man to fish and you feed him for a lifetime." The same holds true here. Teach a man a rule and you help him solve a problem; teach a man to walk with God and you help him solve the rest of his life. Truth be told, you couldn't master enough principles to see yourself safely through this Story. There are too many surprises, ambiguities, exceptions to the rule. Things are hard at work—is it time to make a move? What *has* God called you to do with your life? Things are hard at home—is this just a phase your son is going through, or should you be more concerned? You can't seem to shake this depression—is it medical or something darker? What does the future hold for you—and how should you respond?

Only by walking with God can we hope to find the path that leads to life. *That* is what it means to be a disciple. After all—aren't we "followers of Christ"? Then by all means, let's actually follow him. Not ideas about him. Not just his principles. Him.

(*Waking the Dead*, 96–97)

All sorts of awful things can seem to issue from your heart—anger, lust, fear, petty jealousies. If you think it's you, a reflection of what's really going on in your heart, it will disable you. It could stop your journey dead in its tracks. What you've encountered is either the voice of your flesh or an attempt of the Enemy to distress you by throwing all sorts of thoughts your way and blaming you for it. You must proceed on this assumption: your heart is good. If it seems that some foul thing is at work there, say to yourself, *Well then—this is not my heart. My heart is good. I reject this.* Remember Paul in Romans 7? This is not me. *This is not me.* And carry on in your journey. Over time you'll grow familiar with the movements of your heart, and who is trying to influence you there.

We do the same with any counsel or word that presents itself as being from God, but contradicts what he has said to us in his written Word. We walk with wisdom and revelation. When I hear something that seems really unwise, I test it again and again before I launch out. The flesh will try to use your "freedom" to get you to do things you shouldn't do. And now that the Enemy knows you are trying to walk with God and tune in to your heart, he'll play the ventriloquist and try to deceive you there. Any "word" or suggestion that brings discouragement, condemnation, accusation—that is not from God. Neither is confusion, nor any counsel that would lead you to disobey what you do know. Reject it all, and carry on in your journey. Yes, of course, God needs to convict us of sin, warn us of wrong movements in the soul—but the voice of God is never condemning (Rom. 8:1), never harsh or accusing. His conviction brings a desire for repentance; Satan's accusation kills our hearts (2 Cor. 7:10).

(*Waking the Dead*, 105–6)

Our life is a story. A rather long and complicated story that has unfolded over time. There are many scenes, large and small, and many "firsts." Your first step; your first word; your first day of school. There was your first best friend; your first recital; your first date; your first love; your first kiss; your first heartbreak. If you stop and think of it, your heart has lived through quite a story thus far. And over the course of that story your heart has learned many things. Some of what you learned is true; much of it is not. Not when it comes to the core questions about your heart and the heart of God. Is your heart good? Does your heart really matter? What has life taught you about that? Imagine for a moment that God is walking softly beside you. You sense his presence, feel his warm breath. He says, "Tell me your sorrows." What would you say in reply?

"And I will ask the Father, and he will give you another Counselor to be with you forever—the Spirit of truth" (John 14:16–17). Come again? How would you feel if your spouse or a friend said to you, "I think you need some counseling, and so I've arranged for it. You start tomorrow; it'll probably take years"? I've got five bucks that says you'd get more than a little defensive. The combination of our pride—*I don't need any therapy, thank you very much*—and the fact that it's become a *profession*—Freud and Prozac and all that—has kept most of us from realizing that, in fact, we do need counseling. All of us. Jesus sends us his Spirit as Counselor; that ought to make it clear. In fact, we apparently need quite a lot of counsel—the Spirit isn't just stopping in to give us a tune-up; not even an annual checkup. He has come to stay.

(*Waking the Dead,* 112–13)

Remember, the purpose of this thing called the Christian life is that our hearts might be restored and set free. That's the deal. That's what Jesus came to do, by his own announcement. Jesus wants Life for us, Life with a capital *L*, and that Life comes to us through our hearts. But restoring and releasing the heart is no easy project. God doesn't just throw a switch and poof—it's done. He sends his Counselor to walk with us instead. That tells us it's going to be a *process*. All sorts of damage has been done to your heart over the years, all sorts of terrible things taken in—by sin, by those who should have known better, and by our Enemy, who seeks to steal and kill and destroy the image bearers of God. At best, "hope deferred makes the heart sick" (Prov. 13:12). Certainly there's been a bit of that in your life. "Even in laughter the heart may ache" (Prov. 14:13), which is to say, things may look fine on the outside, but inside it's another story.

We're told to "trust in the LORD" with all our hearts (Prov. 3:5), but frankly, we find it hard to do. Does trust come easily for you? I would *love* to trust God wholeheartedly. Why is it almost second nature to worry about things? We're told to love one another deeply, "from the heart" (1 Peter 1:22), but that's even more rare. Why is it so easy to get angry at, or to resent, or simply to grow indifferent toward the very people we once loved? The answers lie down in the heart. "For it is with your heart that you believe," Paul says (Rom. 10:10). And in Proverbs we read, "The heart of a man is like deep water, but a man of understanding draws it out" (20:5 NASB). Our deepest convictions—the ones that really shape our lives—they are down there somewhere in the depths of our hearts.

(Waking the Dead, 113)

Every great story involves a quest. In J. R. R. Tolkien's *The Hobbit*, Bilbo Baggins ran from the door at a quarter till eleven without even so much as a pocket handkerchief and launched on an adventure that would change his life forever. Alice stepped through the looking glass into Wonderland; Lucy, Edmund, Susan, and Peter stumbled through the wardrobe into Narnia. Abraham left his country, his people, and his father's household to follow the most outlandish sort of promise from a God he'd only just met, and he never came back. Jacob and his sons went to Egypt for some groceries and four hundred years later the Israel nation pulled up stakes and headed for home. Peter, Andrew, James, and John all turned on a dime one day to follow the Master, their fishing nets heaped in wet piles behind them. The Sacred Romance involves for every soul a journey of heroic proportions. And while it may require for some a change of geography, for every soul it means a journey of the heart.

The choice before us now is to journey or to homestead, to live like Abraham, the friend of God, or like Robinson Crusoe, the lost soul cobbling together some sort of existence with whatever he can salvage from the wreckage of the world. Crusoe was no pilgrim; he was a survivor, hunkered down for the duration. He lived in a very, very small world where he was the lead character and all else found its focus in him. Of course, to be fair, Crusoe was stranded on an island with little hope of rescue. We *have* been rescued, but still the choice is ours to stay in our small stories, clutching our household gods and false lovers, or to run in search of life.

(*The Sacred Romance*, 143–44)

Entering into the Sacred Romance begins with eyes to see and ears to hear. Where would we be today if Eve had looked at the serpent with different eyes, if she had seen at once that the beautiful creature with the charming voice and the reasonable proposition was in fact a fallen angel bent on the annihilation of the human race? Failure to see things as they truly are resulted in unspeakable tragedy. From that point on, the theme of blindness runs throughout Scripture. It's not merely a matter of failing to recognize temptation when we meet it; like Elisha's servant, we often fail to see the drama of redemption as well (2 Kings 6:15–17).

Needless to say, Elisha's servant suddenly saw from a whole different perspective. I (John) think it's safe to assume he also experienced a bit of emotional relief—a recovery of heart. What for him had undoubtedly been a harrowing encounter became an exciting adventure.

The apostle Paul experienced an even greater surprise on the road to Damascus. Thinking he was doing God a favor, he was hell-bent on crushing a tiny religious movement called the Way. But he had the plot and the characters completely confused. Paul, known at that time as Saul, was playing the role of Defender of the Faith, when in fact he was Persecutor of Christ. It took a bout of blindness to bring things into focus, and when the scales fell from his eyes, he never saw things the same way again. Paul later explained to the Romans that human sin and suffering are the result of foolish and darkened hearts, brought on by a refusal to see the Sacred Romance. It should come as no surprise that his most fervent prayer for the saints was that the scales would fall from the eyes of our hearts so that we might not miss the Sacred Romance (Eph. 1:18–19).

(The Sacred Romance, 145–46)

| # We Are Faced with a Decision That Grows with Urgency

We are faced with a decision that grows with urgency each passing day: Will we leave our small stories behind and venture forth to follow our Beloved into the Sacred Romance? The choice to become a pilgrim of the heart can happen any day and we can begin our journey from any place. We are here, the time is now, and the Romance is always unfolding. The choice before us is not to make it happen. As G.K. Chesterton said, "An adventure is, by its nature, a thing that comes to us. It is a thing that chooses us, not a thing that we choose." Lucy wasn't looking for Narnia when she found it on the other side of the wardrobe; in a way, it found her. Abraham wasn't wandering about looking for the one true God; he showed up with an extraordinary invitation. But having had their encounters, both could have chosen otherwise. Lucy could have shut the wardrobe door and never mentioned what had happened there. Abraham could have opted for life in Haran. The choice before us is a choice to *enter in*.

(*The Sacred Romance*, 148–49)

So much of the journey forward involves a letting go of all that once brought us life. We turn away from the familiar abiding places of the heart, the false selves we have lived out, the strengths we have used to make a place for ourselves and all our false loves, and we venture forth in our hearts to trace the steps of the One who said, "Follow me." In a way, it means that we stop *pretending*: that life is better than it is, that we are happier than we are, that the false selves we present to the world are really us. We respond to the Haunting, the wooing, the longing for another life. Pilgrim begins his adventure toward redemption with a twofold turning: a turning *away* from attachment and a turning *toward* desire. He wanted life and so he stuck his fingers in his ears and ran like a madman ("a fool," to use Paul's term) in search of it. The freedom of heart needed to journey comes in the form of detachment. As Gerald May writes in *Addiction and Grace,*

> *Detachment* is the word used in spiritual traditions to describe freedom of desire. Not freedom *from* desire, but freedom *of* desire . . . An authentic spiritual understanding of detachment devalues neither desire nor the objects of desire. Instead, it "aims at correcting one's own anxious grasping in order to free oneself for committed relationship to God." According to Meister Eckhart, detachment "enkindles the heart, awakens the spirit, stimulates our longings, and shows us where God is."

With an awakened heart, we turn and face the road ahead, knowing that no one can take the trip for us, nor can anyone plan our way.

(*The Sacred Romance,* 149)

We shall not cease from exploration
And the end of all our exploring
Will be to arrive where we started
And know the place for the first time. (T. S. Eliot)

Look, I am making all things new! (Jesus of Nazareth)

See! The winter is past; the rains are over and gone.
Flowers appear on the earth; the season of singing has
come. (Song 2:11–12)

I was walking in the woods and fields behind our house one evening four months after Brent's death. My heart was so aware of the loss—not only of Brent, but in some ways, of everything that mattered. I knew that one by one, I would lose everyone I cared about and the life I am still seeking. In the east, a full moon was rising, bright and beautiful and enormous as it seems when it is just above the horizon. Toward the west, the clouds were turning peach and pink against a topaz sky. Telling myself to long for eternity feels like telling myself to let go of all I love—forever. It feels like accepting the teaching of Eastern religions, a *denial* of life and all God created. We lose it all too soon, before we can even begin to live and love. But what if? What if nature is speaking to us? What if sunrise and sunset tell the tale every day, remembering Eden's glory, prophesying Eden's return? What if it shall all be restored?

(*The Journey of Desire*, 107–8)

"A bove all else, guard your heart." We usually hear this with a sense of "Keep an eye on that heart of yours," in the way you'd warn a deputy watching over some dangerous outlaw, or a bad dog the neighbors let run. "Don't let him out of your sight." Having so long believed our hearts are evil, we assume the warning is to keep us out of trouble. So we lock up our hearts and throw away the key and then try to get on with our living. But that isn't the spirit of the command at all. It doesn't say guard your heart because it's criminal; it says guard your heart because it is the wellspring of your life, because it is a *treasure*, because everything else depends on it. How kind of God to give us this warning, like someone's entrusting to a friend something precious to him, with the words: "Be careful with this—it means a lot to me."

Above all else? Good grief—we don't even do it once in a while. We might as well leave our life savings on the seat of the car with the windows rolled down—we're that careless with our hearts. "If not for my careless heart," sang Roy Orbison, and it might be the anthem for our lives. Things would be different. I would be farther along. My faith would be much deeper. My relationships so much better. My life would be on the path God meant for me . . . if not for my careless heart. We live completely backward. "All else" is above our hearts. I'll wager that caring for your heart isn't even a category you think in. "Let's see—I've got to get the kids to soccer, the car needs to be dropped off at the shop, and I need to take a couple of hours for *my heart* this week." It probably sounds unbiblical, even after all we've covered.

Seriously now—what do you do on a daily basis to care for your heart? Okay, that wasn't fair. How about weekly? *Monthly?*

(*Waking the Dead,* 207–8)

Winter tarries long at six thousand feet. Here in the Rocky Mountains, spring comes late and fitfully. We had snow again last week—the second week in May. I've come to accept that spring here is really a wrestling match between winter and summer. It makes for a long time of waiting. You see, the flowers are pretty much gone in September. The first of October, the aspens start turning gold and drop their leaves in a week or two. Come November, all is gray. Initially, I don't mind. The coming of winter has its joys, and there are Thanksgiving and Christmastime to look forward to.

But after the new year, things begin to drag on. Through February and then March, the earth remains lifeless. The whole world lies shadowed in brown and gray tones, like an old photograph. Winter's novelty is long past, and by April we are longing for some sign of life—some color, some hope. It's too long.

And then, just this afternoon, I rounded the corner into our neighborhood, and suddenly, the world was green again. What had been rock and twig and dead mulch was a rich oriental carpet of green. I was shocked, stunned. How did it happen? As if in disbelief, I got out of my car and began to walk through the woods, touching every leaf. The birds are back as well, waking us in the morning with their glad songs. It happened suddenly. In the twinkling of an eye.

My surprise is telling. It seems natural to long for spring; it is another thing to be completely stunned by its return. I am truly and genuinely surprised, as if my reaction were, *Really? What are you doing here?* And then I realized, *I thought I'd never see you again.* I think in some deep place inside, I had accepted the fact that winter is what is really true . . . And so I am shocked by the return of spring. And I wonder, *Can the same thing happen for my soul?*

(*The Journey of Desire,* 108–9)

Can it really happen? Can things in our lives be green again? No matter what our creeds may tell us, our hearts have settled into another belief. We have accepted the winter of this world as the final word and tried to get on without the hope of spring. *It will never come*, we have assumed, *and so I must find whatever life here I can.* We have been so committed to arranging for our happiness that we have missed the signs of spring. We haven't given any serious thought to what might be around the corner. Were eternity to appear tomorrow, we would be as shocked as I have been with the return of spring this week, only more so. Our practical agnosticism would be revealed. Pascal declared,

> Our imagination so powerfully magnifies time, by continual reflections upon it, and so diminishes eternity . . . for want of reflection, that we make a nothing of eternity and an eternity of nothing.

But of course we aspire to happiness we can enjoy now. Our hearts have no place else to go. We have made a nothing of eternity. If I told you that your income would triple next year, and that European vacation you've wanted is just around the corner, you'd be excited, hopeful. The future would look promising. It seems possible, *desirable.* But our ideas of heaven, while possible, aren't all that desirable. Whatever it is we think is coming in the next season of our existence, we don't think it is worth getting all that excited about. We make a nothing of eternity by enlarging the significance of this life and by diminishing the reality of what the next life is all about.

(*The Journey of Desire*, 110–11)

Forever and ever? That's it? That's the "good news"? And then we sigh and feel guilty that we are not more "spiritual." We lose heart, and we turn once more to the present to find what life we can. Eternity ends up having no bearing on our search for life whatsoever. It feels like the end of the search. And since we're not all that sure about what comes after, we search hard now. Remember, *we can only hope for what we desire.* How can the church service that never ends be more desirable than the richest experiences of life here? It would be no small difference if you knew in your heart that the life you prize is just around the corner, that your deepest desires have been whispering to you all along about what's coming. You see, Scripture tells us that God has "set eternity" in our hearts (Eccl. 3:11). Where in our hearts? In our *desires.*

The return of spring brings such relief and joy and anticipation. Life has returned, and with it sunshine, warmth, color, and the long summer days of adventure together. We break out the lawn chairs and the barbecue grill. We tend the garden and drink in all the beauty. We head off for vacations. Isn't this what we most deeply long for? To leave the winter of the world behind, what Shakespeare called "the winter of our discontent," and find ourselves suddenly in the open meadows of summer?

(*The Journey of Desire,* 111)

I n heaven, things are not stained or broken; everything is as it was meant to be. Think for a moment of the wonder of this. Isn't every one of our sorrows on earth the result of things *not* being as they were meant to be? And so when the kingdom of God comes to earth, wonderful things begin to unfold. Look at the evidence; watch what happens to people as they are touched by the kingdom of God through Jesus. As he went about "preaching the good news of the kingdom," Jesus was also "healing every disease and sickness among the people" (Matt. 4:23). When he "spoke to them about the kingdom of God," he "healed those who needed healing" (Luke 9:11).

What happens when we find ourselves in the kingdom of God? The disabled jump to their feet and start doing a jig. The deaf go out and buy themselves stereo equipment. The blind are headed to the movies. The dead are not at all dead anymore, but very much alive. They show up for dinner. In other words, human brokenness in all its forms is healed. The kingdom of God brings *restoration.* Life is restored to what it was meant to be. "In the beginning," back in Eden, all of creation was pronounced good because all of creation was exactly as God meant for it to be. For it to be good again is not for it to be destroyed, but healed, renewed, brought back to its goodness.

Those glimpses we see in the miracles of Jesus were the firstfruits. When he announces the full coming of the kingdom, Jesus says, "Look, I am making *all things* new!" (Rev. 21:5 NLT, emphasis added). He does not say, "I am making all new things." He means that the things that have been so badly broken will be restored and then some. "You mean I'll get a new pair of glasses?" my son Sam asked. "Or do you mean I'll get a new pair of eyes, so I won't need glasses?" What do you think? Jesus didn't hand out crutches to help the disabled.

(The Journey of Desire, 113–14)

When the Bible tells us that Christ came to "redeem mankind" it offers a whole lot more than forgiveness. To simply forgive a broken man is like telling someone running a marathon, "It's okay that you've broken your leg. I won't hold that against you. Now finish the race." That would be cruel, to leave him disabled that way. No, there is much more to our redemption. The core of Christ's mission is foretold in Isaiah 61:

> The Spirit of the Sovereign LORD is on me,
> because the LORD has anointed me
> to preach good news to the poor.
> He has sent me to bind up the brokenhearted,
> to proclaim freedom for the captives
> and release from darkness for the prisoners. (v. 1)

The Messiah will come, he says, to bind up and heal, to release and set free. What? *Your heart.* Christ comes to restore and release you, your soul, the true you. This is *the* central passage in the entire Bible about Jesus, the one he chooses to quote about himself when he steps into the spotlight in Luke 4 and announces his arrival. So take him at his word—ask him in to heal all the broken places within you and unite them into one whole and healed heart. Ask him to release you from all bondage and captivity, as he promised to do. As George MacDonald prayed, "Gather my broken fragments to a whole . . . Let mine be a merry, all-receiving heart, but make it a whole, with light in every part." But you can't do this at a distance; you can't ask Christ to come into your wound while you remain far from it. You have to go there with him.

(*Wild at Heart,* 128–29)

Abiding in the love of God is our only hope, the only true home for our hearts. It's not that we mentally acknowledge that God loves us. It's that we let our hearts come home to him, and stay in his love. MacDonald says it this way:

> When our hearts turn to him, that is opening the door to him . . . then he comes in, not by our thought only, not in our idea only, but he comes himself, and of his own will. Thus the Lord, the Spirit, becomes the soul of our souls . . . Then indeed we *are*; then indeed we have life; the life of Jesus has . . . become life in us . . . we are one with God forever and ever. (*The Heart of George MacDonald*)

Or as St. John of the Cross echoes,

> O how gently and how lovingly dost thou lie awake in the depth and centre of my soul, where thou in secret and in silence alone, as its sole Lord, abidest, not only as in Thine own house or in Thine own chamber, but also as within my own bosom, in close and intimate union. (*Living Flame of Love*)

This deep intimate union with Jesus and with his Father is the source of all our healing and all our strength. It is, as Leanne Payne says, "the central and unique truth of Christianity."

(*Wild at Heart*, 130–31)

The devil no doubt has a place in our theology, but is he a category we even think about in the daily events of our lives? Has it ever crossed your mind that not every thought that crosses your mind comes from you? We are being lied to all the time. Yet we never stop to say, "Wait a minute . . . who else is speaking here? Where are those ideas coming from? Where are those *feelings* coming from?" If you read the saints from every age before the Modern Era—that pride-filled age of reason, science, and technology we all were thoroughly educated in—you'll find that they take the devil very seriously indeed. As Paul says, "We are not unaware of his schemes" (2 Cor. 2:11). But we, the enlightened, have a much more commonsense approach to things. We look for a psychological or physical or even political explanation for every trouble we meet.

Who caused the Chaldeans to steal Job's herds and kill his servants? Satan, clearly (Job 1:12, 17). Yet do we even give him a passing thought when we hear of terrorism today? Who kept that poor woman bent over for eighteen years, the one Jesus healed on the Sabbath? Satan, clearly (Luke 13:16). But do we consider him when we are having a headache that keeps us from praying or reading Scripture? Who moved Ananias and Sapphira to lie to the apostles? Satan again (Acts 5:3). But do we really see his hand behind a fallout or schism in ministry? Who was behind that brutal assault on your own strength, those wounds you've taken? As William Gurnall said, "It is the image of God reflected in you that so enrages hell; it is this at which the demons hurl their mightiest weapons."

There is a whole lot more going on behind the scenes of our lives than most of us have been led to believe.

(*Wild at Heart*, 152–53)

As far as I know," wrote Frederick Buechner in *Telling the Truth: The Gospel as Tragedy, Comedy, and Fairy Tale,* "there has never been an age that has not produced fairy tales." There is something deeply true about a fairy tale. It is a timeless form of storytelling because it captures a timeless story. Fairy tales employ universal symbolism that captures both our deepest fears and our highest hopes. They help us understand the meaning of life in a way nothing else does. Buechner added,

> Maybe the first thing to say is that it is a world full of darkness and danger and ambiguity . . . There are fierce dragons who guard the treasure and wicked fairies who show up at royal christenings. To take the wrong turning of the path is to risk being lost in the forest forever, and an awful price has to be paid for choosing the wrong casket or the wrong door. It is a world of dark and dangerous quest where the suitors compete for the hand of the king's daughter with death to the losers, or the young prince searches for the princess who has slept for a hundred years, or the scarecrow, the tin man, and the lion travel many a mile in search of the wizard who will make them whole, and all of them encounter on their way great perils that are all the more perilous because they are seldom seen for what they are.
>
> Good and evil meet and do battle in the fairy-tale world much as they meet and do battle in our world, but in fairy tales the good live happily ever after. That is the major difference.

(*The Sacred Romance Workbook & Journal,* 62–63)

> Be strong and courageous, because you will lead these people to inherit the land I swore to their forefathers to give them. Be strong and very courageous . . . Have I not commanded you? Be strong and courageous. Do not be terrified; do not be discouraged, for the LORD your God will be with you wherever you go. (Josh. 1:6–7, 9)

Joshua knew what it was to be afraid. For years he had been second in command, Moses' right-hand man. But now it was his turn to lead. The children of Israel weren't just going to waltz in and pick up the Promised Land like a quart of milk; they were going to have to fight for it. And Moses was not going with them. If Joshua was completely confident about the situation, why would God have had to tell him over and over and over again not to be afraid? In fact, God gives him a special word of encouragement: "As I was with Moses, so I will be with you; I will never leave you nor forsake you" (Josh. 1:5). How was God "with Moses"? As a mighty warrior. Remember the plagues? Remember all those Egyptian soldiers drowned with their horses and chariots out there in the Red Sea? It was after that display of God's strength that the people of Israel sang, "The LORD is a warrior; the LORD is his name" (Ex. 15:3). God fought for Moses and for Israel; then he covenanted to Joshua to do the same, and they took down Jericho and every other enemy.

(*Wild at Heart*, 167)

The most dangerous man on earth is the man who has reck-
oned with his own death. All men die; few men ever really
live. Sure, you can create a safe life for yourself . . . and end your
days in a rest home babbling on about some forgotten misfortune.
I'd rather go down swinging. Besides, the less we are trying to "save
ourselves," the more effective a warrior we will be. Listen to G. K.
Chesterton on courage:

> Courage is almost a contradiction in terms. It means
> a strong desire to live taking the form of a readiness to
> die. "He that will lose his life, the same shall save it"
> is not a piece of mysticism for saints and heroes. It is
> a piece of everyday advice for sailors or mountaineers.
> It might be printed in an Alpine guide or a drill book.
> The paradox is the whole principle of courage; even of
> quite earthly or quite brutal courage. A man cut off by
> the sea may save his life if he will risk it on the
> precipice. He can only get away from death by con-
> tinually stepping within an inch of it. A soldier sur-
> rounded by enemies, if he is to cut his way out, needs
> to combine a strong desire for living with a strange
> carelessness about dying. He must not merely cling to
> life, for then he will be a coward, and will not escape.
> He must not merely wait for death, for then he will be
> a suicide, and will not escape. He must seek his life in
> a spirit of furious indifference to it; he must desire life
> like water and yet drink death like wine.

(*Wild at Heart,* 169)

He heals the brokenhearted and binds up their wounds.
(Ps. 147:3)

Yes, we have all been wounded in this battle. And we will be wounded again. But something deeper has also happened to us than mere wounds.

I expect that all of us at one time or another have said, "Well, part of me wants to, and another part of me doesn't." You know the feeling—part of you pulled one direction, part of you the other. Part of me loves writing and genuinely looks forward to a day at my desk. But not all of me. Sometimes I'm also afraid of it. Part of me fears that I will fail—that I am simply stating what is painfully obvious, or saying something vital but incoherent. I'm drawn to it, and I also feel ambivalent about it. Come to think of it, I feel that way about a lot of things. Part of me wants to go ahead and dive into friendship, take the risk. I'm tired of living alone. Another part says, *Stay away—you'll get hurt. Nobody really cares anyway.* Part of me says, *Wow! Maybe God really is going to come through for me.* Another voice rises up and says, *You are on your own.*

Don't you feel sometimes like a house divided?

Take your little phobias. Why are you afraid of heights or intimacy or public speaking? All the discipline in the world wouldn't get you to go skydiving, share something really personal in a small group, or take the pulpit next Sunday. Why do you hate it when people touch you or criticize you? And what about those little "idiosyncrasies" you can't give up to save your life? Why do you bite your nails? Why do you work so many hours? Why do you get irritated at these questions? You won't go out unless your makeup is perfect—why is that? Other women don't mind being seen in their grubbies. Something in you "freezes" when your dad calls— what's that all about? You clean and organize; you demand perfection—did you ever wonder *why?*

(*Waking the Dead,* 128–30)

There is a civil war waged between the new heart and the old nature. Romans 7–8 describes it quite well. Part of me doesn't want to love my neighbor—not when his son just backed his car into my Jeep and smashed it up. I want to take the little brat to court. Part of me knows that prayer is essential; another part of me would rather turn on the TV and check out. And that whole bit about long-suffering—no way. Part of me wants to just get drunk. And that is the part I must crucify daily, give no ground to, make no alliance with. It's not the true me (Rom. 7:22). It's my battle with the flesh. We all know that battle well. But that is not what I'm wanting to explore here.

No, there's something else we are describing when we say, "Well, part of me wants to and part of me doesn't." It's more than a figure of speech. We might not know it, but something really significant is being revealed in those remarks. There are these places that we cannot seem to get beyond. Everything is going along just fine, and then—boom. Something suddenly brings you to tears or makes you furious, depressed, or anxious, and you cannot say why. I'll tell you why.

We are not wholehearted.

(*Waking the Dead*, 130)

When Isaiah promised that the Messiah will come to heal the brokenhearted, he was not speaking poetically. The Bible does use metaphor, as when Jesus says, "I am the gate" (John 10:9). Of course, he is not an *actual* gate like the kind you slammed yesterday; he has no hinges on his body, no knob you turn. He is using metaphor. But when Isaiah talks about the brokenhearted, God is not using metaphor. The Hebrew is *leb shabar* (*leb* for "heart," *shabar* for "broken"). Isaiah uses the word *shabar* to describe a bush whose "twigs are dry, they are broken off" (27:11); to describe the idols of Babylon lying "shattered on the ground" (21:9), as a statue shatters into a thousand pieces when you knock it off the table; or to describe a broken bone (38:13). God is speaking literally here. He says, "Your heart is now in many pieces. I want to heal it."

The heart can be broken—literally. Just like a branch or a statue or a bone. Can you name any precious thing that *can't?* Certainly, we've seen that the mind can be broken—or what are all those mental institutions for? Most of the wandering, muttering "homeless" people pushing a shopping cart along have a broken mind. The will can be broken too. Have you seen photos of concentration camp prisoners? Their eyes are cast down; something in them is defeated. They will do whatever they are told. But somehow we have overlooked the fact that this treasure called the heart can also be broken, *has* been broken, and now lies in pieces down under the surface. When it comes to "habits" we cannot quit or patterns we cannot stop, anger that flies out of nowhere, fears we cannot overcome, or weaknesses we hate to admit—much of what troubles us comes out of the broken places in our hearts crying out for relief.

Jesus speaks as though we are all the brokenhearted. We would do well to trust his perspective on this.

(*Waking the Dead,* 131–34)

Okay . . . I know this whole question of "what has God promised us in *this* life?" is fraught with problems. It's a question that's got heresy on both sides. So, let me make a few things clear:

I am not advocating a "name it and claim it" theology, whereby we can have anything and everything we want if we just claim it in Jesus' name. After all, Jesus said, "In this world you will have trouble" (John 16:33).

Nor am I advocating a "prosperity" doctrine that claims God wants everyone to be rich and healthy. "The poor you will always have with you" (Matt. 26:11).

What I *am* saying is that Christ does not put his offer of Life to us totally in the future. That's the other mistake. "'I tell you the truth,' Jesus said to them, 'no one who has left home or wife or brothers or parents or children for the sake of the kingdom of God will fail to receive many times as much *in this age* and, in the age to come, eternal life'" (Luke 18:29–30, emphasis added).

Jesus doesn't locate his offer to us only in some distant future, after we've slogged our way through our days here on earth. He talks about a life available to us *in this age*. So does Paul: "Godliness has value for all things, holding promise *for both the present life* and the life to come" (1 Tim. 4:8, emphasis added).

There is a Life available to us now. Let's find it.

(*A Guidebook to Waking the Dead,* 13)

One of the deepest ways a woman bears the image of God is in her mystery. By mystery we don't mean "forever beyond your knowing," but "something to be explored." "It is the glory of God to conceal a matter," says the book of Proverbs, "to search out a matter is the glory of kings" (25:2). God yearns to be known. But he wants to be *sought after* by those who would know him. He says, "You will seek me and find me when you seek me with all your heart" (Jer. 29:13). There is dignity here; God does not throw himself at any passerby. He is no harlot. If you would know him you must love him; you must seek him with your whole heart. This is crucial to any woman's soul, not to mention her sexuality. "You cannot simply have me. You must seek me, pursue me. I won't let you in unless I know you love me."

Is not the Trinity a great mystery? Not something to be solved, but to be known with ever-deepening pleasure and awe, something to be enjoyed. Just like God, a woman is not a problem to be solved, but a vast wonder to be enjoyed. This is so true of her sexuality. Few women can or even want to "just do it." Foreplay is crucial to her heart, the whispering and loving and exploring of each other that culminates in intercourse. That is a picture of what it means to love her *soul.* She yearns to be known, and that takes time and intimacy. It requires an unveiling. As she is sought after, she reveals more of her beauty. As she unveils her beauty, she draws us to know her more deeply.

Whatever else it means to be feminine, it is depth and mystery and complexity, with beauty as the very essence.

Every woman has a beauty to unveil.

Every woman.

(*Captivating,* 41–42)

L ife on the road takes us into our heart, for *only when we are present in the deep sentences can God speak to them*. That's why the Story is a journey; it has to be lived, it cannot simply be talked about. When we face trials, our most common reaction is to ask God, "Why won't you relieve us?" And when he doesn't, we resignedly ask, "What do you want me to do?" Now we have a new question: "Where is the Romance headed?"

There is another great "revealing" in our life on the road. We run our race, we travel our journey, in the words of Hebrews, before "a great cloud of witnesses" (12:1). When we face a decision to fall back or press on, the whole universe holds its breath—angels, demons, our friends and foes, and the Trinity itself—watching with bated breath to see what we will do. We are still in the drama of Act III and the heart of God is still on trial. The question that lingers from the fall of Satan and the fall of man remains: Will anyone trust the great heart of the Father, or will we shrink back in faithless fear?

As we grow into the love of God and the freedom of our own hearts, we grow in our ability to cast our vote on behalf of God. Our acts of love and sacrifice, the little decisions to leave our false loves behind, and the great struggles of our heart reveal to the world our true identity: We really are the sons and daughters of God.

(*The Sacred Romance*, 154–55)

I t's better to stay in the safety of the camp than venture forth on a wing and a prayer. Who knows what dangers lie ahead? This was the counsel of the ten faithless spies sent in to have a look at the Promised Land when the Jews came out of Egypt. Only two of the twelve, Joshua and Caleb, saw things differently. Their hearts were captured by a vision of what might be and they urged the people to press on. But their voices were drowned by the fears of the other ten spies and Israel wandered for another forty years. Without the anticipation of better things ahead, we will have no heart for the journey.

One of the most poisonous of all Satan's whispers is simply, "Things will never change." That lie kills expectation, trapping our heart forever in the present. To keep desire alive and flourishing, we must renew our vision for what lies ahead. Things will not always be like this. Jesus has promised to "make all things new." Eye has not seen, ear has not heard all that God has in store for his lovers, which does not mean "we have no clue so don't even try to imagine," but rather, *you cannot outdream God.* Desire is kept alive by imagination, the antidote to resignation. We will need imagination, which is to say, we will need *hope.*

Julia Gatta describes impatience, discouragement, and despair as the "noonday demons" most apt to beset the seasoned traveler. As the road grows long we grow weary; impatience and discouragement tempt us to forsake the way for some easier path. These shortcuts never work, and the guilt we feel for having chosen them only compounds our feelings of despair.

(*The Sacred Romance,* 156–57)

F aith looks back and draws courage; hope looks ahead and keeps desire alive. And meantime? In the meantime we need one more item for our journey. To appreciate what it may be, we have to step back and ask, what is all this for? The resurrection of our heart, the discovery of our role in the Larger Story, entering into the Sacred Romance—why do we pursue these things? If we say we seek all of this for our own sake, we're right back where we started: lost in our own story. Jesus said that when a person lives merely to preserve his life, he eventually loses it altogether. Rather, he said, give your life away and discover life as it was always meant to be. "Self-help is no help at all. Self-sacrifice is the way, my way, to finding yourself, your true self" (Matt. 16:25, *The Message*). Self-preservation, the theme of every small story, is so deeply wrong because it violates the Trinity, whose members live to bring glory *to the others*. The road we travel will take us into the battle to restore beauty in all things, chief among them the hearts of those we know. We grow in glory so that we might assist others in doing so; we give our glory to increase theirs. In order to fulfill the purpose of our journey, we will need a passion to increase glory; we will need *love*.

Memory, imagination, and a passion for glory—these we must keep close at hand if we are to see the journey to its end. But the road is not entirely rough. There are oases along the way. It would be a dreadful mistake to assume that our Beloved is only waiting for us at the end of the road. Our communion with him sustains us along our path.

(*The Sacred Romance*, 158)

Every courtship, at least every healthy one, is moving toward a deeper heart intimacy that is the ground for the consummation of the relationship spiritually, emotionally, and physically. The first question in the orthodox confessions of faith tests our awareness of this wonderful truth when it asks, "What is the chief end and purpose of man?" And the answer: "To know God and enjoy knowing him forever."

If we hear that answer as creatures of the Enlightenment, that is to say, the Age of Reason, the answer does not take our breath away.

But listen with me to excerpts from a conversation between two lovers:

Lover: "How beautiful you are, my darling! Oh, how beautiful! Your eyes are doves."

Beloved: "How handsome you are, my lover! Oh, how charming! And our bed is verdant."

Lover: "Show me your face, let me hear your voice; for your voice is sweet, and your face is lovely . . . Your mouth is like the best wine."

Beloved: "May the wine go straight to my lover, flowing gently over lips and teeth. I belong to my lover, and [your] desire is for me. Come, my lover, let us go to the countryside, let us spend the night in the villages . . ."

Is this not a conversation that truly does begin to take our breath away? Do we not find ourselves wanting to follow these lovers to the country just to be close to such passion? This is not a conversation from the latest dime-store romance but from the Song of Solomon. God does not give us this look through the bedroom window at the love affair between Solomon and the Queen of Sheba just to be voyeuristic. As we turn from the window and look into his eyes, we realize that this is the kind of passion he feels for us and desires from us in return—an intimacy much more sensuous, much more exotic than sex itself.

(*The Sacred Romance*, 159–61)

The older Christian wedding vows contained these amazing words: "With my body, I thee worship." Maybe our forefathers weren't so prudish after all; maybe they understood sex far better than we do. To give yourself over to another, passionately and nakedly, to adore that person body, soul, and spirit—we know there is something special, even sacramental about sex. It requires trust and abandonment, guided by a wholehearted devotion. What else can this be but worship? After all, God employs explicitly sexual language to describe faithfulness (and unfaithfulness) to him. For us creatures of the flesh, sexual intimacy is the closest parallel we have to real worship. Even the world knows this. Why else would sexual ecstasy become the number one rival to communion with God? The best impostors succeed because they are nearly indistinguishable from what they are trying to imitate. We worship sex because we don't know how to worship God. But we will.

We have grown cynical, as a society, about whether intimacy is really possible. To the degree that we have abandoned soul-oneness, we have sought out merely sex, physical sex, to ease the pain. But the full union is no longer there; the orgasm comes incomplete; its heart has been taken away. Many have been deeply hurt. Sometimes, we must learn from what we have not known, let it teach us what *ought* to be.

God's design was that the two shall become one flesh. The physical oneness was meant to be the expression of a total interweaving of being. Is it any wonder that we crave this? Our alienation is removed, if only for a moment, and in the paradox of love, we are at the same time known and yet taken beyond ourselves.

(*The Journey of Desire*, 134–35)

It is a mystery almost too great to mention, but God is the expression of the very thing we seek in each other. For do we not bear God's image? Are we not a living portrait of God? Indeed we are, and in a most surprising place—in our *gender*. "So God created man in his own image, in the image of God he created him; male and female he created them" (Gen. 1:27). Follow me closely now. Gender—masculinity and femininity—is how we bear the image of God. "I thought that there was only one kind of soul," said a shocked friend. "And God sort of poured those souls into male or female bodies." Many people believe something like that. But it contradicts the Word of God. We bear his image as men and women, and God does not have a body. So it must be at the level of the soul—the eternal part of us—that we reflect God. The text is clear; it is *as a man* or *as a woman* that the image is bestowed.

God wanted to show the world something of his strength. Is he not a great warrior? Has he not performed the daring rescue of his beloved? And this is why he gave us the sculpture that is man. Men bear the image of God in their dangerous, yet inviting strength. Women, too, bear the image of God, but in a much different way. Is not God a being of great mystery and beauty? Is there not something tender and alluring about the essence of the Divine? And this is why he gave us the sculpture that is woman.

(*The Journey of Desire*, 136)

God is the source of all masculine power; God is also the fountain of all feminine allure. Come to think of it, he is the wellspring of everything that has ever romanced your heart. The thundering strength of a waterfall, the delicacy of a flower, the stirring capacity of music, the richness of wine. The masculine and the feminine that fill all creation come from the same heart. What we have sought, what we have tasted in part with our earthly lovers, we will come face-to-face with in our True Love. For the incompleteness that we seek to relieve in the deep embrace of our earthly love is never fully healed. The union does not last, whatever the poets and pop artists may say. Morning comes and we've got to get out of bed and off to our day, incomplete once more. But oh, to have it healed forever; to drink deeply from that fount of which we've had only a sip; to dive into that sea in which we have only waded.

And so a man like Charles Wesley can pen these words: "Jesus, Lover of my soul, let me to thy bosom fly," while Catherine of Siena can pray, "O fire surpassing every fire because you alone are the fire that burns without consuming! . . . Yet your consuming does not distress the soul but fattens her with insatiable love." The French mystic Madam Guyon can write, "I slept not all night, because Thy love, O my God, flowed in me like delicious oil, and burned as a fire . . . I love God far more than the most affectionate lover among men loves his earthly attachment."

(*The Journey of Desire*, 137–38)

I magine the stories that we'll hear. And all the questions that shall finally have answers. "What were you thinking when you drove the old Ford out on the ice?" "Did you hear that Betty and Dan got back together? But of course you did—you were probably involved in that, weren't you?" "How come you never told us about your time in the war?" "Did you ever know how much I loved you?" And the answers won't be one-word answers, but story after story, a feast of wonder and laughter and glad tears.

The setting for this will be a great party, the wedding feast of the Lamb. Now, you've got to get images of Baptist receptions entirely out of your mind—folks milling around in the church gym, holding Styrofoam cups of punch, wondering what to do with themselves. You've got to picture an Italian wedding or, better, a Jewish wedding. They roll up the rugs and push back the furniture. There is *dancing*: "Then maidens will dance and be glad, young men and old as well" (Jer. 31:13). There is *feasting*: "On this mountain the LORD Almighty will prepare a feast of rich food for all peoples" (Isa. 25:6). (Can you imagine what kind of cook God must be?) And there is *drinking*—the feast God says he is preparing includes "a banquet of aged wine—the best of meats and the finest of wines." In fact, at his Last Supper our Bridegroom said he will not drink of "the fruit of the vine until the kingdom of God comes" (Luke 22:18). Then he'll pop a cork.

> And the people came together
> and the people came to dance
> and they danced like a wave upon the sea. (Yeats)

(*The Journey of Desire*, 141–42)

S omehow," notes Os Guinness, "we human beings are never happier than when we are expressing the deepest gifts that are truly us." Now, some children are gifted toward science, and others are born athletes. But whatever their specialty, *all* children are inherently creative. Give them a barrel of Legos and a free afternoon and my boys will produce an endless variety of spaceships and fortresses and who knows what. It comes naturally to children; it's in their *nature*, their design as little image bearers. A pack of boys let loose in a wood soon becomes a major Civil War reenactment. A chorus of girls, upon discovering a trunk of skirts and dresses, will burst into the *Nutcracker Suite*. The right opportunity reveals the creative nature.

This is precisely what happens when God shares with mankind his own artistic capacity and then sets us down in a paradise of unlimited potential. It is an act of creative *invitation*, like providing Monet with a studio for the summer, stocked full of brushes and oils and empty canvases. Or like setting Martha Stewart loose in a gourmet kitchen on a snowy winter weekend, just before the holidays. You needn't provide instructions or motivation; all you have to do is release them to be who they are, and remarkable things will result. As the poet Hopkins wrote, "What I do is me: for that I came."

Oh, how we long for this—for a great endeavor that draws upon our every faculty, a great "life's work" that we could throw ourselves into. "God has created us and our gifts for a place of his choosing," says Guinness, "and we will only be ourselves when we are finally there." Our creative nature is essential to who we are as human beings—as image bearers—and it brings us great joy to live it out with freedom and skill. Even if it's a simple act like working on your photo albums or puttering in the garden—these, too, are how we have a taste of what was meant to rule over a small part of God's great kingdom.

(*The Journey of Desire*, 152–54)

| # Do Whatever Brings You Back to Your Heart and the Heart of God

Against the flesh, the traitor within, a warrior uses discipline. We have a two-dimensional version of this now, which we call a "quiet time." But most men have a hard time sustaining any sort of devotional life because it has no vital connection to recovering and protecting their strength; it feels about as important as flossing. But if you saw your life as a great battle and you *knew* you needed time with God for your very survival, you would do it. Maybe not perfectly—nobody ever does and that's not the point anyway—but you would have a reason to seek him. We give a half-hearted attempt at the spiritual disciplines when the only reason we have is that we "ought" to. But we'll find a way to make it work when we are convinced we're history if we don't.

Time with God each day is not about academic study or getting through a certain amount of Scripture or any of that. It's about connecting with God. We've got to keep those lines of communication open, so use whatever helps. Sometimes I'll listen to music; other times I'll read Scripture or a passage from a book; often I will journal; maybe I'll go for a run; then there are days when all I need is silence and solitude and the rising sun. The point is simply to do *whatever brings me back to my heart and the heart of God.*

The discipline, by the way, is never the point. The whole point of a "devotional life" is *connecting with God.* This is our primary antidote to the counterfeits the world holds out to us.

(*Wild at Heart,* 171–72)

Y ou will be wounded. Just because this battle is spiritual doesn't mean it's not real; it is, and the wounds a man can take are in some ways more ugly than those that come in a firefight. To lose a leg is nothing compared to losing heart; to be crippled by shrapnel need not destroy your soul, but to be crippled by shame and guilt may. You will be wounded by the Enemy. He knows the wounds of your past, and he will try to wound you again in the same place. But these wounds are different; these are honor-wounds.

Blaine was showing me his scars the other night at the dinner table. "This one is where Samuel threw a rock and hit me in the forehead. And this one is from the Tetons when I fell into that sharp log. I can't remember what this one was from; oh, here's a good one—this one is from when I fell into the pond while chasing Luke. This one is a really old one when I burned my leg on the stove camping." He's proud of his scars; they are badges of honor to a boy . . . and to a man. We have no equivalent now for a Purple Heart of spiritual warfare, but we will. One of the noblest moments that await us will come at the wedding feast of the Lamb. Our Lord will rise and begin to call those forward who were wounded in battle for his name's sake and they will be honored, their courage rewarded. I think of Henry V's line to his men,

> He that outlives this day, and comes safe home,
> Will stand a tip-toe when the day is named,
> And rouse him at the name of Crispian . . .
> Then will he strip his sleeve and show his scars,
> And say, "These wounds I had on Crispin's day."
> Old men forget; yet all shall be forgot,
> But he'll remember with advantages
> What feats he did that day; then shall our names . . .
> Be in their flowing cups freshly remember'd.

(*Wild at Heart*, 176–77)

Once upon a time (as the story goes) there was a beautiful maiden, an absolute enchantress. She might be the daughter of a king or a common servant girl, but we know she is a princess at heart. She is young with a youth that seems eternal. Her flowing hair, her deep eyes, her luscious lips, her sculpted figure—she makes the rose blush for shame; the sun is pale compared to her light. Her heart is golden, her love as true as an arrow. But this lovely maiden is unattainable, the prisoner of an evil power who holds her captive in a dark tower. Only a champion may win her; only the most valiant, daring, and brave warrior has a chance of setting her free. Against all hope he comes; with cunning and raw courage he lays siege to the tower and the sinister one who holds her. Much blood is shed on both sides; three times the knight is thrown back, but three times he rises again. Eventually the sorcerer is defeated; the dragon falls; the giant is slain. The maiden is his; through his valor he has won her heart. On horseback they ride off to his cottage by a stream in the woods for a rendezvous that gives passion and romance new meaning.

Why is this story so deep in our psyche? Every little girl knows the fable without ever being told. She dreams one day her prince will come. Little boys rehearse their part with wooden swords and cardboard shields. And one day the boy, now a young man, realizes that he wants to be the one to win the beauty. Fairy tales, literature, music, and movies all borrow from this mythic theme. Sleeping Beauty, Cinderella, Helen of Troy, Romeo and Juliet, Antony and Cleopatra, Arthur and Guinevere, Tristan and Isolde. From ancient fables to the latest blockbuster, the theme of a strong man coming to rescue a beautiful woman is universal to human nature. It is written in our hearts, one of the core desires of every man and every woman.

(*Wild at Heart,* 180–81)

The question is not, *Are* we spiritually oppressed, but *Where* and *How?*

Think of it—why does every story have a villain?

Little Red Riding Hood is attacked by a wolf. Dorothy must face and bring down the Wicked Witch of the West. Qui-Gon Jinn and Obi-Wan Kenobi go hand to hand against Darth Maul. To release the captives of the Matrix, Neo battles the powerful "agents." Frodo is hunted by the Black Riders. (The Morgul blade that the Black Riders pierced Frodo with in the battle on Weathertop—it was aimed at his heart). Beowulf kills the monster Grendel, and then he has to battle Grendel's mother. Saint George slays the dragon. The children who stumbled into Narnia are called upon by Aslan to battle the White Witch and her armies so that Narnia might be free.

Every story has a villain because *yours* does. You were born into a world at war. When Satan lost the battle against Michael and his angels, "he was hurled to the earth, and his angels with him" (Rev. 12:9). That means that right now, on this earth, there are hundreds of thousands, if not millions, of fallen angels, foul spirits, bent on our destruction. And what is Satan's mood? "He is filled with fury, because he knows that his time is short" (v. 12). So what does he spend every day and every night of his sleepless, untiring existence doing? "Then the dragon was enraged at the woman and went off to make war against . . . those who obey God's commandments and hold to the testimony of Jesus" (v. 17). He has you in his crosshairs, and he isn't smiling.

You have an enemy. He is trying to steal your freedom, kill your heart, destroy your life.

(*Waking the Dead*, 150–51)

> The devil has more temptations than an actor has costumes for the stage. And one of his all-time favorite disguises is that of a lying spirit, to abuse your tender heart with the worst news he can deliver—that you do not really love Jesus Christ and that you are only pretending, you are only deceiving yourself. (William Gurnall)

Satan is called in Scripture the Father of Lies (John 8:44). His very first attack against the human race was to lie to Eve and Adam about God, and where life is to be found, and what the consequences of certain actions would and would not be. He is a master at this. He suggests to us—as he suggested to Adam and Eve—some sort of idea or inclination or impression, and what he is seeking is a sort of "agreement" on our part. He's hoping we'll buy into whatever he's saying, offering, insinuating. Our first parents bought into it, and look what disaster came of it. The Evil One is still lying to us, seeking our agreement every single day.

Your heart is good. Your heart matters to God. Those are the two hardest things to hang on to. I'm serious—try it. Try to hold this up for even a day. *My heart is good. My heart matters to God.* You will be amazed at how much accusation you live under. You have an argument with your daughter on the way to school; as you drive off, you have a nagging sense of, *Well, you really blew that one.* If your heart agrees—*Yeah, I really did*—without taking the issue to Jesus, then the Enemy will try to go for more. *You're always blowing it with her.* Another agreement is made. *It's true. I'm such a lousy parent.* Keep this up and your whole day is tanked in about five minutes. The Enemy will take any small victory he can get. It moves from *You did a bad thing* to *You are bad.* After a while it just becomes a cloud we live under, accept as normal.

(*Waking the Dead,* 152–53)

Any movement toward freedom and life, any movement toward God or others, *will be opposed.* Marriage, friendship, beauty, rest—the thief wants it all.

> So, it becomes the devil's business to keep the Christian's spirit imprisoned. He knows that the believing and justified Christian has been raised up out of the grave of his sins and trespasses. From that point on, Satan works that much harder to keep us bound and gagged, actually imprisoned in our own grave clothes. He knows that if we continue in this kind of bondage . . . we are not much better off than when we were spiritually dead. (A.W. Tozer)

Sadly, many of these accusations will actually be spoken by Christians. Having dismissed a warfare worldview, they do not know who is stirring them to say certain things. "Satan rose up against Israel and incited David to take a census of Israel" (1 Chron. 21:1). The Enemy used David, who apparently wasn't watching for it, to do his evil. He tried to use Peter too. "From that time on Jesus began to explain to his disciples that he must go to Jerusalem and suffer many things . . . Peter took him aside and began to rebuke him. 'Never, Lord!' he said. 'This shall never happen to you!' Jesus turned and said to Peter, 'Get behind me, Satan!'" (Matt. 16:21–23). Heads up—these words will come from anywhere. Be careful what or who you are agreeing with.

When we make those agreements with the demonic forces suggesting things to us, we come under their influence. It becomes a kind of permission we give the Enemy, sort of like a contract.

Some foul spirit whispers, *I'm such a stupid idiot,* and they agree with it; then they spend months and years trying to sort through feelings of insignificance. They'd end their agony if they'd treat it for the warfare it is, break the agreement they've made, and send the Enemy packing.

(Waking the Dead, 154–55)

Remember, when Jesus boiled his whole mission down to healing the brokenhearted and setting prisoners free from darkness, he was referring to *all* of us. Our modern, scientific, Enlightenment worldview has simply removed spiritual warfare as a practical category, and so it shouldn't surprise us that we can't see spiritual strongholds after we say they don't really exist.

If you deny the battle raging against your heart, well, then, the thief just gets to steal and kill and destroy. Some friends of mine started a Christian school together a few years ago. It had been their shared dream for nearly all their adult lives. After years of praying and talking and dreaming, it finally happened. Then the assault came . . . but they would not see it as such. It was "hassles" and "misunderstanding" at first. As it grew worse, it became a rift between them. A mutual friend warned them of the warfare, urged them to fight it as such. "No," they insisted, "this is about *us*. We just don't see eye-to-eye." I'm sorry to say their school shut its doors a few months ago, and the two aren't speaking to each other. Because they refused to fight it for the warfare it was, they got taken out. I could tell you many, many stories like that.

There is no war is the subtle—but pervasive—lie sown by an Enemy so familiar to us we don't even see him. For too long he has infiltrated the ranks of the church, and we haven't even recognized him.

(*Waking the Dead*, 159–60)

I was reading the prophet Jeremiah a few weeks ago when I ran across a passage that referred to God as "the Lord Almighty." To be honest, it didn't resonate. There's something too religious about the phrase; it sounds churchy, sanctimonious. The *Lawd Almiiiighty*. It sounds like something your grandmother would say when you came into her kitchen covered in mud. I found myself curious about what the *actual* phrase means in Hebrew. Might we have lost something in the translation? So I turned to the front of the version I was using for an explanation. Here is what the editors said:

> Because for most readers today the phrases "the Lord of hosts" and "God of hosts" have little meaning, this version renders them "the Lord Almighty" and "God Almighty." These renderings convey the sense of the Hebrew, namely, "he who is sovereign over all the 'hosts' (powers) in heaven and on earth, especially over the 'hosts' (armies) of Israel."

No, they don't. They don't even come close. The Hebrew means "the God of angel armies," "the God of the armies who fight for his people." *The God who is at war.* Does "Lord Almighty" convey "the God who is at war"? Not to me, it doesn't. Not to anyone I've asked. It sounds like "the God who is up there but still in charge." Powerful, in control. The *God of angel armies* sounds like the one who would roll up his sleeves, take up sword and shield to break down gates of bronze, and cut through bars of iron to rescue me.

(*Waking the Dead*, 160)

If for all practical purposes we believe that this life is our best shot at happiness, if this is as good as it gets, we will live as desperate, demanding, and eventually despairing men and women. We will place on this world a burden it was never intended to bear. We will try to find a way to sneak back into the Garden and when that fails, as it always does, our heart fails as well. If truth be told, most of us live as though this life *is* our only hope.

In his wonderful book *The Eclipse of Heaven*, A. J. Conyers put it quite simply: "We live in a world no longer under heaven." All the crises of the human soul flow from there. All our addictions and depressions, the rage that simmers just beneath the surface of our Christian facade, and the deadness that characterizes so much of our lives has a common root: We think this is as good as it gets. Take away the hope of arrival and our journey becomes the Battan death march. The best human life is unspeakably sad. Even if we manage to escape some of the bigger tragedies (and few of us do), life rarely matches our expectations. When we do get a taste of what we really long for, it never lasts. Every vacation eventually comes to an end. Friends move away. Our careers don't quite pan out. Sadly, we feel guilty about our disappointment, as though we ought to be more grateful.

Of course we're disappointed—we're made for so much more. "He has also set eternity in the hearts" (Eccl. 3:11). Our longing for heaven whispers to us in our disappointments and screams through our agony. "If I find in myself desires which nothing in this world can satisfy," C. S. Lewis wrote, "the only logical explanation is that I was made for another world."

(*The Sacred Romance*, 179–80)

The crisis of hope that afflicts the church today is a crisis of *imagination*. Catholic philosopher Peter Kreeft writes:

> Medieval imagery (which is almost totally biblical imagery) of light, jewels, stars, candles, trumpets, and angels no longer fits our ranch-style, supermarket world. Pathetic modern substitutes of fluffy clouds, sexless cherubs, harps and metal halos (not halos of *light*) presided over by a stuffy divine Chairman of the Bored are a joke, not a glory. Even more modern, more up-to-date substitutes—Heaven as a comfortable feeling of peace and kindness, sweetness and light, and God as a vague grandfatherly benevolence, a senile philanthropist—are even more insipid. Our pictures of Heaven simply do not move us; they are not moving pictures. It is this aesthetic failure rather than intellectual or moral failures in our pictures of Heaven and of God that threatens faith most potently today. Our pictures of Heaven are dull, platitudinous and syrupy; therefore, so is our faith, our hope, and our love of Heaven. (*Everything You Wanted to Know About Heaven*)

If our pictures of heaven are to move us, they must be moving pictures. So go ahead—dream a little. Use your imagination. Picture the best possible ending to your story you can. If that isn't heaven, something better is. When Paul says, "No eye has seen, no ear has heard, no mind has conceived what God has prepared for those who love him" (1 Cor. 2:9), he simply means we cannot out-dream God. What is at the end of our personal journeys? Something beyond our wildest imagination. But if we explore the secrets of our heart in the light of the promises of Scripture, we can discover clues. As we have said, there is in the heart of every man, woman, and child an inconsolable longing for intimacy, for beauty, and for adventure. What will heaven offer to our heart of hearts?

(*The Sacred Romance*, 180–81)

There is the joy of having someone save a place for us. We walk into a crowded room at church or at a dinner party and someone across the way waves us over, pointing to a chair he's held on to especially for us. For a moment we feel a sense of relief, a taste of being on the inside. Now consider Jesus' words in John 14:2—"I am going . . . to prepare a place for you." Christ promises that he is saving a place in heaven especially for each of us. When we walk into the crowded excitement of the wedding feast of the Lamb, with the sound of a thousand conversations, laughter and music, the clinking of glasses, and one more time our heart leaps with the hope that we might be let into the sacred circle, we will not be disappointed. We'll be welcomed to the table by our Lover himself. No one will have to scramble to find another chair, to make room for us at the end of the table, or rustle up a place setting. There will be a seat with our name on it, held open at Jesus' command for us and no other.

(*The Sacred Romance,* 182–83)

Heaven is the beginning of an adventure in intimacy, "a world of love," as Jonathan Edwards wrote, "where God is the fountain." The Holy Spirit, through the human authors of Scripture, chose the imagery of a wedding feast for a reason. It's not just any kind of party; it is a *wedding* feast. What sets this special feast apart from all others is the unique intimacy of the wedding night. The Spirit uses the most secret and tender experience on earth—the union of husband and wife—to convey the depth of intimacy that we will partake with our Lord in heaven. He is the Bridegroom and the church is his bride. In the consummation of love, we shall know him and be known.

(*The Sacred Romance,* 183)

The Road goes ever on and on
Down from the door where it began.
Now far ahead the Road has gone,
And I must follow, if I can,
Pursuing it with eager feet,
Until it joins some larger way. (J. R. R. Tolkien)

The Sacred Romance calls to us every moment of our lives. It whispers to us on the wind, invites us through the laughter of good friends, reaches out to us through the touch of someone we love. We've heard it in our favorite music, sensed it at the birth of our first child, been drawn to it while watching the shimmer of a sunset on the ocean. It is even present in times of great personal suffering—the illness of a child, the loss of a marriage, the death of a friend. Something calls to us through experiences like these and rouses an inconsolable longing deep within our heart, wakening in us a yearning for intimacy, beauty, and adventure. This longing is the most powerful part of any human personality. It fuels our search for meaning, for wholeness, for a sense of being truly alive. However we may describe this deep desire, it is the most important thing about us, our heart of hearts, the passion of our life. And the voice that calls to us in this place is none other than the voice of God.

(*The Sacred Romance,* 195)

Where do we go from here? "This life," wrote Jonathan Edwards, "ought to be spent by us only as a journey towards heaven." That's the only story worth living in now. The road goes out before us and our destination awaits. In the imagery of Hebrews, a race is set before us and we must run for all we're worth. Our prayers will have been answered if we've helped to lift some of the deadweight so that your heart may rise to the call, hear it more clearly, respond with "eager feet." Our final thoughts echo the advice found in Hebrews 12:2–3:

> Keep your eyes on *Jesus*, who both began and finished this race we're in. Study how he did it. Because he never lost sight of where he was headed—that exhilarating finish in and with God—he could put up with anything along the way: cross, shame, whatever. And now he's *there*, in the place of honor, right alongside God. When you find yourselves flagging in your faith, go over that story again, item by item, that long litany of hostility he plowed through. *That* will shoot adrenaline into your souls! (Eugene Peterson's translation from *The Message*)

Jesus remembered where he was headed, and he wanted to get there with all his heart. These two themes, memory and desire, will make all the difference in our journey ahead. Without them, we will not run well, if we run at all.

(*The Sacred Romance,* 196–97)

During a long layover at O'Hare, I studied the man who sells popcorn from a little stand in one of the terminal hallways. He sat silently on a stool as thousands of people rushed by. Occasionally, every fifteen minutes or so, someone would stop and buy a bag. He would scoop the popcorn from the bin, take the money, and make change—all without a word being spoken between them. When the brief encounter was over, he would resume his place on the stool, staring blankly, his shoulders hunched over. I wondered at his age; he seemed well past fifty. How long had that been his profession? Could he possibly make a living at it? His face wore a weary expression of resignation tinged with shame. *Adam*, I thought, *what happened?* Did he know how far his situation was from his true design? Somehow he knew, even if he didn't know the Story. His sadness was testimony to it.

Some people love what they do. They are the fortunate souls, who have found a way to link what they are truly gifted at (and therefore what brings them joy) with a means of paying the bills. But most of the world merely toils to survive, and no one gets to use his gifts all the time. On top of that, there is the curse of thorns and thistles, the futility that tinges all human efforts at the moment. As a result, we've come to think of work as a result of the Fall. You can see our cynicism in the fact that we've chosen the cartoon character Dilbert as the icon of our working days. His is a hopeless life of futility and anonymity in the bowels of some large corporation. We don't even know what he does—only that it's meaningless. We identify with him, feeling at some deep level the apparent futility of our lives. Even if we are loved, it is not enough. We yearn to be *fruitful*, to do something of meaning and value that flows naturally out of the gifts and capacities of our own soul. But of course—we were meant to be the kings and queens of the earth.

(*The Journey of Desire*, 154–55)

In Romans 8, Paul says something outrageous. He says that all our sufferings are "not worth comparing" with the glory that will be revealed in us. The human race has seen an unspeakable amount of suffering. What can possibly make that seem like nothing? "The glory that will be revealed in us" (8:18). The Great Restoration. Paul then goes on to say, "The creation waits in eager expectation for the sons of God to be revealed" (v. 19). The release of a fully restored creation is being more or less held back, waiting upon *our* restoration. Only when we have been restored can we take our place again as the kings and queens of creation. Or did you not know? The day is coming when Christ will appoint you as one of his regents over his great and beautiful universe. This has been his plan all along.

> When the Son of Man comes in his glory, and all the angels with him, he will sit on his throne in heavenly glory. All the nations will be gathered before him, and he will separate the people one from another as a shepherd separates the sheep from the goats. Then the King will say to those on his right, "Come, you who are blessed by my Father; take your inheritance, *the kingdom prepared for you since the creation of the world.*" (Matt. 25:31–34, emphasis added)

> Who then is the faithful and wise servant, whom the master has put in charge of the servants in his household to give them their food at the proper time? It will be good for that servant whose master finds him doing so when he returns. I tell you the truth, *he will put him in charge of all his possessions.* (Matt. 24:45–47, emphasis added)

> And they will *reign* for ever and ever. (Rev. 22:5, emphasis added)

> (*The Journey of Desire,* 156–57)

Let's come back for a moment to original glory, the glory of God given to us when we were created in his image. So much light could be shed on our lives if we would explore what we were *meant* to be before things started going wrong. What was it that we were created to *do?* What was our original job description?

> God said, "Let us make man in our image, in our like-ness, and let them rule over the fish of the sea and the birds of the air, over the livestock, over all the earth, and over all the creatures that move along the ground." So God created man in his own image, in the image of God he created him; male and female he created them. God blessed them and said to them, "Be fruitful and increase in number; fill the earth and subdue it. Rule." (Gen. 1:26–28)

And let them *rule.* Like a foreman runs a ranch or like a skip-per runs his ship. Better still, like a king rules a kingdom, God appoints us as the governors of his domain. We were created to be the kings and queens of the earth (small *k*, small *q*). Hebrew scholar Robert Alter has looked long and hard at this passage, mining it for its riches. He says the idea of *rule* means "a fierce exercise of mastery." It is active, engaged, passionate. It is *fierce.*

(*Waking the Dead,* 165–66)

After his resurrection, Jesus sends us *all* out to do what he did: "As the Father has sent me, so I send you" (John 20:21 NRSV). And he gives us his authority to do it: "All authority in heaven and on earth has been given to me. Therefore go" (Matt. 28:18–19). Why else would he have given us his authority if we weren't supposed to *use* it?

The attitude of so many Christians today is anything *but* fierce. We're passive, acquiescent. We're acting as if the battle is over, as if the wolf and the lamb are now fast friends. Good grief—we're beating swords into plowshares as the armies of the Evil One descend upon us. We've bought the lie of the Religious Spirit, which says, "You don't need to fight the Enemy. Let Jesus do that." It's nonsense. It's unbiblical. It's like a private in Vietnam saying, "My commander will do all the fighting for me; I don't even need to fire my weapon." We are *commanded* to "resist the devil, and he will flee from you" (James 4:7). We are told, "Your enemy the devil prowls around like a roaring lion looking for someone to devour. Resist him" (1 Peter 5:8–9); "Fight the good fight" (1 Tim. 1:18); "Rescue those being led away to death" (Prov. 24:11).

Seriously, just this morning a man said to me, "We don't need to fight the Enemy. Jesus has won." *Yes*, Jesus has won the victory over Satan and his kingdom. *However*, the battle is not over. Look at 1 Corinthians 15:24–25: "Then the end will come, when he [Jesus] hands over the kingdom to God the Father after he has destroyed all dominion, authority and power. For he must reign until he has put all his enemies under his feet." *After* he has destroyed the rest of the Enemy's works. *Until* then, he must reign by bringing his enemies under his feet. Jesus is still at war, and he calls us to join him.

(Waking the Dead, 167–68)

You awake to find yourself in the midst of a great and terrible war. It is, in fact, our most desperate hour. Your King and dearest Friend calls you forth. Awake, come fully alive, your good heart set free and blazing for him and for those yet to be rescued. You have a glory that is needed. You are given a quest, a mission that will take you deep into the heart of the kingdom of darkness, to break down gates of bronze and cut through bars of iron so that your people might be set free from their bleak prisons. He asks that you heal them. Of course, you will face many dangers; you will be hunted.

Would you try and do this *alone?*

Something stronger than fate *has* chosen you. Evil *will* hunt you. And so a fellowship *must* protect you. Honestly, though he is a very brave and true hobbit, Frodo hasn't a chance without Sam, Merry, Pippin, Gandalf, Aragorn, Legolas, and Gimli. He has no real idea what dangers and trials lie ahead. The dark mines of Moria; the Balrog that awaits him there; the evil orcs called the Urak-hai that will hunt him; the wastes of the Emyn Muil. He will need his friends. And you will need yours. You must cling to those you have; you must search wide and far for those you do not yet have. *You must not go alone.* From the beginning, right there in Eden, the Enemy's strategy has relied upon a simple aim: divide and conquer. Get them isolated, and take them out.

(*Waking the Dead,* 186–87)

I am not letting men off the hook. God knows, we have a lot more repenting to do. I *am* saying that you won't begin to understand the long and sustained assault on femininity, on women, until you see it as part of something much larger. The most wicked force the world has ever known. The Enemy bears a special hatred for Eve. If you believe he has any role in the history of this world, you cannot help but see it.

The Evil One had a hand in all that has happened to you. If he didn't arrange for the assault directly—and certainly human sin has a large enough role to play—then he made sure he drove the message of the wounds home into your heart. He is the one who has dogged your heels with shame and self-doubt and accusation. He is the one who offers the false comforters to you in order to deepen your bondage. He is the one who has done these things in order to prevent your restoration. For that is what he fears. He fears who you are; what you are; what you might become. He fears your beauty and your life-giving heart.

You really won't understand your life as a woman until you understand this:

> You are passionately loved by the God of the universe.
> You are passionately hated by his Enemy.

And so, dear heart, it is time for your restoration. For there is One greater than your Enemy, One who has sought you out from the beginning of time. He has come to heal your broken heart and restore your feminine soul.

(*Captivating,* 89–91)

The purposes of Jesus Christ are not finished when one of his precious ones is forgiven. Not at all. Would a good father feel satisfied when his daughter is rescued from a car accident, but left in ICU? Doesn't he want her to be healed as well? So God has much more in mind for us. Listen to this passage from Isaiah:

> The Spirit of the Sovereign LORD is on me,
>> because the LORD has anointed me
>> to preach good news to the poor.
> He has sent me to bind up the brokenhearted,
>> to proclaim freedom for the captives
>> and release from darkness for the prisoners,
> to proclaim the year of the LORD's favor
>> and the day of vengeance of our God,
> to comfort all who mourn,
>> and provide for those who grieve in Zion—
> to bestow on them a crown of beauty
>> instead of ashes,
> the oil of gladness
>> instead of mourning,
> and a garment of praise
>> instead of a spirit of despair. (61:1–3)

Of all the Scriptures Jesus could have chosen, this is the one he picked on the day he first publicly announced his mission. It must be important to him. It must be central. What does it mean? It has something to do with healing hearts, setting someone free.

Now that is an offer worth considering. What if it were true? I mean, what if Jesus really *could* and *would* do this for your broken heart? Read it again, and ask, *Jesus, is this true for me? Would you do this for me?* He can, and he will . . . if you'll let him.

(Captivating, 94–95)

Jesus ran because he wanted to, not simply because he had to or because the Father told him to. He ran "for the joy set before him," which means he ran out of *desire*. To use the familiar phrase, his heart was fully in it. We call the final week of our Savior's life his Passion Week. Look at the depth of his desire, the fire in his soul. Consumed with passion, he clears the temple of the charlatans who have turned his Father's house into a swap meet (Matt. 21:12). Later, he stands looking over the city that was to be his bride but now lies in the bondage of her adulteries and the oppression of her taskmasters. "O Jerusalem, Jerusalem," he cries, ". . . how often I have *longed* to gather your children together, as a hen gathers her chicks under her wings, but you were not willing" (Matt. 23:37, emphasis added). As the final hours of his greatest struggle approach, his passion intensifies. He gathers with his closest friends like a condemned criminal sitting down to his last meal. He alone knows what is about to unfold. "I have *eagerly desired* to eat this Passover with you," he says, "before I suffer" (Luke 22:15, emphasis added). Then on he presses, through the intensity of Gethsemane and the passion of the Cross. Is it possible he went through any of it halfheartedly?

(*The Sacred Romance,* 197–98)

The whole life of the good Christian," said Augustine, "is a holy longing." Sadly, many of us have been led to feel that somehow we ought to want less, not more. We have this sense that we should atone for our longings, apologize that we feel such deep desire. Shouldn't we be more content? Perhaps, but contentment is never wanting *less*; that's the easy way out. Anybody can look holy if she's killed her heart; the real test is to have your heart burning within you and have the patience to enjoy what there is now to enjoy, while waiting with eager anticipation for the feast to come. In Paul's words, we "groan inwardly as we wait eagerly" (Rom. 8:23). Contentment can only happen as we increase desire, let it run itself out toward its fulfillment, and carry us along with it. And so George Herbert prayed,

> Immortal Heat, O let thy greater flame
> Attract the lesser to it: let those fires,
> Which shall consume the world, first make it tame;
> And kindle in our hearts such true desires,
> As may consume our lusts, and make thee way.
> Then shall our hearts pant thee. (*Love*)

There may be times when all we have to go on is a sense of duty. But in the end, if that is all we have, we will never make it. Our Hero is the example. He's run on before us and he's made it; he's there now. His life assures us it can be done, but only through passionate desire *for the joy set before us.*

(*The Sacred Romance,* 199–200)

As our soul grows in the love of God and journeys forth toward him, our heart's capacities also grow and expand: "Thou shalt enlarge my heart" (Ps. 119:32 KJV).

But the sword cuts both ways. While our heart grows in its capacity for pleasure, it grows in its capacity to know pain. The two go hand in hand. What, then, shall we do with disappointment? We can be our own enemy, depending on how we handle the heartache that comes with desire. To want is to suffer; the word *passion* means to suffer. This is why many Christians are reluctant to listen to their hearts: They know that their dullness is keeping them from feeling the pain of life. Many of us have chosen simply not to want so much; it's safer that way. It's also godless. That's stoicism, not Christianity. Sanctification is an awakening, the rousing of our souls from the dead sleep of sin into the fullness of their capacity for life.

Desire often feels like an enemy, because it wakes longings that cannot be fulfilled in the moment. In the words of T. S. Eliot,

> April is the cruelest month, breeding
> Lilacs out of the dead land, mixing
> Memory and desire. (*The Waste Land*)

Spring awakens a desire for the summer that is not yet. Awakened souls are often disappointed, but our disappointment can lead us onward, actually increasing our desire and lifting it toward its true passion.

(*The Sacred Romance,* 200)

Simone Weil was absolutely right—beauty and affliction are the only two things that can pierce our hearts. Because this is so true, we must have a measure of beauty in our lives proportionate to our affliction. No, more. Much more. Is this not God's prescription for us? Just take a look around. The sights and sounds, the aromas and sensations—the world is overflowing with beauty. God seems to be rather enamored with it. Gloriously wasteful. Apparently, he feels that there ought to be plenty of it in our lives.

I am at a loss to say what I want to say regarding beauty. Somehow, that is as it ought to be. Our experience of beauty transcends our ability to speak about it, for its magic lies beyond the power of words.

I want to speak of beauty's healing power, of how it comforts and soothes, yet also how it stirs us, how it moves and inspires. All that sounds ridiculous. You know your own experiences of beauty. Let me call upon them then. Think of your favorite music, or tapestry, or landscape. "We have had a couple of inspiring sunsets this week." A dear friend sent this in an e-mail: "It was as if the seams of our atmosphere split for a bit of heaven to plunge into the sea. I stood and applauded . . . simultaneously I wanted to kneel and weep." Yes—that's it. All I want to do is validate those irreplaceable moments, lift any obstacle you may have to filling your life with greater and greater amounts of beauty.

We need not fear indulging here. The experience of beauty is unique to all the other pleasures in this: there is no possessive quality to it. Just because you love the landscape doesn't mean you have to acquire the real estate. Simply to behold the flower is enough; there is nothing in me that wants to consume it. Beauty is the closest thing we have to fullness without possessing on this side of eternity. It heralds the Great Restoration. Perhaps that is why it is so healing—beauty is pure gift. It helps us in our letting go.

(*The Journey of Desire*, 191–92)

The time has come for us to quit playing chess with God over our lives. We cannot win, but we can delay the victory, dragging on the pain of grasping and the poison of possessing. You see, there are two kinds of losses in life. The first is shared by all mankind—the losses that come to us. Call them what you will—accidents, fate, acts of God. The point is that we have no control over them. We do not determine when, where, what, or even how. There is no predicting these losses; they happen *to* us. We choose only how we respond. The second kind is known only to the pilgrim. They are losses that we *choose*. A chosen loss is different from repentance, when we give up something that was never ours to have. With a chosen loss, we place on the altar something very dear to us, something innocent, whose only danger is in its goodness, that we might come to love it too much. It is the act of *consecration*, where little by little or all at once, we give over our lives to the only One who can truly keep them.

Spiritual surrender is not resignation. It is not choosing to care no longer. Nor is it Eastern mysticism, an attempt to get beyond the suffering of this life by going completely numb. As my dear friend Jan describes, "It is surrender *with* desire, or *in* desire." Desire is still present, felt, welcomed even. But the will to secure is made subject to the divine will in an act of abandoned trust. Think of Jesus in the Garden of Gethsemane.

(*The Journey of Desire*, 192–93)

Right above my bed I think I shall hang a sign that says, GOD EXISTS. You see, I wake most mornings an unbeliever. It seems that during the night, I slip into forgetfulness, and by the time the new day comes, I am lost. The deep and precious truths that God has brought to me over the years and even just yesterday seem a thousand miles away. It doesn't happen every morning, but enough to make it an ongoing reality. And I know I am not alone in this. As George MacDonald confessed in *Diary of an Old Soul,*

> Sometimes I wake, and lo, I have forgot,
> And drifted out upon an ebbing sea!
> My soul that was at rest now resteth not,
> For I am with myself and not with thee;
> Truth seems a blind moon in a glaring morn,
> Where nothing is but sick-heart vanity.

Forgetting is no small problem. Of all the enemies our hearts must face, this may be the worst because it is insidious. Forgetfulness does not come against us like an enemy in full battle formation, banners waving. Nor does it come temptingly, seductively, the lady in red. It works slowly, commonly, unnoticed. My wife had a beautiful climbing rose vine that began to fill an arbor in her garden. We enjoyed the red blossoms it produced every summer. But last year, something happened. The vine suddenly turned brown, dropped its flowers, and died within the course of a week. After all that loving care we couldn't figure out what went wrong. A call to the nursery revealed that a worm had gotten into the stalk of the vine and eaten away at the life from the inside. Such is the work of forgetfulness. It cuts us off from our life so slowly, we barely notice, until one day the blooms of our faith are suddenly gone.

(The Journey of Desire, 199–200)

W e're certainly warned about forgetfulness in Scripture, both in word and by example. In the Old Testament, the pattern is so predictable, we come to expect it. God delivers his people from the cruel whips of Egypt by a stunning display of his power and his care—the plagues, the Passover, the Red Sea. The Israelites celebrate with singing and dancing. Three days later, they are complaining about the water supply. God provides sweet water from the bitter desert springs of Marah. They complain about the food. God drops breakfast out of the sky, every morning. Then it's the water again. God provides it from a rock. Enemies attack; God delivers. On and on it goes, for forty years. As they stand on the brink of the Promised Land, God issues a final warning:

> Only be careful, and watch yourselves closely so that you do not forget the things your eyes have seen *or let them slip from your heart* as long as you live. (Deut. 4:9, emphasis added)

They do, of course, let it slip from their hearts. All of it. This becomes the pattern for the entire history of Israel. God shows up; he does amazing things; the people rejoice. Then they forget and go whoring after other gods. They fall under calamity and cry out for deliverance. God shows up; he does amazing things; the people rejoice—you get the picture. Things aren't changed much in the New Testament, but the contrast is greater, and the stakes are even higher. God shows up *in person*, and before he leaves, he gives us the sacraments along with this plea: *Do this to remember me.* They don't—remember him, that is. Paul is "shocked" by the Galatians: they are "turning away so soon from God, who in his love and mercy called you to share the eternal life he gives through Christ" (1:6 NLT). He has to send Timothy to the Corinthians, to "remind you of what I teach about Christ Jesus in all the churches wherever I go" (1 Cor. 4:17 NLT).

(*The Journey of Desire,* 200)

Unveiling our beauty really just means unveiling our feminine hearts.

It's scary, for sure. That is why it is our greatest expression of faith, because we are going to have to trust Jesus—really trust him. We'll have to trust him that we *have* a beauty, that what he has said of us is true. And we'll have to trust him with how it goes when we offer it, because that is out of our control. We'll have to trust him when it hurts, and we'll have to trust him when we are finally seen and enjoyed. That's why unveiling our beauty is *how* we live by faith.

Unveiling our beauty is our greatest expression of hope. We hope it will matter, that our beauty really does make a difference. We hope there is a greater and higher Beauty, hope we are reflecting that Beauty, and hope it will triumph. Our hope is that all is well because of Jesus, and that all will be well because of him. So we unveil beauty in hope. And finally, we unveil beauty in the hope that Jesus is *growing* our beauty. Yes, we are not yet what we long to be. But we are under way. Restoration has begun. To offer beauty now is an expression of hope that it will be completed.

And unveiling beauty is our greatest expression of love, because it is what the world most needs from us. When we choose not to hide, when we choose to offer our hearts, we are choosing to love. Jesus offers, he invites, he is present. That is how he loves. That is how we love—sincerely, as the Scripture says, "from the heart" (1 Peter 1:22). Our focus shifts from self-protection to the hearts of others. We offer Beauty so that their hearts might come alive, be healed, know God. That is love.

(*Captivating,* 147)

F or what shall we do when we wake one day to find we have lost touch with our heart and with it the very refuge where God's presence resides?

Starting very early, life has taught all of us to ignore and distrust the deepest yearnings of our heart. Life, for the most part, teaches us to suppress our longing and live only in the external world where efficiency and performance are everything. We have learned from parents and peers, at school, at work, and even from our spiritual mentors that something else is wanted from us other than our heart, which is to say, that which is most deeply *us*. Very seldom are we ever invited to live out of our heart. If we are wanted, we are often wanted for what we can offer functionally. If rich, we are honored for our wealth; if beautiful, for our looks; if intelligent, for our brains. So we learn to offer only those parts of us that are approved, living out a carefully crafted performance to gain acceptance from those who represent life to us. We divorce ourselves from our heart and begin to live a double life. Frederick Buechner expresses this phenomenon in his biographical work, *Telling Secrets*:

> [Our] original shimmering self gets buried so deep we hardly live out of it at all . . . rather, we learn to live out of all the other selves which we are constantly putting on and taking off like coats and hats against the world's weather.

> (*The Sacred Romance,* 5)

Communion with God is replaced by activity for God. There is little time in this outer world for deep questions. Given the right plan, everything in life can be managed . . . except your heart.

The inner life, the story of our heart, is the life of the deep places within us, our passions and dreams, our fears and our deepest wounds. It is the unseen life, the mystery within—what Buechner calls our "shimmering self." It cannot be managed like a corporation. The heart does not respond to principles and programs; it seeks not efficiency, but passion. Art, poetry, beauty, mystery, ecstasy: These are what rouse the heart. Indeed, they are the language that must be spoken if one wishes to communicate with the heart. It is why Jesus so often taught and related to people by telling stories and asking questions. His desire was not just to engage their intellects but to capture their hearts.

Indeed, if we will listen, a Sacred Romance calls to us through our heart every moment of our lives. It whispers to us on the wind, invites us through the laughter of good friends, reaches out to us through the touch of someone we love. We've heard it in our favorite music, sensed it at the birth of our first child, been drawn to it while watching the shimmer of a sunset on the ocean. The Romance is even present in times of great personal suffering: the illness of a child, the loss of a marriage, the death of a friend. Something calls to us through experiences like these and rouses an inconsolable longing deep within our heart, wakening in us a yearning for intimacy, beauty, and adventure.

This longing is the most powerful part of any human personality. It fuels our search for meaning, for wholeness, for a sense of being truly alive. However we may describe this deep desire, it is the most important thing about us, our heart of hearts, the passion of our life. And the voice that calls to us in this place is none other than the voice of God.

We cannot hear this voice if we have lost touch with our heart.

(*The Sacred Romance,* 6–7)

The religious technocrats of Jesus' day confronted him with what they believed were the standards of a life pleasing to God. The external life, they argued, the life of ought and duty and service, was what mattered. "You're dead wrong," Jesus said. "In fact, you're just plain dead [whitewashed tombs]. What God cares about is the inner life, the life of the heart" (Matt. 23:25–28). Throughout the Old and New Testaments, the life of the heart is clearly God's central concern. When the people of Israel fell into a totally external life of ritual and observance, God lamented, "These people . . . honor me with their lips, but their hearts are far from me" (Isa. 29:13).

Our heart is the key to the Christian life.

The apostle Paul informs us that hardness of heart is behind all the addictions and evils of the human race (Rom. 1:21–25). Oswald Chambers writes, "It is by the heart that God is perceived [known] and not by reason . . . so that is what faith is: God perceived by the heart." This is why God tells us in Proverbs 4:23, "Above all else, guard your heart, for it is the wellspring of life." He knows that to lose heart is to lose everything. Sadly, most of us watch the oil level in our car more carefully than we watch over the life of our heart.

In one of the greatest invitations ever offered to man, Christ stood up amid the crowds in Jerusalem and said, "If anyone is thirsty, let him come to me and drink. Whoever believes in me, as the Scripture has said, streams of living water will flow from within him" (John 7:37–38). If we aren't aware of our soul's deep thirst, his offer means nothing. But, if we will recall, it was from the longing of our hearts that most of us first responded to Jesus. Somehow, years later, we assume he no longer calls to us through the thirst of our heart.

(*The Sacred Romance,* 9)

Aren't there times in your life that if you could, you would love to return to? I grew up in Los Angeles but spent my boyhood summers in Oregon where both my mother's and my father's parents lived. There was a beauty and innocence and excitement to those days. Woods to explore, rivers to fish, grandparents to fuss over me. My parents were young and in love, and the days were full of adventures I did not have to create or pay for, but only live in and enjoy. We all have places in our past when life, if only for a moment, seemed to be coming together in the way we knew in our hearts it was always meant to be.

> There was a time when meadow, grove, and stream,
> The earth, and every common sight,
> To me did seem
> Appareled in celestial light,
> The glory and the freshness of a dream . . .
> Heaven lies about us in our infancy;
> Shades of the prison-house begin to close
> Upon the growing boy,
> But he beholds the light, and whence it flows.
> He sees it in his joy; . . .
> At length the man perceives it die away,
> And fade into the light of common day. (*Ode,
> Intimations of Immortality from Recollection of
> Childhood*)

Wordsworth caught a glimpse of the secret in his childhood, saw in it hints from the realm unknown. We simply must learn the lesson of these moments, or we will not be able to bring our hearts along in our life's journey. For if these moments pass, never to be recovered again, then the life we prize is always fading from view, and our hearts with it.

(The Journey of Desire, 5–6)

The heart," Blaise Pascal said, "has its reasons which reason knows nothing of." Something in us longs, hopes, maybe even at times believes that this is not the way things were supposed to be. Our desire fights the assault of death upon life. And so people with terminal illnesses get married. Prisoners in a concentration camp plant flowers. Lovers long divorced still reach out in the night to embrace one who is no longer there. It's like the phantom pain experienced by those who have lost a limb. Feelings still emanate from that region where once was a crucial part of them. Our hearts know a similar reality. At some deep level, we refuse to accept the fact that this is the way things are, or must be, or always will be.

Simone Weil was right; there are only two things that pierce the human heart: beauty and affliction. Moments we wish would last forever and moments we wish had never begun. The playwright Christopher Fry wrote,

> The inescapable dramatic situation for us all is that we have no idea what our situation is. We may be mortal. What then? We may be immortal. What then? We are plunged into an existence fantastic to the point of nightmare, and however hard we rationalize, or however firm our religious faith, however closely we dog the heels of science or wheel among the starts of mysticism, we cannot really make head or tail of it. ("A Playwright Speaks: How Lost, How Amazed, How Miraculous We Are")

And what does Fry say we do with our dilemma? The worst of all possible reactions:

> We get used to it. We get broken into it so gradually we scarcely notice it.

(The Journey of Desire, 8–9)

The mind takes in and processes information. But it remains, for the most part, indifferent. It is your mind that tells you it is now 2:00 A.M. and your daughter has not returned, for the car is not in the driveway. Your heart wrestles with whether or not this is cause for worry. The heart lives in the far more bloody and magnificent realities of living and dying and loving and hating. That's why those who live from their minds are detached from life. Things don't seem to touch them very much; they puzzle at the way others are so affected by life, and they conclude others are emotional and unstable. Meanwhile, those who live from the heart find those who live from the mind . . . unavailable. Yes, they are physically present. So is your computer. This is the sorrow of many marriages, and the number one disappointment of children who feel entirely missed or misunderstood by their parents.

Yes, the heart is the source of our emotions. But we have equated the heart *with* emotion, and put it away for a messy and even dangerous guide. No doubt, many people have made a wreck of their lives by following an emotion without stopping to consider whether it was a good idea to do so. Neither adultery nor murder is a rational act. But equating the heart *with* emotion is the same nonsense as saying that love is a feeling. Surely, we know that love is more than *feeling* loving; for if Christ had followed his emotions, he would not have gone to the cross for us. Like any man would have been, he was afraid; in fact, he knew that the sins of the world would be laid upon him, and so he had even greater cause for hesitation (Mark 14:32–35). But in the hour of his greatest trial, his love overcame his fear of what loving would cost him.

Emotions are the *voice* of the heart, to borrow Chip Dodd's phrase. Not the heart, but its voice.

(*Waking the Dead*, 41–42)

The Arrows strike at the most vital places in our hearts, the things we care most about. The deepest questions we ever ask are directly related to our hearts' greatest needs and the answers life gives us shape our images of ourselves, of life, and of God. *Who am I?* The Romance whispers that we are someone special, that our heart is good because it is made for someone good; the Arrows tell us we are a dime a dozen, worthless, even dark and twisted, dirty. *Where is life to be found?* The Romance tells us life will flourish when we give it away in love and heroic sacrifice. The Arrows tell us that we must arrange for what little life there may be, manipulating our world and all the while watching our backs. "God is good," the Romance tells us. "You can release the well-being of your heart to him." The Arrows strike back, "Don't ever let life out of your control," and they seem to impale with such authority, unlike the gentle urges of the Romance, that in the end we are driven to find some way to contain them. The only way seems to be to kill our longing for the Romance, much in the same way we harden our heart to someone who hurts us. *If I don't want so much*, we believe, *I won't be so vulnerable.* Instead of dealing with the Arrows, we silence the longing. That seems to be our only hope. And so we lose heart.

Which is the truer message? If we try to hang on to the Romance, what are we to do with our wounds and the awful tragedies of life? How can we keep our heart alive in the face of such deadly Arrows? How many losses can a heart take? If we deny the wounds or try to minimize them, we deny a part of our heart and end up living a shallow optimism that frequently becomes a demand that the world be better than it is. On the other hand, if we embrace the Arrows as the final word on life, we despair, which is another way to lose heart. To lose hope has the same effect on our heart as it would be to stop breathing.

(*The Sacred Romance*, 32–33)

I s there a reality that corresponds to the deepest desires of our heart? Who gets the last word—the Romance or the Arrows? We need to know, so we are constantly, every moment of our lives, trying to make sense out of our experiences. We look for coherence, a flow, an assurance that things fit together. Our problem is that most of us live our lives like a movie we've arrived at twenty minutes late. The action is well under way and we haven't a clue what's happening. Who are these people? Who are the good guys and who are the bad guys? Why are they doing that? What's going on? We sense that something really important, perhaps even glorious, is taking place, and yet it all seems so *random*. Beauty catches us by surprise and makes us wish for more, but then the Arrows come and we are pierced.

No wonder it's so hard to live from our heart! We find ourselves in the middle of a story that is sometimes wonderful, sometimes awful, often a confusing mixture of both, and we haven't the slightest clue how to make sense of it all. Worse, we try to interpret the meaning of life with only fragments, isolated incidents, feelings, and images without reference to the story of which these scenes are merely a part. It can't be done, because, as Julia Gatta pointed out, "Experience, no matter how accurately understood, can never furnish its own interpretation." So we look for someone to interpret life for us. Our interpreters will usually be the primary people in our lives when we are young, our parents or grandparents or another key figure. They shape our understanding of the story in which we find ourselves and tell us what to do with the Romance, the Arrows, and our hearts.

(*The Sacred Romance*, 35–36)

The Religious Man or Woman is a popular story option in which we try to reduce the wildness of life by constructing a system of promises and rewards, a contract that will obligate God to grant us exemption from the Arrows. It really doesn't matter what the particular group bargain is—doctrinal adherence, moral living, or some sort of spiritual experience—the desire is the same: taming God in order to tame life. Never mind those deep yearnings of the soul; never mind the nagging awareness that God is not cooperating. If the system isn't working, it's because we're not doing it right. There's always something to work on, with the promise of abundant life just around the corner. Plenty of churches and leaders are ready to show you how to cut a deal.

These stories comprise what James McClendon calls the "tournament of narratives" in our culture, a clash of many small dramas competing for our heart. Through baseball and politics and music and sex and even church, we are searching desperately for a Larger Story in which to live and find our role. All of these smaller stories offer a taste of meaning, adventure, or connectedness. But none of them offer the real thing; they aren't large enough. Our loss of confidence in a Larger Story is the reason we demand immediate gratification. We need a sense of being alive now, for now is all we have. Without a past that was planned for us and a future that waits for us, we are trapped in the present. There's not enough room for our souls in the present.

(*The Sacred Romance*, 42–43)

We have lived for so long with a "propositional" approach to Christianity, we have nearly lost its true meaning. As Mary Stewart Van Leeuwen says,

> Much of it hinges on your view of scripture. Are you playing proof-text poker with Genesis plus the Gospels and Paul's epistles, with everything else just sort of a big mystery in between—except maybe Psalms and Proverbs, which you use devotionally? Or do you see scripture as being a cosmic drama—creation, fall, redemption, future hope—dramatic narratives that you can apply to all areas of life? (*Prism* interview)

For centuries prior to our Modern Era, the church viewed the gospel as a Romance, a cosmic drama whose themes permeated our own stories and drew together all the random scenes in a redemptive wholeness. But our rationalistic approach to life, which has dominated Western culture for hundreds of years, has stripped us of that, leaving a faith that is barely more than mere fact-telling. Modern evangelicalism reads like an IRS 1040 form: It's true, all the data is there, but it doesn't take your breath away. As British theologian Alister McGrath warns, the Bible is not primarily a doctrinal sourcebook: "To reduce revelation to principles or concepts is to suppress the element of mystery, holiness and wonder to God's self-disclosure. 'First principles' may enlighten and inform; they do not force us to our knees in reverence and awe, as with Moses at the burning bush, or the disciples in the presence of the risen Christ" (*A Passion for Truth*).

(*The Sacred Romance,* 45)

[We live our lives before] the wild, dangerous, unfettered and free character of the living God. (Walter Brueggemann)

The unknown Romancing or the Message of the Arrows—which captures the essence of life? Should we keep our hearts open to the Romance or concentrate on protecting ourselves from the Arrows? Should we live with hopeful abandon, trusting in a larger story whose ending is good, or should we live in our small stories and glean what we can from the Romance while trying to avoid the Arrows?

Perhaps God, as the Author of the Story we're all living in, would tilt the scale in a favorable direction if we knew we could trust him. And therein lies our dilemma. There seems to be no direct correlation between the way we live our lives and the resulting fate God has in store for us, at least on this earth. Abraham's grandson, Jacob, lives the life of a manipulator and is blessed. Jesus lives for the sake of others and is crucified. And we never quite know when we're going to run into the uncertainty of the part God has written for us in his play, whether our character has significant lines yet to speak or will even survive the afternoon.

(*The Sacred Romance,* 47)

The question lodged deep in our hearts, hidden from our conscious minds, is: "Do you care for me, God?"

What's under that question?

Blaise Pascal, in his *Pensées*, says, "The heart has its reasons which reason knows nothing of." What's under that question is our personal stories, often punctuated by the Message of the Arrows: parents who were emotionally absent; bedtimes without words or hugs; ears that were too big and noses that were too small; others chosen for playground games while we were not; and prayers about all these things seemingly met with silence. And embedded in our stories, deep down in our heart, in a place so well guarded that they have rarely if ever been exposed to the light of day, are other grief-laden and often angry questions: "God, why did you allow this to happen to me? Why did you make me like this? What will you allow to happen next?" In the secret places of our heart, we believe God is the One who did not protect us from these things or even the One who perpetrated them upon us. Our questions about him make us begin to live with a deep apprehension that clings anxiously to the depths of our hearts . . . "Do you really care for me, God?"

This is the question that has shipwrecked many of our hearts, leaving them grounded on reefs of pain and doubt, no longer free to accompany us on spiritual pilgrimage. We might be able to rationalize away that question by telling ourselves that we need to be more careful, or that sometimes others are just bad. We can even breathe a sigh of relief when we realize that trouble has come from our own sin. But even the careful, legalistic, and constricted lifestyle that arises out of thinking we can avoid trouble through our own devices shipwrecks when the Arrows seem to strike us out of nowhere. What are we to make of God's wildness in allowing these things to happen?

(*The Sacred Romance,* 49–50)

We use a phrase to try to console ourselves after what we think is an irrecoverable loss: "All good things come to an end." I hate that phrase. It's a lie. Even our troubles and our heartbreaks tell us something about our true destiny. The tragedies that strike us to the core and elicit the cry, "This isn't the way it was supposed to be!" are also telling the truth—it *isn't* the way it was supposed to be. Pascal writes,

> Man is so great that his greatness appears even in knowing himself to be miserable. A tree has no sense of its misery. It is true that to know we are miserable is to be miserable; but to know we are miserable is also to be great. Thus all the miseries of man prove his grandeur; they are the miseries of a dignified personage, the miseries of a dethroned monarch . . . What can this incessant craving, and this impotence of attainment mean, unless there was once a happiness belonging to man, of which only the faintest traces remain, in that void which he attempts to fill with everything within his reach? (*Pensées*)

Should the king in exile pretend he is happy there? Should he not seek his own country? His miseries are his ally; they urge him on. And so let them grow, if need be. But do not forsake the secret of life; do not despise those kingly desires. We abandon the most important journey of our lives when we abandon desire. We leave our hearts by the side of the road and head off in the direction of fitting in, getting by, being productive, what have you. Whatever we might gain—money, position, the approval of others, or just absence of the discontent itself—it's not worth it. "What good will it be for a man if he gains the whole world, yet forfeits his soul?" (Matt. 16:26).

(*The Journey of Desire*, 12–13)

The battles God calls us to, the woundings and cripplings of soul and body we all receive, cannot simply be ascribed to our sin and foolishness, or even to the sin and foolishness of others. When Jesus and the disciples were on the road one day, they came upon a man who had been blind since birth. "Rabbi, who sinned, this man or his parents?" they asked him. "Neither this man nor his parents sinned," said Jesus, "but this happened so that the work of God might be displayed in his life." And with that, Jesus spat on the ground, made some mud to place on the man's eyes, and healed him (John 9:1–7).

Many of us who are reading these words have not yet received God's healing. The display of God's works through our wounds, losses, and sufferings is yet to be revealed. And so, we groan and we wonder.

(*The Sacred Romance,* 61)

When we were young, most of us loved adventure. There is something about the unknown that draws us, which is why we like stories so much. But I like to leave the theater at the end of the play, knowing that the dilemma of evil has been resolved by the characters on the stage or screen. Like Peter, Susan, Lucy, and Edmund, to find ourselves not as spectators but as central characters in the play itself is somewhat daunting. The stakes are truly high, sometimes literally life or death, and God rarely if ever yells, "Cut!" just as the dangerous or painful scene descends upon us. No stunt doubles come onto the set to take our places. Many of us feel that we have been playing these kinds of scenes ever since we were children. We wonder if the hero will ever show up to rescue us.

We would like to picture goodness as being synonymous with safety. When we think of God being good, we perhaps picture someone like Al on the popular TV program *Home Improvement*. He is someone who carefully plans out each task ahead of time and has all the proper tools and safety equipment in place; someone who has thought out every possible danger ahead of time and made allowances to ensure our safety as his workmate; someone who goes to bed early, gets plenty of rest, and wears flannel shirts as a mark of his reliability.

Being in partnership with God, though, often feels much more like being Mel Gibson's sidekick in the movie *Lethal Weapon*. In his determination to deal with the bad guy, he leaps from seventh-story balconies into swimming pools, surprised that we would have any hesitation in following after him. Like Indiana Jones's love interests in the movies, we find ourselves caught up in an adventure of heroic proportions with a God who both seduces us with his boldness and energy and repels us with his willingness to place us in mortal danger, suspended over pits of snakes.

(*The Sacred Romance*, 56–57)

I think even a quick read of the Old Testament would be enough to convince you that *war* is a central theme of God's activity. There is the Exodus, where God goes to war to set his captive people free. Blood. Hail. Locusts. Darkness. Death. Plague after plague descends on Egypt like a boxer's one-two punch, like the blows of some great ax. Pharaoh releases his grip, but only for a moment. The fleeing slaves are pinned against the Red Sea when Egypt makes a last charge, hurtling down on them in chariots. God drowns those soldiers in the sea, every last one of them. Standing in shock and joy on the opposite shore, the Hebrews proclaim, "The LORD is a warrior!" (Ex. 15:3). Yahweh is a warrior.

Then it's war to get *to* the Promised Land. Moses and company have to do battle against the Amalekites; again God comes through, and Moses shouts, "The LORD will be at war against the Amalekites from generation to generation" (Ex.17:16). Yahweh will be at war. Indeed. You ain't seen nothin' yet. Then it's war to get *into* the Promised Land—Joshua and the battle of Jericho, and all that. After the Jews gain the Promised Land, it's war after war to *keep* it. Israel battles the Canaanites, the Philistines, the Midianites, the Egyptians again, the Babylonians—and on and on it goes. Deborah goes to war; Gideon goes to war; King David goes to war. Elijah wars against the prophets of Baal; Jehoshaphat battles the Edomites. Are you getting the picture?

(Waking the Dead, 14–15)

Many people think the theme of war ends with the Old Testament. Not at all. Jesus says, "I did not come to bring peace, but a sword" (Matt. 10:34). In fact, his birth involved another battle in heaven (Rev. 12:1–5, 7–8, 17).

The birth of Christ was an act of war, an *invasion*. The Enemy knew it and tried to kill him as a babe (Matt. 2:13). The whole life of Christ is marked by battle and confrontation. He kicks out demons with a stern command. He rebukes a fever and it leaves Peter's mother-in-law. He rebukes a storm and it subsides. He confronts the Pharisees time and again to set God's people free from legalism. In a loud voice he wakes Lazarus from the dead. He descends to hell, wrestles the keys of hell and death from Satan, and leads a train of captives free (Eph. 4:8–9; Rev. 1:18). And when he returns, I might point out, Jesus will come mounted on a steed of war, with his robe dipped in blood, armed for battle (Rev. 19:11–15).

War is not just one among many themes in the Bible. It is *the* backdrop for the whole Story, the context for everything else. God is at war. He is trampling out the vineyards where the grapes of wrath are stored. And what is he fighting for? Our freedom and restoration. The glory of God is man fully alive. In the meantime, Paul says, *arm yourselves*, and the first piece of equipment he urges us to don is the belt of truth (Eph. 6:10–18). We arm ourselves by getting a good, solid grip on our situation, by getting some clarity on the battle over our lives. God's intentions toward us are life; those intentions are opposed. Forewarned is forearmed, as the saying goes.

(*Waking the Dead,* 15–16)

THE UNWAVERING INTENSITY
OF DESIRE

I am haunted by the stories of people who make the summit of
Everest. Such incredible devotion is required, such total focus
of body, soul, and spirit. Reaching the top of the world's tallest
mountain becomes for those who try the central driving force of
their lives. The goal is so remarkable and the journey so uncertain.
Many climbers have been lost on the mountain. Those who reach
the summit and return safely are among a rare and elite group of
mountaineers in the world. Why do they do it? *How* do they do it?

John Krakauer recounted the desperate tale of the ill-fated '96
expedition in his book *Into Thin Air*: "There were many, many
fine reasons not to go, but attempting to climb Everest is an
intrinsically irrational act—a triumph of desire over sensibility." It
is a feat begun in desire that can be accomplished only through
desire. Krakauer explained how one of his climbing partners
attained the summit: "Yasuko had been propelled up the mountain by the unwavering intensity of her desire."

Desire—it's the only way you will ever make it. Take marriage,
for instance. Or singleness. Either makes for a far more difficult
and arduous ascent than Everest, in large part because it does not
seem so. The struggles are not heightened and focused into one
month of do or die; rather, they stretch on across a lifetime. So it
is with any act of faith or of hope—anything, in other words, that
makes a life worth living. How can we possibly sustain such an
intrinsically irrational act as love if we've killed our desire?

(*The Journey of Desire*, 18–19)

Choosing love will open spaces of immense beauty and joy for you, but you will be hurt. You already know this. You have retreated from love countless times in your life because of it. We all have. We have been and will be hurt by the loss of loved ones, by what they have done to us and we to them. Even in the bliss of love there is a certain exquisite pain: the pain of too much beauty, of overwhelming magnificence. Further, no matter how perfect a love may be, it is never really satisfied . . . In both joy and pain, love is boundless. (Gerald May, *The Awakened Heart*)

Desire is the source of our most noble aspirations and our deepest sorrows. The pleasure and the pain go together; indeed, they emanate from the same region in our hearts. We cannot live without the yearning, and yet the yearning sets us up for disappointment—sometimes deep and devastating disappointment. One storm claimed the lives of eight of Krakauer's companions in the Everest disaster of 1996. Should they not have tried? Many have said they were foolish even to begin. Do we reach for nothing in life because our reaching opens us up to tragedy? Because of its vulnerable nature, desire begins to feel like our worst enemy.

(*The Journey of Desire,* 19)

Despair," wrote James Houston, "is the fate of the desiring soul." Or as Scripture says, "Hope deferred makes the heart sick" (Prov. 13:12 NLT). How agonizing it can be to awaken desire! Over the past year I have wrestled deeply with what it means to go on. God has come to me again and again, insisting that I not give up the dream. I have ranted and railed, fought him and dismissed him. It feels crazy to desire anymore. What does it mean to live the rest of my life without my closest friend? I think of Lewis and Clark, those inseparable wilderness explorers, how we cannot think of one without the other. Lewis said of his companion, "I could neither hope, wish, nor expect from a union with any man on earth, more perfect support or further aid in the discharge of my mission, than that, which I am confident I shall derive from being associated with yourself." I know I shall never find another like him.

But I am not alone in this. Most of you will by this time have lost a parent, a spouse, even a child. Your hopes for your career have not panned out. Your health has given way. Relationships have turned sour. We all know the dilemma of desire, how awful it feels to open our hearts to joy, only to have grief come in. They go together. We know that. What we don't know is what to do with it, how to live in this world with desire so deep in us and disappointment lurking behind every corner. After we've taken a few Arrows, dare we even desire? Something in me knows that to kill desire is to kill my heart altogether.

(*The Journey of Desire,* 22–23)

Remember that little guy I told you about, with the shiny boots and a pair of six-shooters? The best part of the story is that it wasn't all pretend. I had a place to live out those dreams. My grandfather, my father's father, was a cowboy. He worked his own cattle ranch in eastern Oregon. And though I was raised in the suburbs, the redemption of my life and the real training grounds for my own masculine journey took place on that ranch, where I spent my boyhood summers. Oh, that every boy should be so lucky. To have your days filled with tractors and pickup trucks, horses and roping steers, fishing in the ponds. I was Huck Finn for three wonderful months every year. How I loved it when my grandfather—"Pop" is what I called him—would look at me, his thumbs tucked in his belt, smile, and say, "Saddle up."

One afternoon Pop took me into town, to my favorite store. It was a combination feed and tack/hardware/ranch supply shop. It smelled of hay and linseed oil, of leather and gunpowder and kerosene—all the things that thrill a boy's heart. That summer Pop was having a problem with an overrun pigeon population on the ranch. He hated the dirty birds, feared they were carrying diseases to the cattle. "Flying rats" is what he called them. Pop walked straight over to the firearms counter, picked out a BB rifle and a quart-sized milk carton with about a million BBs in it, and handed them to me. The old shopkeeper looked a bit surprised as he stared down at me, squinting over his glasses. "Isn't he a bit young for that?" Pop put his hand on my shoulder and smiled. "This is my grandson, Hal. He's riding shotgun for me."

I may have walked into that feed store a squirrely little kid, but I walked out as Sheriff Wyatt Earp. I had an identity and a place in the story. I was invited to be dangerous. If a boy is to become a man, if a man is to know he is one, this is not an option. A man *has* to know where he comes from, and what he's made of.

(*Wild at Heart,* 20-21)

What Is Your Image of Jesus as a Man?

Maybe it would be better to turn our search to the headwaters, to that mighty root from which these branches grow. Who is this One we allegedly come from, whose image every man bears? What is he like? In a man's search for his strength, telling him that he's made in the image of God may not sound like a whole lot of encouragement at first. To most men, God is either distant or he is weak—the very thing they'd report of their earthly fathers. Be honest now—what is your image of Jesus *as a man?* "Isn't he sort of meek and mild?" a friend remarked. "I mean, the pictures I have of him show a gentle guy with children all around. Kind of like Mother Teresa." Yes, those are the pictures I've seen myself in many churches. In fact, those are the *only* pictures I've seen of Jesus. As I've said before, they leave me with the impression that he was the world's nicest guy. Mister Rogers with a beard. Telling me to be like him feels like telling me to go limp and passive. Be nice. Be swell. Be like Mother Teresa.

I'd much rather be told to be like William Wallace.

(*Wild at Heart*, 22)

In the gospel of John, Jesus extends the offer to anyone who realizes that his life just isn't touching his deep desire: "If you are thirsty, come to me! If you believe in me, come and drink! For the Scriptures declare that rivers of living water will flow out from within" (John 7:37–38 NLT). His message wasn't something new, but it confounded the religious leaders of the day. Surely, those scripturally learned Jews must have recalled God's long-standing invitation to them, spoken seven hundred years earlier through the prophet Isaiah,

> Come, all you who are thirsty,
>   come to the waters;
> and you who have no money,
>   come, buy and eat!
> Come, buy wine and milk
>   without money and without cost.
> Why spend money on what is not bread,
>   and your labor on what does not satisfy?
> Listen, listen to me, and eat what is good,
>   and your soul will delight in the richest of fare.
>   (55:1–2)

Somehow, the message had gotten lost by the time Jesus showed up on the scene. The Jews of his day were practicing a very soul-killing spirituality, a lifeless religion of duty and obligation. Desire was out of the question. No wonder they feared Jesus. He came along and started *appealing* to desire. To the weary, Jesus speaks of rest. To the lost, he speaks of finding your way. Again and again and again, Jesus takes people back to their desires. "Ask and it will be given to you; seek and you will find; knock and the door will be opened to you" (Matt. 7:7). These are outrageous words, provocative words. *Ask, seek, knock*—these words invite and *arouse* desire. What is it that you *want?* They fall on deaf ears if there is nothing you want, nothing you're looking for, nothing you're hungry enough to bang on a door over.

(*The Journey of Desire*, 37–38)

Eternal life—we tend to think of it in terms of existence that never comes to an end. And the existence it seems to imply—a sort of religious experience in the sky—leaves us wondering if we *would* want it to go on forever. But Jesus is quite clear that when he speaks of eternal life, what he means is life that is absolutely wonderful and can never be diminished or stolen from you. He says, "I have come that they may have life, and have it to the full" (John 10:10). Not, "I have come to threaten you into line," or "I have come to exhaust you with a long list of demands." Not even, "I have come primarily to forgive you." But simply, *My purpose is to bring you life in all its fullness.* Dallas Willard writes in *The Divine Conspiracy,*

> Jesus offers himself as God's doorway into the life that is truly life. Confidence in him leads us today, as in other times, to become his apprentices in eternal living. "Those who come through me will be safe," he said. "They will go in and out and find all they need. I have come into their world that they may have life, and life to the limit."

In other words, eternal life is not primarily *duration* but *quality* of life, "life to the limit." It cannot be stolen from us, and so it does go on. But the focus is on the life itself. "In him was life," the apostle John said of Jesus, "and that life was the light of men" (John 1:4).

(*The Journey of Desire,* 38–39)

Deep within the Arrows stay, poisoning our self-perceptions, until someone comes along with the power to take them away, free us from all the false selves we use to weather the world's weather, and restore to us our true identity. Identity is not something that falls on us out of the sky. For better or for worse, identity is *bestowed*. We are who we are in relation to others. But far more important, we draw our identity from our impact on those others—*if* and *how* we affect them. We long to know that we make a difference in the lives of others, to know that we matter, that our presence cannot be replaced by a pet, a possession, or even another person. The awful burden of the false self is that it must be constantly maintained.

We think we have to keep doing something in order to be desirable. Once we find something that will bring us some attention, we have to keep it going or risk the loss of the attention.

And so we live with the fear of not being chosen and the burden of maintaining whatever it is about us that might get us noticed and the commitment never to be seen for who we really are. We develop a *functional* self-image, even if it is a negative one. The little boy paints his red wagon a speckled gray with whatever Father left in the can after putting a new coat on the backyard fence. "Look what I did!" he says, hoping for affirmation of the wonderful impact his presence has on the world. The angry father shames him: "What do you think you're doing? You've ruined it." The boy forms an identity: *My impact is awful; I foul good things up. I am a fouler.* And he forms a commitment never to be in a place where he can foul things up again. Years later, his colleagues wonder why he turned down an attractive promotion. The answer lies in his identity, an identity he received from the impact he had on the most important person in his world and his fear of ever being in such a place again.

(*The Sacred Romance,* 86, 88)

The Bible uses a number of metaphors to describe our relationship to God at various stages. If you'll notice, they ascend in a stunning way:

Potter and clay. At this level we are merely aware that our lives are shaped—even broken—by a powerful hand. There isn't much communication, just the sovereignty of God at work.

Shepherd and sheep. At this stage we feel provided for, watched over, cared about. But beyond that, a sheep has little by way of true intimacy with the Shepherd. They are altogether different creatures.

Master and servant. Many, many believers are stuck in this stage, where they are committed to obey, but the relationship is mostly about receiving orders and instructions and carrying them out.

Father and child. This is certainly more intimate than being a servant; children get the run of the house, they get to climb on Daddy's lap. These fortunate souls understand God's fatherly love and care for them. They feel "at home" with God.

Friends. This stage actually opens up a deeper level of intimacy as we walk together with God, companions in a shared mission. We know what's on his heart; he knows what's on ours. There is a maturity and intimacy to the relationship.

Bridegroom and bride (lovers). Here, the words of the Song of Songs could also describe our spiritual intimacy, our union and oneness with God. Madame Guyon wrote, "I love God far more than the most affectionate lover among men loves his earthly attachment."

Where would you put your relationship with God? Why did you choose that "level"? Has it always been that way?

(The Journey of Desire Journal & Guidebook, 150)

The gospel says that we, who are God's beloved, created a cosmic crisis. It says we, too, were stolen from our True Love and that he launched the greatest campaign in the history of the world to get us back. God created us for intimacy with him. When we turned our back on him he promised to come for us. He sent personal messengers; he used beauty and affliction to recapture our hearts. After all else failed, he conceived the most daring of plans. Under the cover of night he stole into the Enemy's camp incognito, the Ancient of Days disguised as a newborn. The Incarnation, as Phil Yancey reminds us, was a daring raid into enemy territory. The whole world lay under the power of the Evil One and we were held in the dungeons of darkness. God risked it all to rescue us. Why? What is it that he sees in us that causes him to act the jealous lover, to lay siege both on the kingdom of darkness and on our own idolatries as if on Troy—not to annihilate, but to win us once again for himself? This fierce intention, this reckless ambition that shoves all conventions aside, willing literally to move heaven and earth—what does he want from us?

We've been offered many explanations. From one religious camp we're told that what God wants is obedience, or sacrifice, or adherence to the right doctrines, or morality. Those are the answers offered by conservative churches. The more therapeutic churches suggest that no, God is after our contentment, or happiness, or self-actualization, or something else along those lines. He is concerned about all these things, of course, but they are not his primary concern. What he is after is *us*—our laughter, our tears, our dreams, our fears, our heart of hearts. How few of us truly believe this. We've never been wanted for our heart, our truest self, not really, not for long. The thought that God wants our heart seems too good to be true.

(*The Sacred Romance*, 91)

And so Screwtape reveals the Enemy's ploy—first make humans flabby, with small passions and desires, then offer a sop to those diminished passions so that their experience is one of contentment. They know nothing of great joy or great sorrow. They are merely *nice*.

Christianity has come to the point where we believe that there is no higher aspiration for the human soul than to be nice. We are producing a generation of men and women whose greatest virtue is that they don't offend anyone. Then we wonder why there is not more passion for Christ. How can we hunger and thirst after righteousness if we have ceased hungering and thirsting altogether? As C. S. Lewis said, "We castrate the gelding and bid him be fruitful."

The greatest enemy of holiness is not passion; it is apathy. Look at Jesus. He was no milksop. His life was charged with passion. After he drove the crooks from the temple, "his disciples remembered that it is written: 'Zeal for your house will consume me'" (John 2:17). This isn't quite the pictures we have in Sunday school, Jesus with a lamb and a child or two, looking for all the world like Mr. Rogers with a beard. The world's nicest guy. He was something far more powerful. He was holy.

(*The Journey of Desire*, 53–54)

I f the way to avoid the murderous rage and deceptive allures of desire is to kill it, if deadness is next to godliness, then Jesus had to be the deadest person ever. But he is called the *living* God. "It is a dreadful thing," the writer of Hebrews says, "to fall into the hands of the living God . . . For our 'God is a consuming fire'" (10:31; 12:29). And what is this consuming fire? His jealous love (Deut. 4:24). God is a deeply, profoundly passionate person. Zeal consumes him. It is the secret of his life, the writer of Hebrews says. The "joy set before him" enabled Jesus to endure the agony of the Cross (Heb. 12:2). In other words, his profound desire for something greater sustained him at the moment of his deepest trial. We cannot hope to live like him without a similar depth of passion. Many people find that the dilemma of desire is too much to live with, and so they abandon, they disown their desire. This is certainly true of a majority of Christians at present. Somehow we believe that we can get on without it. We are mistaken.

(*The Journey of Desire,* 54–55)

God is a romantic at heart, and his jealousy is for the hearts of his people and for their freedom. As Francis Frangipane so truly states, "Rescue is the constant pattern of God's activity."

> For Zion's sake I will not keep silent,
>> for Jerusalem's sake I will not remain quiet,
> till her righteousness shines out like the dawn,
>> her salvation like a blazing torch . . .
> As a bridegroom rejoices over his bride,
>> so will your God rejoice over you. (Isa. 62:1, 5)

And though she has committed adultery against him, though she has fallen captive to his enemy, God is willing to move heaven and earth to win her back. He will stop at nothing to set her free:

> Who is this coming from Edom,
>> from Bozrah, with his garments stained crimson?
> Who is this, robed in splendor,
>> striding forward in the greatness of his strength?
> "It is I, speaking in righteousness, mighty to save."
> Why are your garments red,
>> like those of one treading the winepress?
> "I have trodden the winepress alone;
>> from the nations no one was with me.
> I trampled them in my anger
>> and trod them down in my wrath;
> their blood spattered my garments,
>> and I stained all my clothing.
> For the day of vengeance was in my heart,
>> and the year of my redemption has come. (Isa. 63:1–4)

Whoa. Talk about a Braveheart. This is one fierce, wild, and passionate guy. I have never heard anyone in church talk like that. But this is the God of heaven and earth. The Lion of Judah.

(Wild at Heart, 34–35)

God has a beauty to unveil. There's a reason that a man is captivated by a woman. Eve is the crown of creation. If you follow the Genesis narrative carefully, you'll see that each new stage of creation is better than the one before. First, all is formless, empty and dark. God begins to fashion the raw materials, like an artist working with a rough sketch or a lump of clay. Light and dark, land and sea, earth and sky—it's beginning to take shape. With a word, the whole floral kingdom adorns the earth. Sun, moon, and stars fill the sky. Surely and certainly, his work expresses greater detail and definition. Next come fish and fowl, porpoises and red-tailed hawks. The wild animals are next, all those amazing creatures. A trout is a wonderful creature, but a horse is truly magnificent. Can you hear the crescendo starting to swell, like a great symphony building and surging higher and higher?

Then comes Adam, the triumph of God's handiwork. It is not to any member of the animal kingdom that God says, "You are my very image, the icon of my likeness." Adam bears the likeness of God in his fierce, wild, and passionate heart. And yet, there is one more finishing touch. There is Eve. Creation comes to its high point, its climax with her. She is God's finishing touch. And all Adam can say is, "Wow." Eve embodies the beauty and the mystery and the tender vulnerability of God. As the poet William Blake said, "The naked woman's body is a portion of eternity too great for the eye of man."

(*Wild at Heart*, 36–37)

Have you no other daughters?" "No," said the man. "There is a little stunted kitchen wench which my late wife left behind her, but she cannot be the bride." The King's son said he was to send her up to him; but the stepmother answered, "Oh no, she is much too dirty, she cannot show herself!" But he absolutely insisted on it, and Cinderella had to be called. She first washed her hands and face clean, and then went and bowed down before the King's son, who gave her the golden slipper. Then she seated herself on a stool, drew her foot out of the heavy wooden shoe, and put it into the slipper, which fit like a glove. And when she rose up and the King's son looked at her face, he recognized the beautiful maiden who had danced with him and cried, "This is the true bride!" The stepmother and two sisters were horrified and became pale with rage; he, however, took Cinderella on his horse and rode away with her.

I love this part of the story—to see the heroine unveiled in all her glory. To have her, *finally*, rise up to her full height. Mocked, hated, laughed at, spit upon—Cinderella is the one the slipper fits; she's the one the prince is in love with; *she's* the true bride. Just as we are.

(*Waking the Dead*, 71–72)

The thought of *me* being called out of hiding is unnerving. I don't think I want to be seen. Many years ago, during my life in the theater, I received a standing ovation for a performance. The audience was literally on its feet, cheering. What actor doesn't crave a standing ovation? So you know what I did? I *ran*. Literally. As soon as the curtain went down I bolted for the door, so I wouldn't have to talk to anyone. I didn't want to be seen. I know, it's weird, but I'll bet you feel the same about being unveiled.

You probably can't imagine there being a glory to your life, let alone one that the Enemy fears. But remember—things are not what they seem. *We* are not what we seem. You probably believed that your heart was bad too. I pray that fog of poison gas from the pit of hell is fading away in the wind of God's truth. And there is more. Not only does Christ say to you that your heart is good, he invites you now out of the shadows to unveil your glory. You have a role you never dreamed of having.

There's the beautiful scene toward the end of Joseph's life where he, too, is unveiled. The very brothers who sold him into slavery as a boy are standing before what they believe is an angry Egyptian lord, equal in power to Pharaoh himself, their knees knocking. The silver cup of this dreaded lord was found stashed away in their luggage as they headed out of town—placed there by Joseph himself as a ruse. Now Joseph interrogates them till they squirm, deepening the plot by using an interpreter as if he doesn't understand Hebrew, pressing them hard. Finally, unable to hold back his tears, he *reveals* himself: "I am Joseph; does my father still live? . . . So you shall tell my father of all my glory in Egypt . . . and you shall hurry and bring my father down here" (Gen. 45:3, 13 NKJV). This is who I really am! Tell him about my glory! Amazing.

(*Waking the Dead*, 72–73)

The story of Eve holds such rich treasures for us to discover. The essence and purpose of a woman are unveiled here in the story of her creation. These profound, eternal, mythic themes are written not just here in the coming of Eve, but in the soul of every woman after. Woman is the crown of creation—the most intricate, dazzling creature on earth. She has a crucial role to play, a destiny of her own.

And she, too, bears the image of God. But in a way that only the feminine can speak. What can we learn from her? God wanted to reveal something about himself, so he gave us Eve. When you are with a woman, ask yourself, *What is she telling me about God?* It will open up wonders for you.

First, you'll discover that God is relational to his core, that he has a heart for romance. Second, that he longs to share adventures with us—adventures we cannot accomplish without him. And finally, that God has a beauty to unveil. A beauty that is captivating and powerfully redemptive.

(*Captivating*, 26)

The Scriptures employ a wide scale of metaphors to capture the many facets of our relationship with God. If you consider them in a sort of ascending order, there is a noticeable and breathtaking progression. Down near the bottom of the totem pole we are the clay and he is the Potter. Moving up a notch, we are the sheep and he is the Shepherd, which is a little better position on the food chain but hardly flattering; sheep don't have a reputation as the most graceful and intelligent creatures in the world. Moving upward, we are the servants of the Master, which at least lets us into the house, even if we have to wipe our feet, watch our manners, and not talk too much. Most Christians never get past this point, but the ladder of metaphors is about to make a swift ascent. God also calls us his children and himself our heavenly Father, which brings us into the possibility of real intimacy— love is not one of the things a vase and its craftsman share together, nor does a sheep truly know the heart of the shepherd, though it may enjoy the fruits of his kindness. Still, there is something missing even in the best parent-child relationship. Friendship levels the playing field in a way family never can, at least not until the kids have grown and left the house. Friendship opens a level of communion that a five-year-old doesn't know with his mother and father. And "friends" are what he calls us.

But there is still a higher and deeper level of intimacy and partnership awaiting us at the top of this metaphorical ascent. We are lovers. The courtship that began with a honeymoon in the Garden culminates in the wedding feast of the Lamb. "I will take delight in you," he says to us, "as a bridegroom rejoices over his bride, so will I rejoice over you," so that we might say in return, "I am my beloved's and his desire is for me."

(*The Sacred Romance,* 96)

We are the sons and daughters of God, even more, the Beloved, pursued by God himself. We might think that, having our heart and mind bolstered by these images of beauty and truth, we would live our lives with courage and energy that arise out of the exuberant hope we have in the future. But there is another voice that whispers in our ear a very different message: a message in a minor and condemning key; a key that dilutes or even erases the truths John has portrayed so well. Some of this music in minor key we can ascribe to the pathos of living on this side of the Fall. Along with the creation itself, we will experience an inner groaning until Christ returns to wipe away every tear and establish his kingdom with us in joy and laughter.

But what is the source of the persistent accusations in our head and heart? It is a voice that speaks to us in tones and words vaguely familiar. The words and accusations that slide almost unnoticed into our consciousness are words we have heard before, sometimes from parents, peers, or the enemies of our youth. The voice (sometimes voices) that accuses us is so familiar we have learned to think of it as our own. Many of us have learned to use the voice to help us control life's unknowns—or so we think. It is a voice that constantly questions the wisdom of hope and the life of faith and love that flows from it.

It is the voice of our adversary.

(*The Sacred Romance*, 99–100)

Our enemy is the angel Lucifer, son of the morning, one of the first and highest angels God created. He is the antagonist in the Sacred Romance—the great villain. All other villains are only a shadow of him. He is the one God gave a place of honor and trust "among the fiery stones" of the courts of heaven and who sees God face-to-face even to this day. He is one who spurned God's love and lost everything good through the sin of presumption. His desire was, and still is, to possess everything that belongs to God, including the worship of all those whom God loves. And God, as the Author of the great Story in which we are all living, has mysteriously allowed him a certain freedom to harass and oppress the other characters in the play, sometimes in a severe manner.

In some ways, due to his great age and dark wisdom, Satan knows us better than we know ourselves. The one purpose of his heart is the destruction of all that God loves, particularly his beloved. He stalks us day and night, as the Lord tells us through Peter: "Your enemy the devil prowls around like a roaring lion looking for someone to devour" (1 Peter 5:8). Peter makes it clear he is talking especially to believers, saying in verse 9, "Resist him, standing firm in the faith, because you know that *your brothers* throughout the world are undergoing the same kind of sufferings" (emphasis added).

(*The Sacred Romance*, 101–2)

God and Satan each have a design, a battle plan, to capture our heart's devotion. The intimacy, beauty, and adventure of the Sacred Romance are placed and nurtured in the deepest longings of our heart by God himself. God's grand strategy, birthed in his grace toward us in Christ, and nurtured through the obedience of disciplined faith, is to release us into the redeemed life of our heart, knowing it will lead us back to him even as the North Star guides a ship across the vast unknown surface of the ocean.

If we were to find ourselves living with total freedom, Jesus informs us through his summary of the law in Luke 10:26–28, we would find ourselves loving God with all of our heart and our neighbors as ourselves. Jesus said further, "You will know the truth [me], and the truth will set you free."

The Enemy knows this as well, and his strategy to capture us is simply the opposite: to disconnect us from our heart and the heart of God toward us by any means possible. It is what he no doubt had to do to his own heart to bear the loss of heaven.

(*The Sacred Romance,* 107)

The core of Satan's plan for each of us is not found in tempting us with obvious sins like shoplifting or illicit sex. These things he uses more as maintenance strategies. His grand tactic in separating us from our heart is to sneak in as the Storyteller through our fears and the wounds we have received from life's Arrows. He weaves a story that becomes our particular "Message of the Arrows." Counting on our vanity and blindness, he seduces us to try to control life by living in the smaller stories we all construct to one degree or another. He accuses God to us and us to God. He accuses us through the words of parents and friends and God himself. He calls good evil and evil good and always helps us question whether God has anything good in mind in his plans for us. He steals our innocence as children and replaces it with a blind naïveté or cynicism as adults.

At the same time Satan is at work reinterpreting our own individual stories in order to make God our enemy, he is also at work dismantling the Sacred Romance—the Larger Story God is telling—so that there is nothing visible to take our breath away. He replaces the love affair with a religious system of dos and don'ts that parches our hearts and replaces our worship and communion services with entertainment. Our experience of life deteriorates from the passion of a grand love affair, in the midst of a life-and-death battle, to an endless series of chores and errands, a busyness that separates us from God, each other, and even from our own thirstiness.

Part of Satan's grand strategy of separating us from our heart, once Jesus has drawn us to an awareness of being his sons and daughters through believing faith, is to convince us that our heart's desires are *at core* illegitimate.

(*The Sacred Romance,* 107–9)

We've exchanged that great hymn "Onward, Christian Soldiers" for a subtle but telling substitute, a song that is currently being taught to thousands of children in Sunday school each week, which goes something like this (sung in a very happy, upbeat tune):

> I may never march in the infantry,
> ride in the cavalry,
> shoot the artillery,
> I may never fly over the enemy
> but I'm in the Lord's army, yes sir!

There is no battle and there is no war and there is no Enemy and your life is not at stake and you are not desperately needed this very hour, but you're in the Lord's army. Yes, sir. Doing *what?* may I ask.

The reason I bring this up is that if you want the real deal, if you want the life and freedom that Jesus offers, then you are going to have to break free of this religious fog in particular. "It is for freedom that Christ has set us free. Stand firm, then, and do not let yourselves be burdened again by a yoke of slavery" (Gal. 5:1). So here's a bottom-line test to expose the Religious Spirit: If it doesn't bring freedom and it doesn't bring life, it's not Christianity. If it doesn't restore the image of God and rejoice in the heart, it's not Christianity.

The ministry of Jesus is summarized by one of those who knew him best when Peter brings the gospel to the gentiles: "God anointed Jesus of Nazareth with the Holy Spirit and power, and . . . he went around doing good and healing all who were under the power of the devil, because God was with him" (Acts 10:38). The stream of Spiritual Warfare was essential to Jesus' life and ministry. It follows that it must be essential to ours if we would be his followers.

(*Waking the Dead*, 162–63)

Having abandoned desire, we have lost hope. C. S. Lewis summed it up: "We can only hope for what we desire." No desire, no hope. Now, desire doesn't always translate into hope. There are many things I desire that I have little hope for. I desire to have lots more money than I do, but I see little reason to think it will come. But there isn't one thing I hope for that I don't *also* desire. This is Lewis's point. Bland assurances of the sweet by-and-by don't inflame the soul. Our hopes are deeply tied to our real desires, and so killing desire has meant a hopeless life for too many. It's as if we've already entered Dante's *Inferno*, where the sign over hell reads, "Abandon hope, all ye who enter here."

The effect has been disastrous, not only for individual Christians, but also for the message of the gospel as a whole. People aren't exactly ripping the roofs off churches to get inside. We see the Enemy's ploy: drain all the life and beauty and adventure away from the gospel, bury Christians in duty, and nobody will want to take a closer look. It's so very unappealing.

David Whyte calls this the "devouring animal of our disowned desire." It is the reason behind most affairs in the church. The pastor lives out of duty, trying to deny his thirst for many years. One day, the young secretary smiles at him and it's over. Because he has so long been out of touch with his desire, it becomes overwhelming when it does show up. The danger of disowning desire is that it sets us up for a fall. We are unable to distinguish real life from a tempting imitation. We are fooled by the impostors. Eventually, we find some means of procuring a taste of the life we were meant for.

(*The Journey of Desire,* 64–66)

I was thumbing through a Williams-Sonoma catalog. It calls itself "a catalog for cooks," but really, it's a catalog of the life we wish we had. Everything is beautiful, delicious, elegant. The kitchens portrayed are immaculate—there are no messes. Cooking there would be a joy. The tables are sumptuous with their beautiful china place settings, wine glasses brimming with nectar, gourmet foods deliciously prepared, invitingly presented. Fresh flowers abound. The homes are lovely and spacious; the view out the windows is always a mountain lake, a beach, or perhaps an English garden. Everything is as it ought to be. Glancing through its pages, you get a sense of rest. Life is good. *You see*, the images whisper, *it can be done. Life is within your grasp.* And so the quest continues. But of course. Our address used to be Paradise, remember?

And oh, how we yearn for another shot at it. Flip with me for a moment through the photo album of your heart, and collect a few of your most treasured memories. Recall a time in your life when you felt really special, a time when you *knew* you were loved. The day you got engaged perhaps. Or a childhood Christmas. Maybe a time with your grandparents.

Hold your memory while you gather another, a time of real adventure, such as when you first learned to ride a bike, or galloped on a horse, or perhaps did something exciting on a vacation. Now, we were meant to live in a world like that—every day. Just as our lungs are made to breathe oxygen, our souls are designed to flourish in an atmosphere rich in love and meaning, security and significance, *intimacy* and *adventure*. But we don't live in that world anymore. Far from it. Though we try to resolve the dilemma by disowning our desire, it doesn't work. It is the soul's equivalent of holding our breath. Eventually, we find ourselves gasping for air.

(*The Journey of Desire,* 71–72)

Emasculation happens in marriage as well. Women are often attracted to the wilder side of a man, but once having caught him they settle down to the task of domesticating him. Ironically, if he gives in he'll resent her for it, and she in turn will wonder where the passion has gone. Most marriages wind up there. A weary and lonely woman asked me the other day, "How do I get my husband to come alive?" "Invite him to be dangerous," I said. "You mean, I should let him get the motorcycle, right?" "Yep." She shrank back, disappointment on her face. "I know you're right, but I hate the idea. I've made him tame for years."

Think back to that great big lion in that tiny cage. Why would we put a man in a cage? For the same reason we put a lion there. For the same reason we put God there: he's dangerous. To paraphrase Dorothy Sayers, we've also pared the claws of the Lion *Cub* of Judah. A man is a dangerous thing. Women don't start wars. Violent crimes aren't for the most part committed by women. Our prisons aren't filled with women. Columbine wasn't the work of two young girls. Obviously, something has gone wrong in the masculine soul, and the way we've decided to handle it is to take that dangerous nature away . . . entirely.

(*Wild at Heart,* 82)

That strength so essential to men is also what makes them *heroes*. If a neighborhood is safe, it's because of the strength of men. Slavery was stopped by the strength of men, at a terrible price to them and their families. The Nazis were stopped by men. Apartheid wasn't defeated by women. Who gave their seats up on the lifeboats leaving the *Titanic*, so that women and children would be saved? And have we forgotten—it was a Man who let himself be nailed to Calvary's Cross. This isn't to say women can't be heroic. I know many heroic women. It's simply to remind us that God made men the way they are because we desperately *need* them to be the way they are. Yes, a man is a dangerous thing. So is a scalpel. It can wound or it can save your life. You don't make it safe by making it dull; you put it in the hands of someone who knows what he's doing.

If you've spent any time around horses, you know a stallion can be a major problem. They're strong, very strong, and they've got a mind of their own. Stallions typically don't like to be bridled, and they can get downright aggressive—especially if there are mares around. A stallion is hard to tame. If you want a safer, quieter animal, there's an easy solution: castrate him. A gelding is much more compliant. You can lead him around by the nose; he'll do what he's told without putting up a fuss. There's only one problem: Geldings don't give life. They can't come through for you the way a stallion can. A stallion is dangerous all right, but if you want the life he offers, you have to have the danger too. They go together.

(*Wild at Heart,* 83–84)

"I'm just a sinner, saved by grace." "I'm just clothes for God to put on." "There sure isn't any good thing in me." It's so common this mind-set, this idea that we are no-good wretches, ready to sin at a moment's notice, incapable of goodness, and certainly far from any glory.

It's also unbiblical.

The passage people think they are referring to is Romans 7:18, where Paul says, "For I know that in me (that is, in my flesh,) dwelleth no good thing" (KJV). Notice the distinction he makes. He does *not* say, "There is nothing good in me. Period." What he says is that "*in my flesh* dwelleth no good thing." The flesh is the old nature, the old life, crucified with Christ. The flesh is the very thing God removed from our hearts when he circumcised them by his Spirit. In Galatians Paul goes on to explain, "Those who belong to Christ Jesus have crucified the sinful nature [the flesh] with its passions and desires" (5:24). He does *not* say, "I am incapable of good." He says, "*In my flesh* dwelleth no good thing." In fact, just a few moments later, he discovers that "the law of the Spirit of life in Christ Jesus has made me free from the law of sin and death" (Rom. 8:2 NKJV).

Yes, we still battle with sin. *Yes*, we still have to crucify our flesh on a daily basis. "For if you live according to the flesh you will die; but if by the Spirit you put to death the deeds of the [sinful nature], you will live" (Rom. 8:13 NKJV). We have to *choose* to live from the new heart, and our old nature doesn't go down without a fight. I'll say more about that later. For now the question on the table is: Does the Bible teach that Christians are nothing but sinners—that there is nothing good in us? The answer is *no!* Christ lives in you. You have a new heart. Your heart is good. That sinful nature you battle *is not who you are.*

(*Waking the Dead*, 75–76)

Twice, in the famous chapter of Romans 7, where Paul presents a first-person angst about our battle against sin, he says, "But this is not my true nature. This is not my heart."

> As it is, *it is no longer I myself* who do it, but sin living in me. I know that nothing good lives in me, that is, in my sinful nature . . . Now if I do what I do not want to do, *it is no longer I* who do it, but it is sin living in me that does it . . . For in my inner being I delight in God's law." (vv. 17–18, 20, emphasis added)

Paul is making a crucial distinction. *This is not me; this is not my true heart.* Listen to how he talks about himself in other places. He opens every letter by introducing himself as "Paul, an apostle." Not as a sinner, but as an apostle, writing to "the saints." Dump the religiosity; think about this *mythically.* Paul, appointed as a Great One in the kingdom, writing to other Great Allies of the kingdom. How bold of him. There is no false humility, no groveling. He says,

> Surely you have heard about the . . . grace that was given to me for you, that is, the mystery made known to me by revelation, as I have already written briefly. In reading this, then, you will be able to understand my insight into the mystery of Christ, which was not made known to men in other generations as it has now been revealed [to me]. (Eph. 3:2–5)

Paul is unashamed to say that he knows things no man before him knew. He even assumes they've heard about him, the mysteries revealed to him. That is part of his glory. His humility comes through clearly, in that he quickly admits that it's all been a gift, and in fact, a gift given to him *for others.*

(Waking the Dead, 76–77)

I (John) just let out a deep sigh. That we even need to explain how beauty is so *absolutely essential* to God only shows how dull we have grown to him, to the world in which we live, and to Eve. Far too many years of our own spiritual lives were lived with barely a nod to beauty, to the central role that beauty plays in the life of God, and in our own lives. How could we have missed this?

Beauty is essential to God. No—that's not putting it strongly enough. Beauty is the essence of God.

The first way we know this is through nature, the world God has given us. Scripture says that the created world is filled with the glory of God (Isa. 6:3). In what way? Primarily through its *beauty.* We had a wet spring here in Colorado, and the wildflowers are coming up everywhere—lupine and wild iris and Shasta daisy and a dozen others. The aspens have their heart-shaped leaves again, trembling in the slightest breeze. Massive thunderclouds are rolling in, bringing with them the glorious sunsets they magnify. The earth in summer is brimming with beauty, beauty of such magnificence and variety and unembarrassed lavishness, ripe beauty, lush beauty, beauty given to us with such generosity and abundance it is almost scandalous.

Nature is not primarily functional. It is primarily beautiful. Stop for a moment and let that sink in. We're so used to evaluating everything (and everyone) by their usefulness, this thought will take a minute or two to dawn on us. Nature is not primarily functional. It is primarily *beautiful.* Which is to say, beauty is in and of itself a great and glorious good, something we need in large and daily doses (for our God has seen fit to arrange for this). Nature at the height of its glory shouts, *Beauty is essential!* revealing that Beauty is the essence of God. The whole world is full of his glory.

(Captivating, 23–24)

I will go before you
and will level the mountains;
I will break down gates of bronze
and cut through bars of iron.
I will give you the treasures of darkness,
riches stored in secret places,
so that you may know that I am the Lord,
the God of Israel, who summons you by name. (Isa. 45:2–3)

God's imagery of going before us lets us know that he desires us to go on a journey. This is not so frightening. Most of us are aware that the Christian life requires a pilgrimage of some sort. We know we are sojourners. What we have sometimes not given much thought to is what kind of a journey we are to be taking.

Not realizing it is a journey of the heart that is called for, we make a crucial mistake. We come to a place in our spiritual life where we hear God calling us. We know he is calling us to give up the less-wild lovers that have become so much a part of our identity, embrace our nakedness, and trust in his goodness.

As we stand at this intersection of God's calling, we look down two highways that appear to travel in very different directions. The first highway quickly takes a turn and disappears from our view. We cannot see clearly where it leads, but there are ominous clouds in the near distance. Standing still long enough to look down this road makes us aware of an anxiety inside, an anxiety that threatens to crystallize into unhealed pain and forgotten disappointment. We check our valise and find no up-to-date road map but only the torn and smudged parchment containing the scribbled anecdotes and travelers' warnings by a few who have traveled the way of the heart before us. They encourage us to follow them, but their rambling journals give no real answers to our queries on how to navigate the highway.

(The Sacred Romance, 127–28)

This is the power of addiction. Whatever the object of our addiction is, it attaches itself to our intense desire for eternal and intimate communion with God and each other in the midst of Paradise—the desire that Jesus himself placed in us before the beginning of the world. Nothing less than this kind of unfallen communion will ever satisfy our desire or allow it to drink freely without imprisoning it and us. Once we allow our heart to drink water from these less-than-eternal wells with the goal of finding the life we were made for, it overpowers our will, and becomes, as Jonathan Edwards said, "like a viper, hissing and spitting at God" and us if we try to restrain it.

"Nothing is less in power than the heart and far from commanding, we are forced to obey it," said Jean Rousseau. Our heart will carry us either to God or to addiction.

"Addiction is the most powerful psychic enemy of humanity's desire for God," says Gerald May in *Addiction and Grace*, which is no doubt why it is one of our adversary's favorite ways to imprison us. Once taken captive, trying to free ourselves through willpower is futile. Only God's Spirit himself can free us or even bring us to our senses.

(*The Sacred Romance*, 133–34)

The Evil One has basically two ploys. If he cannot get us to kill our hearts and bury our desire, then he is delighted to seduce our desire into a trap. Once we give over our desire for life to any object other than God, we become ensnared. Think of the phrase "She's a slave to fashion." We become slaves to any number of things, which at the outset we thought would serve us. In this light, repression of desire is a much less dangerous stage in the process. Addiction is far worse, for as Gerald May explains,

> Our addictions are our own worst enemies. They enslave us with chains that are of our own making and yet that, paradoxically, are virtually beyond our control. Addiction also makes idolaters of us all, because it forces us to worship these objects of attachment, thereby preventing us from truly, freely loving God and one another. (*Addiction and Grace*)

Like the rich young ruler, we find we cannot give up our treasured possessions, whatever they may be, even though God himself is standing before us with a better offer. If you think his sad story is not also your own, you are out of touch with yourself. I remember standing in the East River several summers ago. It was a gorgeous summer evening, and I was about to enjoy some great fly-fishing. I had just begun to cast when God spoke to me. *Put down the rod*, he said. *I'd like to spend some time with you.* I was irritated. *Now?* I replied. *You want to talk to me now? Why not later on the drive home? There's plenty of time in the car.* Good grief. What an addict I am! Thus the father of lies turns our most precious treasure—our longing for God and for his kingdom—into our worst enemy. It is truly diabolical. We wind up serving our desire slavishly, or resenting it, or a little of both.

(*The Journey of Desire*, 84)

I t seems at times that God will go to any length to thwart the very thing we most deeply want. We can't get a job. Our attempt to find a spouse never pans out. The doctors aren't able to help us with our infertility. Isn't this precisely the reason we fear to desire in the first place? Life is hard enough as it is, but to think that God himself is working against us is more than disheartening. As Job cried out, "What do you gain by oppressing me? . . . You hunt me like a lion and display your awesome power against me" (10:3, 16 NLT).

I want to state very clearly that not every trial in our life is specially arranged for us by God. Much of the heartache we know comes from living in a broken world filled with broken people. But there are times when God seems to be set *against* us. Unless we understand our desperate hearts and our incredible tenacity to arrange for the life we want, these events will just seem cruel.

When we lived in Eden, there was virtually no restriction on the pleasure around us. We could eat *freely* from any tree in the Garden. Our desire was innocent and fully satisfied. We had it all, but we threw it away. By mistrusting God's heart, by reaching to take control of what we wanted, Adam and Eve set in motion a process in our hearts, a desperate grasping that can be described only as *addiction*. Desire goes mad within us. Gerald May observes, "Once they gave in to that temptation, their freedom was invaded by attachment. They experienced the need for more. God knew that they would not—*could not*—stop with just the one tree."

Our first parents are banished from Paradise as an act of mercy. The thought of the human race gaining immortality—eating from the Tree of Life—in a fallen state is too horrible to imagine. We would be evil forever.

(*The Journey of Desire*, 91–92)

From the place of our woundedness we construct a false self. We find a few gifts that work for us, and we try to live off them. Stuart found he was good at math and science. He shut down his heart and spent all his energies perfecting his "Spock" persona. There, in the academy, he was safe; he was also recognized and rewarded. "When I was eight," confesses Brennan Manning, "the impostor, or false self, was born as a defense against pain. The impostor within whispered, 'Brennan, don't ever be your real self anymore because nobody likes you as you are. Invent a new self that everybody will admire and nobody will know.'" Notice the key phrase: "as a defense against pain," as a way of saving himself. The impostor is our plan for salvation.

So God must take it all away. He thwarts our plan for salvation; he shatters the false self. Our plan for redemption is hard to let go of; it clings to our hearts like an octopus.

Why would God do something so terrible as to wound us in the place of our deepest wound? Jesus warned us that "whoever wants to save his life will lose it" (Luke 9:24). Christ is not using the word *bios* here; he's not talking about our physical life. The passage is not about trying to save your skin by ducking martyrdom or something like that. The word Christ uses for "life" is the word *psyche*—the word for our soul, our inner self, our heart. He says that the things we do to save our psyche, our self, those plans to save and protect our inner life—those are the things that will actually destroy us. "There is a way that seems right to a man but in the end it leads to death," says Proverbs 16:25. The false self, our plan for redemption, seems so right to us. It shields us from pain and secures us a little love and admiration. But the false self is a lie; the whole plan is built on pretense. It's a deadly trap. God loves us too much to leave us there. So he thwarts us, in many, many different ways.

(*Wild at Heart,* 107–8)

This is a very dangerous moment, when God seems set against everything that has meant life to us. Satan spies his opportunity, and leaps to accuse God in our hearts. *You see,* he says, *God is angry with you. He's disappointed in you. If he loved you he would make things smoother. He's not out for your best, you know.* The Enemy always tempts us back toward control, to recover and rebuild the false self. We must remember that it is out of love that God thwarts our impostor. As Hebrews reminds us, it is the son whom God disciplines, therefore do not lose heart (12:5–6).

God thwarts us to save us. We think it will destroy us, but the opposite is true—we must be saved from what really will destroy us. If we would walk with him in our journey, we must walk away from the false self—set it down, give it up willingly. It feels crazy; it feels immensely vulnerable. We simply accept the invitation to leave all that we've relied on and venture out with God. We can choose to do it ourselves, or we can wait for God to bring it all down.

If you have no clue as to what your false self may be, then a starting point would be to ask those you live with and work with, "What is my effect on you? What am I like to live with (or work with)? What *don't* you feel free to bring up with me?" Drop the fig leaf; come out from hiding. For how long? Longer than you want to; long enough to raise the deeper issues, let the wound surface from beneath it all.

(*Wild at Heart,* 111–12)

Guys are unanimously embarrassed by their emptiness and woundedness; it is for most of us a tremendous source of shame, as I've said. But it need not be. From the very beginning, back before the Fall and the assault, ours was meant to be a desperately dependent existence. It's like a tree and its branches, explains Christ. You are the branches, I am the trunk. From me you draw your life; that's how it was meant to be. In fact, he goes on to say, "Apart from me you can do nothing" (John 15:5). He's not berating us or mocking us or even saying it with a sigh, all the while thinking, *I wish they'd pull it together and stop needing me so much.* Not at all. We are *made* to depend on God; we are made for union with him, and nothing about us works right without it. As C. S. Lewis wrote, "A car is made to run on gasoline, and it would not run properly on anything else. Now God designed the human machine to run on himself. He himself is the fuel our spirits were designed to burn, or the food our spirits were designed to feed on. There is no other."

This is where our sin and our culture have come together to keep us in bondage and brokenness, to prevent the healing of our wound. Our sin is that stubborn part inside that wants, above all else, to be independent. There's a part of us fiercely committed to living in a way where we do not have to depend on anyone—especially God. Then culture comes along with figures like John Wayne and James Bond and all those other "real men," and the one thing they have in common is that they are *loners*; they don't need anyone. We come to believe deep in our hearts that needing anyone for anything is a sort of weakness, a handicap.

(*Wild at Heart*, 121–22)

I f you wanted to learn how to heal the blind and you thought that following Christ around and watching how he did it would make things clear, you'd wind up pretty frustrated. He never does it the same way twice. He spits on one guy; for another, he spits on the ground and makes mud and puts that on his eyes. To a third he simply speaks, a fourth he touches, and for a fifth he kicks out a demon. There are no formulas with God. The way in which God heals our wound is a deeply personal process. He is a person and he insists on working personally. For some, it comes in a moment of divine touch. For others, it takes place over time and through the help of another, maybe several others. As Agnes Sanford says, "There are in many of us wounds so deep that only the mediation of someone else to whom we may 'bare our grief' can heal us."

So much healing took place in my life simply through my friendship with Brent. We were partners, but far more than that, we were friends. We spent hours together fly-fishing, backpacking, hanging out in pubs. Just spending time with a man I truly respected, a real man who loved and respected me—nothing heals quite like that. At first I feared that I was fooling him, that he'd see through it any day and drop me. But he didn't, and what happened instead was validation. My heart knew that if a man I *know* is a man thinks I'm one, too, well then, maybe I am one after all. Remember—masculinity is bestowed by masculinity. But there have been other significant ways in which God has worked—times of healing prayer, times of grieving the wound and forgiving my father. Most of all, times of deep communion with God. The point is this: Healing never happens outside of intimacy with Christ. The healing of our wound flows out of our union with him.

(*Wild at Heart*, 127–28)

The deeper reason we fear our own glory is that once we let others see it, they will have seen the truest us, and that is nakedness indeed. We can repent of our sin. We can work on our "issues." But there is nothing to be "done" about our glory. It's so naked. It's just there—the truest us. It is an awkward thing to shimmer when everyone else around you is not, to walk in your glory with an unveiled face when everyone else is veiling his. For a woman to be truly feminine and beautiful is to invite suspicion, jealousy, misunderstanding. A friend confided in me, "When you walk into a room, every woman looks at you to see—are you prettier than they are? Are you a threat?"

And that is why living from your glory is the only loving thing to do. You cannot love another person from a false self. You cannot love another while you are still hiding. You cannot love another unless you offer her your heart. It takes courage to live from your heart. My friend Jenny said just the other day, "I desperately want to be who I am. I don't want the glory that I marvel at in others anymore. I want to be that glory which God set in me."

Finally, our deepest fear of all . . . we will need to live from it. To admit we do have a new heart and a glory from God, to begin to let it be unveiled and embrace it as true—that means the next thing God will do is ask us to live from it. Come out of the boat. Take the throne. Be what he meant us to be. And that feels risky . . . really risky. But it is also exciting. It is coming fully alive. My friend Morgan declared, "It's a risk worth taking."

(*Waking the Dead*, 87–88)

Either we wake to tackle our "to do" list, get things done, guided by our morals and whatever clarity we may at the moment have (both rather lacking to the need, I might add); or we wake in the midst of a dangerous Story, as God's intimate ally, following him into the unknown.

If you're not pursuing a dangerous quest with your life, well, then, you don't need a Guide. If you haven't found yourself in the midst of a ferocious war, then you won't need a seasoned Captain. If you've settled in your mind to live as though this is a fairly neutral world and you are simply trying to live your life as best you can, then you can probably get by with the Christianity of tips and techniques. Maybe. I'll give you about a fifty-fifty chance. But if you intend to live in the Story that God is telling, and if you want the life he offers, then you are going to need more than a handful of principles, however noble they may be. There are too many twists and turns in the road ahead, too many ambushes waiting only God knows where, too much at stake. You cannot possibly prepare yourself for every situation. Narrow is the way, said Jesus. How shall we be sure to find it? We need God intimately, and we need him desperately.

"You have made known to me the path of life," David said (Ps. 16:11). Yes—that's it. In all the ins and outs of this thing we call living, there is one narrow path to life, and we need help finding it.

(*Waking the Dead*, 95)

A personal walk with God comes to us through wisdom and revelation. You will soon discover that we need both.

> For a moment the King's grief and anger were so great that he could not speak. Then he said: "Come, friends. We must go up the river and find the villains who have done this, with all the speed we may. I will not leave one of them alive." "Sire, with a good will," said Jewel. But Roonwit said, "Sire, be wary in your just wrath. There are strange doings on foot. If there should be rebels in arms further up the valley, we three are too few to meet them. If it would please you to wait while . . ." "I will not wait the tenth part of a second," said the King. "But while Jewel and I go forward, do you gallop as hard as you may to Cair Paravel . . . we must go on and take the adventure that comes to us." "It is the only thing left for us to do, Sire," said the Unicorn. He did not see at the moment how foolish it was for two of them to go on alone; nor did the King. They were too angry to think clearly. But much evil came of their rashness in the end. (C. S. Lewis, *The Last Battle*)

King Tirian of Narnia has a good heart. But he also has an unwise heart—an untrained heart. I'd say that's true for most of us. Our heart has been made good by the work of Christ, but we haven't learned how to live from it. Young and naive it remains. It's as though we've been handed a golden harp or a shining sword. Even the most gifted musician still has to take lessons; even the bravest of warriors must be trained. We are unfamiliar, unpracticed with the ways of the heart. This is actually a very dangerous part of the journey. Launching out with an untrained heart can bring much hurt and ruin, and afterward we will be shamed back into the gospel of Sin Management, having concluded that our heart is bad. It isn't bad; it's just young and unwise.

(*Waking the Dead,* 97–98)

A friend of mine wanted to teach English as a second language in an Asian country, as a way of becoming a sort of undercover missionary. A beautiful dream, one that I'm sure she would have been excellent in fulfilling. But she rushed to the field unprepared in many ways. I don't mean finances and language skills; I mean in the ways of the heart. Lurking down in her soul were some deep and unresolved issues that would set her up for a fall: among them shame and guilt from an abusive past. The team she joined was totally unfamiliar with the new heart, and they doubted its goodness; as with too many Christian ministries, shame and guilt were often used as motivators. Their old covenant theology would play right into Susan's issues, shut down her young heart. Finally, she was unpracticed in spiritual warfare, ill-equipped for what hell would throw at her. The devil is a master at shame and guilt. She went; she got hammered; she came home, defeated. Her friends wonder if she'll ever try it again.

The disaster could have been avoided. Wisdom was crying out: do not rush the field (Luke 14:31); train yourself to discern good and evil (Heb. 5:14); live as though your life is at stake, and the enemy is waiting to outwit you (Matt. 10:16). God has given us all sorts of counsel and direction in his written Word; thank God, we have it written down in black and white. We would do well to be familiar with it, study it with all the intensity of the men who studied the maps of the Normandy coastline before they hit the beaches on D-Day. The more that wisdom enters our hearts, the more we will be able to trust our hearts in difficult situations. Notice that wisdom is not cramming our head with principles. It is developing a discerning *heart*. What made Solomon such a sharp guy was his wise and discerning heart (1 Kings 3:9).

We don't seek wisdom because it's a good idea; we seek wisdom because we're dead if we don't.

(*Waking the Dead*, 99–100)

Wisdom is crucial. But wisdom is not enough. Wisdom is essential . . . and insufficient.

Saul of Tarsus was headed to Damascus, "breathing out murderous threats against the Lord's disciples," with official documents granting him permission to arrest all Christians in the city and have them sent to prison (Acts 9:1–2). Now, you and I know that Jesus changed Saul's agenda rather radically before he ever reached the city—the blinding light, the voice from heaven, the total realignment of his worldview. But the believers in Damascus don't know all this. As they wait in fear for Saul's arrival, God speaks to one of them, a man named Ananias, and tells him to go to the house where Saul is staying, lay hands on him, and pray for him. Understandably, Ananias suggests this is not such a good idea. "Lord . . . I have heard many reports about this man and all the harm he has done to your saints in Jerusalem. And he has come here with authority from the chief priests to arrest all who call on your name" (9:13–14). It's okay, God says, he's my man now. Against wisdom Ananias goes, and the greatest of all the apostles is launched.

The Bible is full of such counterintuitive direction from God. Would you counsel a father to sacrifice his only child, the only hope for the promised nation? Certainly, it wasn't wisdom that compelled a fugitive to walk back into the country where he was wanted for murder, a land where all his kin were held as slaves, march into Pharaoh's palace and demand their release. Was it reasonable to take a fortified city by marching around it blowing trumpets? What's the sense of slashing the ranks of your army from 32,000 to 300, just before battle? It was dangerous advice, indeed, to send the young maiden before her king unbidden, and even worse to send a boy against a trained mercenary. And frankly, it looked like perfect madness for Jesus to give himself up to the authorities, let himself get killed.

(*Waking the Dead*, 100)

E ven Jesus endured assault—not the open accusation that he had a wicked heart, but the more subtle kind, the seemingly "innocent" Arrows that come through "misunderstanding."

> After this, Jesus went around in Galilee, purposely staying away from Judea because the Jews there were waiting to take his life. But when the Jewish Feast of Tabernacles was near, Jesus' brothers said to him, "You ought to leave here and go to Judea, so that your disciples may see the miracles you do. No one who wants to become a public figure acts in secret. Since you are doing these things, show yourself to the world." For even his own brothers did not believe in him. (John 7:1–5)

I think we can relate to that. Did your family believe in you? Or did they believe in the person *they* wanted you to be? Did they even notice your heart at all? Have they been thrilled in your choices, or has their disappointment made it clear that you just aren't what you're supposed to be? At another point in his ministry, Jesus' family shows up to collect him. "Your mother and brothers are standing outside, wanting to see you" (Luke 8:19). They think he's lost it, and they've come to bring him home, poor man. Misunderstanding is damaging, more insidious because we don't identify it as an attack on the heart. How subtly it comes, sowing doubt and discouragement where there should have been validation and support. There must be something wrong with us.

(*Waking the Dead,* 117)

Iow long, O men, will you turn my glory into shame?" (Ps. 4:2). These blows aren't random or incidental. They strike directly at some part of the heart, turn the very thing God created to be a source of celebration into a source of shame. And so you can at least begin to discover your glory by looking more closely at what you were shamed for. Look at what's been assaulted, used, abused. As Bernard of Clairvaux said, "Through the heart's wound, I see its secret."

Let me put it this way: What has life taught you about your God-given glory? What have you believed about your heart over the years? "That it's not worth anyone's time," said a woman. Her parents were too busy to really want to know her. "That it's weak," confided a friend. He suffered several emasculating blows as a boy, and his father simply shamed him for it. "That I shouldn't trust it to anyone." "That it's selfish and self-centered." "That it's bad." And you . . . what have you believed?

Those accusations you heard growing up, those core convictions that formed about your heart, will remain down there until someone comes to dislodge them, run them out of Dodge.

(*Waking the Dead*, 118)

Denial is a favorite method of coping for many Christians. But not with Jesus. He wants truth in the inmost being, and to get it there he's got to *take us into* our inmost being. One way he'll do this is by bringing up an old memory. You'll be driving down the road and suddenly remember something from your childhood. Or maybe you'll have a dream about a long-forgotten person, event, or place. However he brings it up, go with him there. He has something to say to you.

The lessons that have been laid down in pain can be accessed only in pain. Christ must open the wound, not just bandage it over. Sometimes he'll take us there by having an event repeat itself years later, only with new characters in the current situation. We find ourselves overlooked for a job, just as we were overlooked by our parents. Or we experience fear again, just as we felt those lonely nights in our room upstairs. These are all *invitations* to go with him into the deep waters of the heart, uncover the lies buried down there, and bring in the truth that will set us free. Don't just bury it quickly; ask God what he is wanting to speak to.

(*Waking the Dead,* 122)

Yes, dear friends, we are already God's children, and we can't even imagine what we will be like when Christ returns. But we do know that when he comes we will be like him, for we will see him as he really is. (1 John 3:2 NLT)

We have an expression that we use to describe someone who's out of sorts, who's not acting like the person we know her to be: "She's just not herself today." It's a marvelous, gracious phrase, for in a very real way, no one is quite himself today. There is more to us than we have seen. I know my wife is a goddess. I know she is more beautiful than she imagines. I have seen it slip out, seen moments of her glory. Suddenly, her beauty shines through, as though a veil has been lifted.

All of us have moments like this, glimpses of our true creation. They come unexpectedly and then fade again. Life for the most part keeps our glory hidden, cloaked by sin, or sorrow, or merely weariness. When I see an old woman, doubled over with arthritis, the hard years etched into her face, I want to cry, *Eve, what happened?* How truly wonderful it will be to see her in her youth again, the full flower of her beauty restored.

When the disciples saw Jesus on the Mount of Transfiguration, they got a peek at his glory. He was radiant, beautiful, magnificent. He was Jesus, the Jesus they knew and loved—only *more so.* And we shall be glorious as well. Jesus called himself the Son of man to state clearly that he is what mankind was meant to be. What we see in Jesus is our personal destiny.

(*The Journey of Desire,* 116–17)

Early in the morning, Jesus stood on the shore, but the disciples did not realize that it was Jesus. He called out to them, "Friends, haven't you any fish?" "No," they answered. He said, "Throw your net on the right side of the boat and you will find some." When they did, they were unable to haul the net in because of the large number of fish. Then the disciple whom Jesus loved said to Peter, "It is the Lord!" . . . When they landed, they saw a fire of burning coals there with fish on it, and some bread . . . Jesus said to them, "Come and have breakfast." (John 21:4–12)

Now think about this for a minute. You're the Son of God. You've just accomplished the greatest work of your life, the stunning rescue of mankind. You rose from the dead. What would you do next? Have a cookout with a few friends? It seems so unspiritual, so *ordinary*. Do you see that eternal life does not become something totally "other," but rather that life goes on—only as it should be?

Jesus did not vanish into a mystical spirituality, becoming one with the cosmic vibration. Jesus has a body, and it's *his* body. His wounds have been healed, but the scars remain—not gruesome, but lovely, a remembrance of all he did for us. His friends recognize him. They share a bite to eat. This is our future as well—our lives will be healed and we shall go on, never to taste death again.

(*The Journey of Desire,* 118)

Time has come for us to forgive our fathers. Paul warns us that unforgiveness and bitterness can wreck our lives and the lives of others (Eph. 4:31; Heb. 12:15). I am sorry to think of all the years my wife endured the anger and bitterness that I redirected at her from my father. As someone has said, forgiveness is setting a prisoner free and then discovering the prisoner was you. I found some help in Bly's experience of forgiving his own father, when he said, "I began to think of him not as someone who had deprived me of love or attention or companionship, but as someone who himself had been deprived, by his father and his mother and by the culture." My father had his own wound that no one ever offered to heal. His father was an alcoholic, too, for a time, and there were some hard years for my dad as a young man just as there were for me.

Now you must understand: Forgiveness is a choice. It is not a feeling, but an act of the will. As Neil Anderson has written, "Don't wait to forgive until you feel like forgiving; you will never get there. Feelings take time to heal after the choice to forgive is made." We allow God to bring the hurt up from our past, for "if your forgiveness doesn't visit the emotional core of your life, it will be incomplete." We acknowledge that it hurt, that it mattered, and we choose to extend forgiveness to our father. This is *not* saying, "It didn't really matter"; it is *not* saying, "I probably deserved part of it anyway." Forgiveness says, "It was wrong, it mattered, and I release you."

And then we ask God to father us, and to tell us our true name.

(*Wild at Heart,* 131–32)

Your sin has been dealt with. Your Father has removed it from you "as far as the east is from the west" (Ps. 103:12). Your sins have been washed away (1 Cor. 6:11). When God looks at you he does not see your sin. He has not one condemning thought toward you (Rom. 8:1). But that's not all. You have a new heart. That's the promise of the new covenant: "I will give you a new heart and put a new spirit in you; I will remove from you your heart of stone and give you a heart of flesh. And I will put my Spirit in you and move you to follow my decrees and be careful to keep my laws" (Ezek. 36:26–27). There's a reason that it's called good news.

Too many Christians today are living back in the old covenant. They've had Jeremiah 17:9 drilled into them and they walk around believing *my heart is deceitfully wicked*. Not anymore it's not. Read the rest of the book. In Jeremiah 31:33, God announces the cure for all that: "I will put my law in their minds and write it on their hearts. I will be their God, and they will be my people." I will give you a new heart. That's why Paul says in Romans 2:29, "No, a man is a Jew if he is one inwardly; and circumcision is circumcision of the heart, by the Spirit." Sin is not the deepest thing about you. You have a new heart. Did you hear me? Your heart is *good*.

What God sees when he sees you is the *real* you, the true you, the man he had in mind when he made you.

(*Wild at Heart*, 133–34)

True strength does not come out of bravado. Until we are broken, our life will be self-centered, self-reliant; our strength will be our own. So long as you think you are really something in and of yourself, what will you need God for? I don't trust a man who hasn't suffered; I don't let a man get close to me who hasn't faced his wound. Think of the posers you know—are they the kind of man you would call at 2:00 A.M., when life is collapsing around you? Not me. I don't want clichés; I want deep, soulful truth, and that only comes when a man has walked the road I've been talking about. As Frederick Buechner says,

> To do for yourself the best that you have it in you to do—to grit your teeth and clench your fists in order to survive the world at its harshest and worst—is, by that very act, to be unable to let something be done for you and in you that is more wonderful still. The trouble with steeling yourself against the harshness of reality is that the same steel that secures your life against being destroyed secures your life also against being opened up and transformed. (*The Sacred Journey*)

Only when we enter our wound will we discover our true glory. As Robert Bly says, "Where a man's wound is, that is where his genius will be." There are two reasons for this. First, the wound was given in the place of your true strength, as an effort to take you out. Until you go there you are still posing, offering something more shallow and insubstantial. And therefore, second, it is out of your brokenness that you discover what you have to offer the community. The false self is never wholly false. Those gifts we've been using are often quite true about us, but we've used them to hide behind. We thought that the power of our life was in the golden bat, but the power is in *us*. When we begin to offer not merely our gifts but our true selves, that is when we become powerful.

(*Wild at Heart*, 137–38)

> For this people's heart has become calloused;
>> they hardly hear with their ears,
>> and they have closed their eyes.
> Otherwise they might see with their eyes,
>> hear with their ears,
>> understand with their hearts
> and turn, and I would heal them. (Matt. 13:15)

And I would heal them." That's a different offer from: "And I would forgive them." It's a different offer from: "And I will give them a place in heaven." No, Jesus is offering *healing* to us. Look at what he does to people who are broken. How does he handle them? The blind are able to see like a hawk. The deaf are able to hear a pin drop. The lame do hurdles. The corroding skin of the leper is cleansed and made new. The woman with the issue of blood stops hemorrhaging. The paralyzed servant hops out of bed. They are, every last one of them, healed. Now follow this closely: everything Jesus *did* was to illustrate what he was trying to *say*. Here—look at this—this is what I'm offering to do for you. Not just for your body, but more important, for your soul. I can heal your heart. I can restore your soul.

(Waking the Dead, 134–35)

This is what Jesus nearly always does when he comes to mend those rifts in our hearts. He brings his comfort and mercy to those times and places where we suffered the shattering blow, and the heart in that place often feels the same age as it was at the time of the event, even though it might have been decades ago.

It might be a surprise that Christ asks our permission to come in and heal, but you may remember that famous passage from Revelation, "Behold, I stand at the door and knock" (Rev. 3:20 NKJV). He doesn't force his way in, and the principle remains true after we have given Christ the initial access to our hearts that we call salvation. There are rooms we have kept locked up, places he has not had access to by our own will, and in order to experience his healing, we must also give him permission to come in there. *Will you let me heal you?*

The work of Christ in healing the soul is a deep mystery, more amazing than open-heart surgery. A friend described his experience as having Christ "holding the broken parts of my heart in his hands, and bringing them all together, holding them tenderly until his life brought a wholeness or a oneness to what was many pieces." That idea of "binding up" our brokenness involves bringing all the shattered pieces back together into one whole heart. Reintegrating those places broken off by tragedy or assault.

(*Waking the Dead*, 138–40)

Every woman is haunted by Eve in the core of her being. She knows, if only when she passes a mirror, that she is not what she was meant to be. We are more keenly aware of our own short-comings than anyone else. Remembering the glory that was once ours awakens my heart to an ache that has long gone unfulfilled. It's almost too much to hope for, too much to have lost.

You see, every little girl—and every little boy—is asking one fundamental question. But they are very different questions, depending on whether you are a little boy or a little girl. Little boys want to know, *Do I have what it takes?* All that rough-and-tumble, all that daring and superhero dress-up, all of that is a boy seeking to prove that he does have what it takes. He was made in the image of a warrior God. Nearly all a man does is fueled by his search for validation, that longing he carries for an answer to his Question.

Little girls want to know, *Am I lovely?* The twirling skirts, the dress-up, the longing to be pretty and to be seen—that is what that's all about. We are seeking an answer to our Question. I remember when I was a girl of maybe five years old standing on top of the coffee table in my grandparents' living room and singing my heart out. I wanted to capture attention—especially my father's attention. I wanted to be captivating. We all did. But for most of us, the answer to our Question when we were young was "No, there is nothing captivating about you. Get off the cof-fee table." Nearly all a woman does in her adult life is fueled by her longing to be delighted in, her longing to be beautiful, to be irreplaceable, to have her Question answered, "Yes!"

Why does the Question linger so? Why haven't we been able to find and rest in a wonderful, personal answer for our own hearts?

(*Captivating,* 46)

The wounds that we received as young girls did not come alone. They brought messages with them, messages that struck at the core of our hearts, right in the place of our Question. Our wounds strike at the core of our *femininity*. The damage done to our feminine hearts through the wounds we received is made much worse by the horrible things we believe about ourselves as a result. As children, we didn't have the faculties to process and sort through what was happening to us. Our parents were godlike. We believed them to be right. If we were overwhelmed or belittled or hurt or abused, we believed that somehow it was because of *us*— the problem was with *us*.

We can't put words to it, but down deep we fear there is something terribly wrong with us. If we were the princess, then our prince would have come. If we were the daughter of a king, he would have fought for us. We can't help but believe that if we were different, if we were *better*, then we would have been loved as we so longed to be. It must be us.

It's taken a lot of years for me to sort through the wounds and messages that shaped my life. It's been a journey for growing clarity, understanding, and healing. Just last night, as John and I talked about this chapter, I began to realize more clearly what the message of my wounds has been. My mom was overwhelmed with the prospect of having another child—me. The message that landed in my heart was that I was overwhelming; my presence alone caused sorrow and pain. From a father who didn't seem to want to know me or be with me, I got the message, "You don't have a beauty that captivates me. You are a disappointment."

(*Captivating,* 68–71)

As a result of the wounds we receive growing up, we come to believe that some part of us, maybe every part of us, is marred. Shame enters in and makes its crippling home deep within our hearts. Shame is what makes us look away, so we avoid eye contact with strangers and friends. Shame is that feeling that haunts us, the sense that if someone really knew us, they would shake their heads in disgust and run away. Shame makes us feel, no, *believe*, that we do not measure up—not to the world's standards, the church's standards, or our own.

Others seem to master their lives, but shame grips our hearts and pins them down, ever ready to point out our failures and judge our worth. We are lacking. We know we are not all that we long to be, all that God longs for us to be, but instead of coming up for grace-filled air and asking God what he thinks of us, shame keeps us pinned down and gasping, believing that we deserve to suffocate. If we were not deemed worthy of love as children, it is incredibly difficult to believe we are worth loving as adults. Shame says we are unworthy, broken, and beyond repair.

Shame causes us to hide. We are afraid of being truly seen, and so we hide our truest selves and offer only what we believe is wanted. We refuse to bring the weight of our lives, who God has made us to be, to bear on others out of a fear of being rejected.

(*Captivating*, 73–74)

MAUI, MANGOES, CABERNET GRAPES, AND HUMMINGBIRDS

When the curtain goes up on the story of humanity, we see God in a flurry of breathtaking, dramatic actions that we rather blandly call "creation." Remember, we're looking for the motives of his heart. Why is he doing all this? We know he already had the perfect relationship and that he has suffered a betrayal in the heart of heaven simply for the offense of sharing it. Now we see him preparing to woo our hearts with a world that is beautiful and funny and full of adventure. Don't rush ahead to the Fall. Stay here a moment and feel God's happiness with it all. Yosemite and Yellowstone and Maui and the Alps; mangoes and blackberries and cabernet grapes; horses and hummingbirds and rainbow trout. "The morning stars sang together and all the angels shouted for joy" (Job 38:7).

God creates man and woman and sets them in Paradise. How long had he been planning this? Are we merely the replacement for the angels he lost, the first date he can find on the rebound? The first chapter of Ephesians gives a look into God's motives here:

> Long before he laid down earth's foundations, he had us in mind, had settled on us as the focus of his love, to be made whole and holy by his love. Long, long ago he decided to adopt us into his family through Jesus Christ. (What pleasure he took in planning this!) He wanted us to enter into the celebration of his lavish gift-giving by the hand of his beloved Son . . . Long before we first heard of Christ and got our hopes up, he had his eye on us, had designs on us for glorious living. (vv. 4–6, 11 *The Message*)

(*The Sacred Romance,* 76–77)

God begins our courtship with a surprise. Taking the blindfold off, he turns us around and reveals his handmade wedding present. "Here," he says. "It's yours. Enjoy yourselves. Do you like it? Take it for a spin." A lavish gift indeed. What's he up to? Flowers, chocolates, exotic vacations, dinners at the finest restaurants—any person would feel pursued. But what are his intentions? Surprisingly, we see in the first glimpse of God's wildness the goodness of his heart—he gives us our freedom. In order for a true romance to occur, we had to be free to reject him. In *Disappointment with God*, Philip Yancey reminds us that the powers of the Author aren't sufficient to win our hearts.

Power can do everything but the most important thing: it cannot control love . . . In a concentration camp, the guards possess almost unlimited power. By applying force, they can make you renounce your God, curse your family, work without pay, eat human excrement, kill and then bury your closest friend or even your own mother. All this is within their power. Only one thing is not: they cannot force you to love them. This fact may help explain why God sometimes seems shy to use his power. He created us to love him, but his most impressive displays of miracle— the kind we may secretly long for—do nothing to foster that love. As Douglas John Hall has put it, "God's problem is not that God is not able to do certain things. God's problem is that God loves. Love complicates the life of God as it complicates every life."

The wildness of giving us freedom is even more staggering when we remember that God has already paid dearly for giving freedom to the angels. But because of his grand heart he goes ahead and takes the risk, an enormous, colossal risk. The reason he didn't make puppets is because he wanted lovers.

(*The Sacred Romance,* 77–78)

When we first think of being in a relationship with God, we probably picture him as somewhat flashy, even as many of us tried to be (at least us guys) when we were dating. He gave Jacob visions of angels descending and ascending to heaven; he parted the Red Sea for Moses and made the sun stand still for a day so the Israelites could win a battle. He definitely makes an impression. But you kind of wonder what he's like when you're alone with him. Would he just stay the life of the party, still playing to the crowd?

An image from the Scriptures shows us a very different side of God. A picture of the way God desires to commune with us is found in 1 Kings 19, where we find the prophet Elijah worn out and afraid, fleeing from Jezebel. She has been trying to kill him ever since he did the same to her prophets. God tenderly ministers to Elijah, twice bringing him food and water. Elijah, strengthened, travels forty days and forty nights until he reaches Mt. Horeb, where he goes to sleep in a cave. The Lord wakes him and listens to his lament about what it is like to be God's prophet. Elijah is worn out from "doing" and badly in need of restoration of spirit. A great wind strikes the mountain, followed by an earthquake and a fire. And God is in none of these. Finally, Elijah hears a "gentle whisper." And it is in the gentle whisper that he finds God.

(*The Sacred Romance,* 162)

God is not "out there somewhere" in some dramatic way, waiting to commune with us by earthquake or fire or signs in the sky. Instead, he desires to talk with us in the quietness of our own heart through his Spirit, who is in us. It is his voice that has whispered to us about a Sacred Romance. What do you hear when you listen for that gentle, quiet voice?

What I so often hear, or feel, is a restlessness, a distractedness where it seems that dozens if not hundreds of disconnected or scattered thoughts vie for my attention. Bits and pieces of my smaller story, and sometimes major edifices, flash onto the screen: what other people think of me and what I need to do to win them. Anger, ego, lust, and simply blankness of spirit all take turns occupying my heart.

Indeed, when I first listen to my heart, what I often hear is the language and clatter of my old "lovers" and not much else. There seems to be no stillness or rest. If I try to hold still, my soul reacts like a feather in the afternoon breeze, flitting from place to place without purpose or direction. I almost seem invisible in the noise or blankness. Theologians refer to this condition as "ontological lightness," the reality that when I stop "doing" and simply listen to my heart, I am not anchored to anything substantive. I become aware that my very identity is synonymous with activity.

Our whole American culture is infected with ontological lightness, celebrities and pro athletes being the most dramatic examples of this victimization of our souls that ruins us for any substantive love relationship. They are anchored only to their performances, and out of their performances come their identities—and ours who worship them. As soon as they stop performing, their identities—and ours—disappear.

(The Sacred Romance, 162–64)

When we hear the phrase "trust totally in God," most of us probably sigh, hearing it as one more requirement that we have never been able to live up to. But what if we were to listen to our hearts, and hear it as a need to faint, a need to lay down our "doings" and simply make our needs known to Christ, and rest in him?

How do we go about actually "doing" rest?

When Jesus was preparing for his public ministry, as well as his battle with Satan, he went to the desert—away from the synagogue, away from people, away from family and friends. Matthew tells us that God's Spirit led Jesus into the desert to be tempted by the devil. He prepared for spiritual battle by separating himself from all dependency on the provisions of this world, starting with the most basic: food. He fasted for forty days. He abided in prayer, in communion with his Father in heaven. When Satan came to test him with the things of this world, he answered him not with intellectual argument, but rested in the truth of Scripture. And when he had resisted the devil by abiding in the Spirit, angels came and ministered to him.

There is a place on each of our spiritual journeys where the Spirit also desires to lead us into the desert. We hear him calling to us in the restlessness and weariness of our own heart. The first time the Spirit speaks to us, we don't know it is him. We assume we are just not doing enough to be spiritual, and so we renew our religious efforts instead of fainting. Sometimes, like Samuel when God spoke to him in the night, we go through this process two or three times before we realize it is God speaking to us in our heart and follow him into the desert.

(*The Sacred Romance,* 170–71)

In order to learn who we really are, we must have a place in our lives where we are removed from the materialism, entertainment, diversion, and busyness that the Vanity Fair of our society and culture immerse us in. The things sold at the booths in the Fair are tranquilizers that separate us, and protect us, from the emptiness and need of our heart. As we leave these less-wild lovers behind and enter into solitude and silence in our own desert place, the first thing we encounter is not rest, but fear, and a compulsion to return to activity. In *The Ascent to Truth*, Thomas Merton says,

> We look for rest and if we find it, it becomes intolerable. Incapable of the divine activity which alone can satisfy [rest] . . . fallen man flings himself upon exterior things, not so much for their own sake as for the sake of agitation which keeps his spirit pleasantly numb . . . [The distraction] diverts us aside from the one thing that can help us to begin our ascent to truth . . . the sense of our own emptiness.

Our emptiness is often the first thing we find when we face honestly the story going on in our heart. It is the desert's gift to us. George MacDonald encourages us to embrace it as a friend by "leaving the heart an empty cup," and proceeding. But what do we do with our emptiness if we stay with our heart? If we try to pray, our minds fill with busy, disconnected petitions that start with the words, "God, help me to do this or that better, have more faith, read the Bible more." The busy petitions of our minds seem to leave something inside our chest cavity unexpressed, something that is trying to tell us about the way things are.

(*The Sacred Romance,* 172)

Resting in Jesus is not applying a spiritual formula to ourselves as a kind of fix-it. It is the essence of repentance. It is letting our heart tell us where we are in our own story so that Jesus can minister to us out of the Story of his love for us. When, in a given moment, we lay down our false self and the smaller story of whatever performance has sustained us, when we give up everything else but him, we experience the freedom of knowing that he simply loves us where we are. We begin just to *be*, having our identity anchored in him. We begin to experience our spiritual life as the "easy yoke and light burden" Jesus tells us is his experience.

In Matthew 24, Jesus tells us that in the last days, people will have lost the Sacred Romance altogether. Having no anchor, their faith will grow cold and they will be literally swept away in panic, as all but what cannot be shaken is shaken. Only those of us who are securely anchored in him in our heart will be left standing to share the Sacred Romance with those who are lost.

We have come to the shores of heaven together, to the border of the region where our Christianity begins to move from a focus on doing to one of communion with Christ, our Lover and Lord. The spiritual disciplines of silence, solitude, meditation (heart prayer), fasting, and simplicity practiced by Christ and passed on to us by the traditions of the Desert Fathers bring us through our emptiness and thirst into the presence of God. When we begin to abide in God's heart, the blades of grass on heaven's outskirts no longer puncture our feet. Here and there, a fresh and exotic scent reaches us from heaven's very borders.

(*The Sacred Romance,* 174–75)

A story is only as good as its ending. Without a happy ending that draws us on in eager anticipation, our journey becomes a nightmare of endless struggle. Is this all there is? Is this as good as it gets? On a recent flight I was chatting with one of the attendants about her spiritual beliefs. A follower of a New Age guru, she said with all earnestness, "I don't believe in heaven. I believe life is a never-ending cycle of birth and death." *What a horror*, I thought to myself. *This Story had better have a happy ending.* Paul felt the same. If this is as good as it gets, he said, you may as well stop at a bar on the way home and tie one on; go to Nordstrom's and max out all your credit cards; bake a cake and eat the whole thing. "Let us eat and drink, for tomorrow we die" (1 Cor. 15:32).

Our hearts cannot live without hope. Gabriel Marcel says that "hope is for the soul what breathing is for the living organism." In the trinity of Christian graces—faith, hope, and love—love may be the greatest, but hope plays the deciding role. The apostle Paul tells us that faith and love depend on hope, our anticipation of what lies ahead: "Faith and love . . . spring from the hope that is stored up for you in heaven" (Col. 1:5). Our courage for the journey so often falters because we've lost our hope of heaven—the consummation of our Love Story. The reason most men, to quote Thoreau, "live lives of quiet desperation" is that they live without hope.

(*The Sacred Romance,* 177–78)

Christ is not joking when he says that we shall inherit the kingdom prepared for us and we shall reign with him forever. We will take the position for which we have been uniquely made and will rule *as he does*—meaning, with creativity and power.

> The created world itself can hardly wait for what's coming next. Everything in creation is being more or less held back. God reins it in until both creation and all the creatures are ready and can be released at the same moment into the glorious times ahead. (Rom. 8:19–20 *The Message*)

> All creation anticipates the day when it will join God's children in glorious freedom from death and decay. (Rom. 8:21 NLT)

What would you like to do first? Paddle a canoe down the Amazon? Learn to play an instrument? Discover a new universe? You'll have plenty of time for that and more.

> And in the perfect time, O perfect God,
> When we are in our home, our natal home,
> When joy shall carry every sacred load,
> And from its life and peace no heart shall roam,
> What if thou make us able to make like thee—
> To light with moons, to clothe with greenery,
> To hang gold sunsets o'er a rose and purple sea!
> (George MacDonald, *Diary of an Old Soul*)

(Epic, 94–95)

E very woman can tell you about her wound; some came with violence, others came with neglect. Just as every little boy is asking one question, every little girl is, as well. But her question isn't so much about her strength. No, the deep cry of a little girl's heart is, *Am I lovely?* Every woman needs to know that she is exquisite and exotic and *chosen.* This is core to her identity, the way she bears the image of God. *Will you pursue me? Do you delight in me? Will you fight for me?* And like every little boy, she has taken a wound as well. The wound strikes right at the core of her heart of beauty and leaves a devastating message with it: *No. You're not beautiful and no one will really fight for you.* Like your wound, hers almost always comes at the hand of her father.

A little girl looks to her father to know if she is lovely. The power he has to cripple or to bless is just as significant to her as it is to his son. If he's a violent man he may defile her verbally or sexually. The stories I've heard from women who have been abused would tear your heart out. Janet was molested by her father when she was three; around the age of seven he showed her brothers how to do it. The assault continued until she moved away to college. What is a violated woman to think about her beauty? Am I lovely? The message is, *No . . . you are dirty. Anything attractive about you is dark and evil.* The assault continues as she grows up, through violent men and passive men. She may be stalked; she may be ignored. Either way, her heart is violated and the message is driven farther in: *you are not desired; you will not be protected; no one will fight for you.* The tower is built brick by brick, and when she's a grown woman it can be a fortress.

(*Wild at Heart,* 182–83)

There is something mythic in the way a man is with a woman. Our sexuality offers a parable of amazing depth when it comes to being masculine and feminine. The man comes to offer his strength and the woman invites the man into herself, an act that requires courage and vulnerability and selflessness for both of them. Notice first that if the man will not rise to the occasion, nothing will happen. He must move; his strength must swell before he can enter her. But neither will the love consummate unless the woman opens herself in stunning vulnerability. When both are living as they were meant to live, the man enters his woman and offers her his strength. He *spills himself there*, in her, for her; she draws him in, embraces and envelops him. When all is over he is spent; but ah, what a sweet death it is.

And that is how life is created. The beauty of a woman arouses a man to play the man; the strength of a man, offered tenderly to his woman, allows her to be beautiful; it brings life to her and to many. This is far, far more than sex and orgasm. It is a reality that extends to every aspect of our lives. When a man withholds himself from his woman, he leaves her without the life only he can bring. This is never more true than how a man offers—or does not offer—his words. Life and death are in the power of the tongue, says Proverbs (18:21). She is made for and craves words from him.

(*Wild at Heart*, 185)

Where would we be today if Abraham had carefully weighed the pros and cons of God's invitation and decided that he'd rather hang on to his medical benefits, three weeks paid vacation, and retirement plan in Ur? What would have happened if Moses had listened to his mother's advice to "never play with matches" and lived a careful, cautious life steering clear of all burning bushes? You wouldn't have the gospel if Paul had concluded that the life of a Pharisee, while not everything a man dreams for, was at least predictable and certainly more stable than following a voice he heard on the Damascus road. After all, people hear voices all the time, and who really knows whether it's God or just one's imagination. Where would we be if Jesus was not fierce and wild and romantic to the core? Come to think of it, we wouldn't *be* at all if God hadn't taken that enormous risk of us in the first place.

Most men spend the energy of their lives trying to eliminate risk, or squeezing it down to a more manageable size. Their children hear "no" far more than they hear "yes"; their employees feel chained up and their wives are equally bound. If it works, if a man succeeds in securing his life against all risk, he'll wind up in a cocoon of self-protection and wonder all the while why he's suffocating. If it doesn't work, he curses God, redoubles his efforts and his blood pressure. When you look at the structure of the false self men tend to create, it always revolves around two themes: seizing upon some sort of competence and rejecting anything that cannot be controlled. As David Whyte says, "The price of our vitality is the sum of all our fears."

(*Wild at Heart*, 202–3)

To live as an authentic, ransomed, and redeemed woman means to be real and present in this moment. If we continue to hide, much will be lost. We cannot have intimacy with God or anyone else if we stay hidden and offer only who we think we ought to be or what we believe is wanted. We cannot play the *ezer* role we were meant to play if we remain bound by shame and fear, presenting only to the world the face we have learned is safe. *You have only one life to live. It would be best to live your own.*

What have we to offer, really, other than who we are and what God has been pouring into our lives? It was not by accident that you were born; it was not by chance that you have the desires you do. The Victorious Trinity has planned on your being here now, "for such a time as this" (Esth. 4:14). We need you.

> Jesus knew that the Father had put all things under his power, *and that he had come from God and was returning to God*; so he got up from the meal, took off his outer clothing, and wrapped a towel around his waist. After that, he poured water into a basin and began to wash his disciples' feet, drying them with the towel that was wrapped around him. (John 13:3–5, emphasis added)

Jesus knew who he was. He knew where he had come from and where he was going. He knew why he was here.

God really does want you to know who *you* are. He wants you to be able to understand the story of your life, to know where you have come from, and to know where you are going. There is freedom there. Freedom to be and to offer and to love. So, may we take a moment and remind you who you truly are?

(*Captivating*, 216)

Who has kept the new covenant so effectively under wraps that most Christians still believe their hearts are evil? Dear God—they hold to that lie as a core doctrine of their *faith*. To say your heart is good still sounds like heresy. Whose PR campaign made that so effective? And who convinced the church to stay so focused on the Cross that we know next to nothing about the power of the Resurrection and the Ascension? Why has the cross become our central symbol when it wasn't the central symbol for the first four hundred years of the church? Is it any wonder that we think Christianity is primarily about not sinning and waiting to die to go to heaven? What happened to the *life*, the glory of God as man fully alive?

Let me ask you another question: Who did Jesus tangle with more than any other group or type of person? Who started the rumors about him to try to discredit his ministry? Who kept trying to put him on the spot with their loaded questions? And when it became clear they could not shame or intimidate him back into place, where did the open opposition to Christ come from? Who paid Judas the thirty pieces of silver? Who got the crowd to yell for Barabbas when Pilate was ready to let Jesus go?

Religion and its defenders have always been the most insidious enemy of the true faith precisely because they are not glaring opponents; they are *impostors*. A raving pagan is easier to dismiss than an elder in your church. Before Jesus came along, the Pharisees ran the show. Everybody took what they said as gospel— even though it didn't sound like good news at all. But we wrestle not against flesh and blood. The Pharisees and their brethren down through the ages have merely acted—unknowingly, for the most part—as puppets, the mouthpiece of the Enemy.

(*Waking the Dead,* 161)

The Religious Spirit has turned discipleship into a soul-killing exercise of principles. Most folks don't even know they can walk with God, hear his voice. He's stigmatized counseling as a profession for sick patients, and so the wounds of our hearts never get healed. He's taken healing away from us almost entirely, so that we sit in pews as broken people feeling guilty because we can't live the life we're supposed to live. And he takes warfare and mocks it, stigmatizes it as well so that most of the church knows almost nothing about how to break strongholds, set captives free.

Finally, the Religious Spirit makes it next to impossible for a person to break free by spreading the lie that *there is no war*. Be honest—how many Christians do you know who practice spiritual warfare as a normal, necessary, daily part of the Christian life? Some of my dearest friends pull back from this stream and sort of cast a concerned look over me when I suggest it's going on. Onward Christian soldiers, marching as to war? You've got to be kidding me. We're not advancing the kingdom, we're holding car washes. We gave up the hymn not so much for reasons of musical fashion but because we felt ridiculous singing it, as you do when asked to sing "Happy Birthday" in a restaurant to a perfect stranger. We don't sing it 'cause it ain't true. We have acquiesced. We have surrendered without a fight.

(*Waking the Dead*, 162)

We long for beauty, and when the biblical writers speak of heaven, they use the most beautiful imagery they can. You can almost hear the agony of the writer trying to get it right while knowing he falls far short of what he sees. In the book of Revelation, John uses the word *like* again and again. "And He who was sitting was like a jasper stone and a sardius in appearance; and there was a rainbow around the throne, like an emerald in appearance . . . Before the throne there was . . . a sea of glass like crystal" (4:3, 6 NASB). The beauty cannot be captured, only alluded to by the most beautiful things on earth.

I believe the beauty of heaven is why the Bible says we shall be "feasted." It's not merely that there will be no suffering, though that will be tremendous joy in itself; to have every Arrow we've ever known pulled out and every wound dressed with the leaves from the tree of life (Rev. 22:2). But there is more. We will have glorified bodies with which to partake of all the beauty of heaven. As Edwards wrote, "Every faculty will be an inlet of delight." We will eat freely the fruit of the tree of life and drink deeply from the river of life that flows through the city. And the food will satisfy not just our body but our soul. As C.S. Lewis said,

> We do not want merely to *see* beauty, though, God knows, even that is bounty enough. We want something else which can hardly be put into words—to be united with the beauty we see, to pass into it, to receive it into ourselves, to bathe in it, to become part of it. (*The Weight of Glory*)

And so we shall.

(The Sacred Romance, 186–87)

What will we do in heaven? The Sunday comics picture saints lying about on clouds, strumming harps. It hardly takes your breath away. The fact that most Christians have a gut sense that earth is more exciting than heaven points to the deceptive powers of the Enemy and our own failure of imagination. What do we do with the idea of "eternal rest"? That sounds like the slogan of a middle-class cemetery. We know heaven begins with a party, but then what? A long nap after the feast? The typical evangelical response—"We will worship God"—doesn't help either. The answer is certainly biblical, and perhaps my reaction is merely a reflection on me, but it sounds so one-dimensional. Something in my heart says, *That's all? How many hymns and choruses can we sing?*

We will worship God in heaven, meaning all of life will finally be worship, not round after round of "Amazing Grace." The parable of the minas in Luke 19 and the talents in Matthew 25 foreshadow a day when we shall exercise our real place in God's economy, the role we have been preparing for on earth. He who has been faithful in the small things will be given even greater adventures in heaven. We long for adventure, to be caught up in something larger than ourselves, a drama of heroic proportions. This isn't just a need for continual excitement, it's part of our design. Few of us ever sense that our talents are being used to their fullest; our creative abilities are rarely given wings in this life. When Revelation 3 speaks of us being "pillars in the temple of our God," it doesn't mean architecture. Rather, Christ promises that we shall be actively fulfilling our total design in the adventures of the new kingdom.

(*The Sacred Romance,* 187–88)

L ife is now a battle and a journey. As Eugene Peterson reminds us, "We must fight the forces that oppose our becoming whole; we must find our way through difficult and unfamiliar territory to our true home." It's not that there aren't joy and beauty, love and adventure now—there are. The invasion of the kingdom has begun. But life in its fullness has yet to come. So we must take seriously the care of our hearts. We must watch over our desire with a fierce love and vigilance, as if we were protecting our most precious possession. We must do battle with the enemies of our hearts—those sirens that would seduce and shipwreck our desire and those arrows that aim to kill it outright. And we must journey forward, toward God, toward the Great Restoration and the Adventures to come. How awful to reach the end of our life's road and find we haven't brought our hearts along with us.

So let me say it again: life is now a battle and a journey. This is the truest explanation for what is going on, the only way to rightly understand our experience. Life is not a game of striving and indulgence. It is not a long march of duty and obligation. It is not, as Henry Ford once said, "one damn thing after another." Life is a desperate quest through dangerous country to a destination that is, beyond all our wildest hopes, indescribably good. Only by conceiving of our days in this manner can we find our way safely through. You see, different roads lead different places. To find the Land of Desire, you must take the Journey of Desire. You can't get there by any other means. If we are to take up the trail and get on with our quest, we've got to get our hearts back . . . which means getting our desire back.

(*The Journey of Desire,* 164–65)

I continue to be stunned by the level of deadness that most people consider normal and seem to be content to live with. It had been more than a year since Diane and Ted first came to see me for counseling. As with most marriages, the real issues lay buried under years of just getting by, hidden beneath the way we've learned to live with each other so as not to rock the boat. Sadly, this way involves killing large regions of our hearts. And so their struggle toward intimacy required a lot of pain and hard work. But they stuck with it until they began to taste the true life of a real marriage. At this point Diane asked Ted about his deepest desires: "If I could be more of what you wanted in a woman, what do you secretly wish I would offer you?" It's a question that most men are dying to be asked. His response? Clean socks. That's all he could come up with. Life would be better, his marriage would be richer, if Diane would keep his drawer filled with clean socks. I wanted to throw him out the window.

I wasn't angry with Ted because his answer was unbelievably shallow, or because it mocked all that his wife was seeking to offer him. I was angry because *it's just not true*. We are made in the image of God; we carry within us the desire for our true life of intimacy and adventure. To say we want less than that is to lie. Ted may believe that clean socks would satisfy him, but he is deceived. His satisfaction comes at the price of his soul.

When I brought up this very issue with a colleague, he sort of dismissed it all with the comment, "Not everyone longs like you do." I had to admit that much. But we were *meant* to. I thought of *The Weight of Glory*, where Lewis says that "when we consider the unblushing promises of reward and the staggering nature of the rewards promised in the Gospels, it would seem that our Lord finds our desires not too strong, but too weak."

(*The Journey of Desire*, 165–66)

When Neo is set free from the Matrix, he joins the crew of the *Nebuchadnezzar*—the little hovercraft that is the headquarters and ship of the small fellowship called to set the captives free. There are nine of them in all, each a character in his own way, but nonetheless a company of the heart, a "band of brothers," a family bound together in a single fate. Together, they train for battle. Together, they plan their path. When they go back into the Matrix to set others free, each one has a role, a gifting, a glory. They function as a team. And they watch each other's back. Neo is fast, really fast, but he still would have been taken out if it hadn't been for Trinity. Morpheus is more gifted than them all, but it took the others to rescue him.

You see this sort of thing at the center of every great story. Dorothy takes her journey with the Scarecrow, the Tin Woodman, the Lion, and of course, Toto. Maximus rallies his little band and triumphs over the greatest empire on earth. When Captain John Miller is sent deep behind enemy lines to save Private Ryan, he goes in with a squad of eight rangers. And, of course, Jesus had the Twelve. This is written so deeply on our hearts: *You must not go alone.* The Scriptures are full of such warnings, but until we see our desperate situation, we hear it as an optional religious assembly for an hour on Sunday mornings.

Think again of Frodo or Neo or Caspian or Jesus. Imagine you are surrounded by a small company of friends who know you well (characters, to be sure, but they love you, and you have come to love them). They understand that we all are at war, know that the purposes of God are to bring a man or a woman fully alive, and are living by sheer necessity and joy in the Four Streams. They fight for you, and you for them. Imagine you *could* have a little fellowship of the heart. Would you want it if it were available?

(*Waking the Dead,* 187–88)

When he left Rivendell, Frodo didn't head out with a thousand Elves. He had eight companions. Jesus didn't march around backed by hundreds of followers, either. He had twelve men—knuckleheads, every last one of them, but they were a band of brothers. This is the way of the kingdom of God. Though we are part of a great company, we are meant to live in little platoons. The little companies we form must be small enough for each of the members to know one another as friends and allies. Is it possible for five thousand people who gather for an hour on a Sunday morning to really and truly *know* one another? Okay, how about five hundred? One hundred and eighty? It can't be done. They can't possibly be intimate allies. It can be inspiring and encouraging to celebrate with a big ol' crowd of people, but who will fight for your heart?

Who will fight for your heart?

How can we offer the stream of Counseling to one another unless we actually *know* one another, know one another's stories? Counseling became a hired relationship between two people primarily because we couldn't find it anywhere else; we haven't formed the sort of small fellowships that would allow the stream to flow quite naturally. Is it possible to offer rich and penetrating words to someone you barely know, in the lobby of your church, as you dash to pick up the kids? And what about warfare? Would you feel comfortable turning to the person in the pew next to you and, as you pass the offering plate, asking him to bind a demon that is sitting on your head?

(*Waking the Dead,* 190–91)

Where will you find the Four Streams? The Four Streams are something we learn, and grow into, and offer one another, within a small fellowship. We hear each other's stories. We discover each other's glories. We learn to walk with God together. We pray for each other's healing. We cover each other's back. This small core fellowship is the essential ingredient for the Christian life. Jesus modeled it for us *for a reason*. Sure, he spoke to the masses. But he *lived* in a little platoon, a small fellowship of friends and allies. His followers took his example and lived this way too. "They broke bread in their homes and ate together with glad and sincere hearts" (Acts 2:46); "Aquila and Priscilla greet you warmly in the Lord, and so does the church that meets at their house" (1 Cor. 16:19); "Give my greetings to the brothers at Laodicea, and to Nympha and the church in her house" (Col. 4:15).

Church is not a building. Church is not an event that takes place on Sundays. I know, it's how we've come to think of it. "I go to First Baptist." "We are members of St. Luke's." "Is it time to go to church?" Much to our surprise, that is *not* how the Bible uses the term. Not at all. When the Scripture talks about church, it means *community*. The little fellowships of the heart that are outposts of the kingdom. A shared life. They worship together, eat together, pray for one another, go on quests together. They hang out together, in each other's homes. When Peter was sprung from prison, "he went to the house of Mary the mother of John" where the church had gathered to pray for his release (Acts 12:12).

(*Waking the Dead*, 191–92)

Of course, small groups have become a part of the programming most churches offer their people. For the most part, they are disappointing and short-lived—by the very admission of those who try them. There are two reasons. One, you can't just throw a random group of people together for a twelve-week study of some kind and expect them to become intimate allies. The sort of devotion we want and need takes place within a shared life. Over the years our fellowship has gone camping together. We play together; help one another move; paint a room; find work. We throw great parties. We fight for each other, live in the Four Streams. This is how it was meant to be.

I love this description of the early church: "All the believers were one in heart" (Acts 4:32). A camaraderie was being expressed there, a bond, an esprit de corps. It means they all loved the same thing, they all wanted the same thing, and they were bonded together to find it, come hell or high water. And hell or high water *will* come, friends, and this will be the test of whether or not your band will make it: if you are one in heart. Judas betrayed the brothers because his heart was never really with them, just as Cipher betrays the company on the *Nebuchadnezzar* and as Boromir betrays the fellowship of the Ring. My goodness— churches split over the size of the parking lot or what instruments to use during worship. Most churches are *not* "one in heart."

(*Waking the Dead,* 193)

The family is . . . like a little kingdom, and, like most other little kingdoms, is generally in a state of something resembling anarchy. (G. K. Chesterton)

Chesterton could have been talking about a little fellowship (our *true* family, because it is the family of God). It is a royal mess. I will not whitewash this. It is *disruptive*. Going to church with hundreds of other people to sit and hear a sermon doesn't ask much of you. It certainly will never expose you. That's why most folks prefer it. Because community will. It will reveal where you have yet to become holy, right at the very moment you are so keenly aware of how *they* have yet to become holy. It will bring you close and you will be *seen* and you will be *known*, and therein lies the power and therein lies the danger. Aren't there moments when all those little companies, in all those stories, hang by a thread? Galadriel says to Frodo, "Your quest stands upon the edge of a knife. Stray but a little and it will fail, to the ruin of all. Yet hope remains while the Company is true."

We've experienced incredible disappointments in our fellowship. We have, every last one of us, hurt one another. Sometimes deeply. Last year there was a night when Stasi and I laid out a vision for where we thought things should be going—our lifelong dream for redemptive community. We hoped the Company would leap to it with loud hurrahs. "Hurrah for John and Stasi!" Far from it. Their response was more on the level of blank stares. Our dream was mishandled—badly. Stasi was sick to her stomach; she wanted to leave the room and throw up. I was . . . stunned. Disappointed. I felt the dive toward a total loss of heart. The following day I could feel my heart being pulled toward resentment. Its moments like these that usually toll the beginning of the end for most attempts at community.

(*Waking the Dead,* 197–98)

Change a few of the details and you have my story—and yours. We construct a life of safety (I will not be vulnerable *there*) and find some place to get a taste of being enjoyed or at least of being "needed." Our journey toward healing begins when we repent of those ways, lay them down, let them go. They've been a royal disaster anyway. As Frederick Buechner says,

> To do for yourself the best that you have it in you to do—to grit your teeth and clench your fists in order to survive the world at its harshest and worst—is, by that very act, to be unable to let something be done for you and in you that is more wonderful still. The trouble with steeling yourself against the harshness of reality is that the same steel that secures your life against being destroyed secures your life also against being opened up and transformed. (*The Sacred Journey*)

God comes to us and asks, "Will you let me come for you?" Not only does he thwart, but at the same time he calls to us as he did to our friend Susan, "Set it down. Set it down. Turn from your ways to me. I want to come for you."

> Therefore I am now going to allure her;
> I will lead her into the desert
> and speak tenderly to her. (Hos. 2:14)

To enter the journey toward the healing of your feminine heart, all it requires is a "Yes. Okay." A simple turning in the heart. Like the Prodigal we wake one day to see that the life we've constructed is no life at all. We let desire speak to us again; we let our hearts have a voice, and what the voice usually says is, *This isn't working. My life is a disaster. Jesus—I'm sorry. Forgive me. Please come for me.*

(*Captivating*, 98–99)

Of course this is scary.

Responding to the invitations of Jesus often feels like the riskiest thing we've ever done. Just ask Rahab, Esther, Ruth, and Mary. Webster defines "risk" as exposing one's life to the possibility of injury, damage, or loss. The life of the friends of God is a life of profound risk. The risk of loving others. The risk of stepping out and offering, speaking up and following our God-given dreams. The risk of playing the irreplaceable role that is ours to play. Of course it is hard. If it were easy, you'd see lots of women living this way.

So let's come back then to what Peter said when he urged women to offer their beauty to others in love. This is the secret of femininity unleashed:

> Do not give way to fear. (1 Peter 3:6)

The reason we fear to step out is because we know that it might not go well (is that an understatement?). We have a history of wounds screaming at us to play it safe. We feel so deeply that if it doesn't go well, if we are not received well, their reaction becomes the verdict on our lives, on our very beings, on our hearts. We fear that our deepest doubts about ourselves as women will be confirmed. Again. That we will hear yet again the message of our wounds, the piercing negative answers to our Question. That is why we can *only* risk stepping out when we are resting in the love of God. When we have received his verdict on our lives—that we are chosen and dearly loved. That he finds us captivating. Then we are free to offer.

(*Captivating,* 213–14)

He wants the same thing that you want. He wants to be loved. He wants to be known as only lovers can know each other. He wants intimacy with you. Yes, yes, he wants your obedience but only when it flows out of a heart filled with love for him. "Whoever has my commands and obeys them, he is the one who loves me" (John 14:21). Following hard after Jesus is the heart's natural response when it has been captured and fallen deeply in love with him.

Reading George MacDonald several years ago, I came across an astounding thought. You've probably heard that there is in every human heart a place that God alone can fill. (Lord knows we've tried to fill it with everything else, to our utter dismay.) But what the old poet was saying was that there is *also* in God's heart a place that you alone can fill. "It follows that there is also a chamber in God himself, into which none can enter but the one, the individual." You. You are meant to fill a place in the heart of God no one and nothing else can fill. Whoa. He longs for *you*.

God wants to live this life together with you, to share in your days and decisions, your desires and disappointments. He wants intimacy with you in the midst of the madness and mundane, the meetings and memos, the laundry and lists, the carpools and conversations and projects and pain. He wants to pour his love into your heart and he longs to have you pour yours into his. He wants your deep heart; that center place within that is the truest *you*. He is not interested in intimacy with the woman you think you are supposed to be. He wants intimacy with the real you.

(*Captivating,* 120–21)

I f we choose the way of desire, our greatest enemy on the road ahead is not the Arrows, nor Satan, nor our false lovers. The most crippling thing that besets the pilgrim heart is simply forgetfulness, or more accurately, the failure to remember. You *will* forget; this isn't the first book you've read in search of God. What do you remember from the others? If God has been so gracious as to touch you through our words, it will not have been the first time he has touched you. What have you done with all the other times? I have had enough encounters with God to provide a lifetime of conviction—why don't I live more faithfully? Because I forget.

I am humbled by the story of the golden calf. These people, the Jews God has just delivered from Egypt, have seen an eyeful. First came the plagues; then the Passover; then the escape from Pharaoh's armies and last-minute rescue straight through the Red Sea. After that came the manna: breakfast in bed, so to speak, every morning for months. They drank water from a rock. They heard and saw the fireworks at Mt. Sinai and shook in their sandals at the presence of God. I think it's safe to say that this band of ransomed slaves had reasons to believe. Then their leader, Moses, disappears for forty days into the "consuming fire" that enveloped the top of the mountain, which they could see with their own eyes. While he's up there, they blow the whole thing off for a wild bacchanalian party in honor of an idol made from their earrings. My first reaction is arrogant: How could they possibly be so stupid? How could they forget everything they've received straight from the hand of God? My second is a bit more honest: That's me; I could do that; I forget all the time.

(*The Sacred Romance,* 202)

Our acts of remembering must therefore involve both essential truths and dramatic narrative. I believe we need to hold the creeds in one hand and our favorite forms of art in the other. There are films, books, poems, songs, and paintings I return to again and again for some deep reason in my heart. Taking a closer look, I see that they all tell me about some part of the Sacred Romance. They help wake me to a deeper remembrance. As Don Hudson has said, "Art is, in the final analysis, a window on heaven."

Now that we are on our way, Satan will do everything he can to steal the Romance. One way he does this is to leave us only propositions, or worse, "principles," like "the management techniques of Jesus" or "the marketing methods of Jesus." The heart cannot live on facts and principles alone; it speaks the language of story, and we must rehearse the truths of our faith in a way that captures the heart and not just the mind.

Let us return again to that central scene and see what it is the author of Hebrews wants us to see in order to follow our Hero in the race ahead. How did Jesus sustain his passionate heart in the face of brutal opposition? *He never lost sight of where he was headed.* He had a vision for the future that was grounded in the past. In the story of the Last Supper, we are told that Jesus knew "he had come from God and was returning to God," and lived his life of selfless love to the end. He remembered both where he had come from and where he was going (John 13:3). And so must we.

(The Sacred Romance, 204–5)

W e were meant to remember together, in community. We need to tell our stories to others and to hear their stories told. We need to help each other with the interpretation of the Larger Story and our own. Our regular times of coming together to worship are intended to be times of corporate remembrance. "This, God has done," we say; "this, he will do." How different Sunday mornings would be if they were marked by a rich retelling of the Sacred Romance in the context of real lives. This is a far cry from the fact-telling, principle listing, list keeping that characterizes much of modern worship.

One of the reasons modern evangelicalism feels so thin is because it is merely modern; there is no connection with the thousands of years of saints who have gone before. Our community of memory must include not only saints from down the street, but also those from down the ages. Let us hear the stories of John and Teresa from last week, but also those of St. John of the Cross and Teresa of Avila, to name only two. Let us draw from that "great cloud of witnesses" and learn from their journeys, so that our memory may span the story of God's relationship with his people.

Remembering is not mere nostalgia; it is an act of survival, our way of "watching over our hearts with all diligence." In *The Brothers Karamazov*, the gentle Alyosha says, "And even if only one good memory remains with us in our hearts, that alone may serve some day for our salvation."

(*The Sacred Romance*, 207–8)

So I tell you this, and insist on it in the Lord, that you must no longer live as the Gentiles do, in the futility of their thinking. They are darkened in their understanding and separated from the life of God because of the ignorance that is in them due to the hardening of their hearts. Having lost all sensitivity, they have given themselves over to sensuality so as to indulge in every kind of impurity, with a continual lust for more. (Eph. 4:17–19)

The loss of sensitivity that Paul is referring to here is the dullness that most people accept as normal. It actually leads us into sin, to sensuality and lust. The deadened soul requires a greater and greater level of stimulation to arouse it. This is, of course, the downward spiral of any addiction. What began as an attraction to *Playboy* ends up for the porn addict in some really horrific stuff. Just look at the progression of television drama over the past thirty years. What we have now would have been considered shocking, even repulsive, to an earlier audience. Networks have to keep adding more sex, more violence, to keep our attention. We have become so sensual. This is why holiness is not numbness; it is sensitivity. It is being *more* attuned to our desires, to what we were truly made for and therefore what we truly want. Our problem is that we've grown quite used to seeking life in all kinds of things other than God.

"For example, God wants to be our perfect lover, but instead we seek perfection in human relationships and are disappointed when our lovers cannot love us perfectly. God wants to provide our ultimate security, but we seek our safety in power and possessions and then we find we must continually worry about them. We seek satisfaction of our spiritual longing in a host of ways that may have very little to do with God." (*Addiction and Grace*)

And so, Gerald May says, "The more we become accustomed to seeking spiritual satisfaction through things other than God, the more abnormal and stressful it becomes to look for God directly." Our instrument is out of tune from years of misuse.

(*The Journey of Desire*, 175–76)

Everything in you may be saying, "But you don't understand. I *want* to eat that whole box of chocolates (or sleep with my boyfriend, or let my anger really fly). That's what really seems like life to me right now." God says, "I know you do, but it'll kill you in the end. What you think is life is not. That's not the comfort (or the love, or the significance) you are seeking. You'll wind up destroying yourself." The commands of God become our tutor in the healing of our desire. We need the Law because our instrument is out of tune; we're not clear all the time on what it is we *really* desire.

And so the first command comes first. God tells us to love him with all our hearts and all our souls, with all our minds and all our strength. It's not a burden but a rescue, a trail out of the jungles of desire. When we don't look for God as our true life, our desire for him spills over into our other desires, giving them an ultimacy and urgency they were never intended to bear. We become desperate, grasping and arranging and worrying over all kinds of things, and once we get them, they end up ruling us. It's the difference between wants and needs. All we truly need is God. Prone to wander from him, we find we need all sorts of other things. Our desire becomes insatiable because we've taken our longing for the Infinite and placed it upon finite things. God saves us from the whole mimetic mess by turning our hearts back to him.

(*The Journey of Desire*, 176)

| # He Thinks, Wills, Enjoys, Feels, Loves, Desires, and Suffers as Any Other Person

Theologians and Bible teachers have told many of us that God is "impassable," that he does not experience emotion as we humans do. Is that what you find when you read Isaiah or Jeremiah or Hosea? A. W. Tozer pleads in *The Pursuit of God*: "We have almost forgotten that God is a person . . . and in the deep of his mighty nature he thinks, wills, enjoys, feels, loves, desires and suffers as any other person may."

In *Disappointment with God*, Phil Yancey tells of going to a cabin in the mountains in Colorado to face his doubts about God and to read the Bible for himself. What he discovered changed his life:

> Simply reading the Bible, I encountered not a misty vapor but an actual Person. A Person as unique and distinctive and colorful as any person I know. God has deep emotions; he feels delight and frustration and anger . . . As I read through the Bible in my winter aerie, I marveled at how much God lets human beings affect him. I was unprepared for the joy and anguish— in short, the passion—of the God of the Universe. By studying "about" God, by taming him and reducing him to words and concepts that could be filed away in alphabetical order, I had lost the force of the passionate relationship God seeks above all else. The people who related to God best—Abraham, Moses, David, Isaiah, Jeremiah—treated him with startling familiarity. They talked to God as if he were sitting in a chair beside them, as one might talk to a counselor, a boss, a parent, or a lover. They treated him like a person.

(*The Sacred Romance Workbook & Journal*, 95–96)

Henri Nouwen once asked Mother Teresa for spiritual direction. Spend one hour each day in adoration of your Lord, she said, and never do anything you know is wrong. Follow this, and you'll be fine. Such simple yet profound advice. Worship is the act of the abandoned heart adoring its God. It is the union that we crave. Few of us experience anything like this on a regular basis, let alone for an hour each day. But it is what we need. Desperately. Simply showing up on Sunday is not even close to worship. Neither does singing songs with religious content pass for worship. What counts is *the posture of the soul* involved, the open heart pouring forth its love toward God and communing with him. It is a question of desire.

Worship occurs when we say to God, from the bottom of our hearts, "You are the One whom I desire." As Thomas à Kempis prayed, "There is nothing created that can fully satisfy my desires. Make me one with You in a sure bond of heavenly love, for You alone are sufficient to Your lover, and without You all things are vain and of no substance."

I spent a year in the Psalms at the same time I was resting from the duty of Sunday morning. I wasn't studying them with my head; I was praying them from my heart. It gave me a voice for the cry of my soul—the anguish, the weariness, the joy, the sorrow. It's all there. What is remarkable is that no matter where the poet begins, he almost always ends in worship. This is no coincidence. It is where our journey must lead us. In the most often quoted phrase from Augustine, he says, "Our hearts are restless until they find their rest in Thee." He is referring to desire. Our only hope for rest from the incessant craving of our desire is in God, and us united to him. The full union, of course, is coming. We rehearse for the wedding now through worship.

(The Journey of Desire, 177–78)

There is a widespread belief in the church that to be a Christian somehow satisfies our every desire. As one camp song has it, "I'm inright, outright, upright, downright happy all day long." What complete nonsense! Augustine emphasized, "The whole life of the good Christian is a holy longing. What you desire ardently, as yet you do not see." So, "let us long because we are to be filled . . . That is our life, to be exercised by longing." There's the mystery again. Longing leads to fullness somewhere down the road. Meanwhile, being content is not the same thing as being full.

Paul said he had "learned the secret of being content" (Phil. 4:12), and many Christians assume he no longer experienced the thirst of his soul. But earlier in the same epistle, the old saint said that he had *not* obtained his soul's desire, or "already been made perfect." Quite the contrary. He described himself as pressing on, "straining toward what is ahead" (3:12–14). These are not the words of a man who no longer experienced longing because he had arrived. They are the account of a man propelled on his life quest by his desire.

Contentment is not freedom *from* desire, but freedom *of* desire. Being content is not pretending that everything is the way you wish it would be; it is not acting as though you have no wishes. Rather, it is no longer being *ruled* by your desires.

(*The Journey of Desire,* 181–82)

What can this incessant craving, and this impotence of attainment mean, unless there was once a happiness belonging to man, of which only the faintest traces remain, in that void which he attempts to fill with everything within his reach? But it is in vain he seeks from absent objects the relief things present cannot give, and which neither of them can give; because, in a soul that will live forever, there is an infinite void that nothing can fill, but an infinite unchangeable being. (*Pensées*)

You can be satisfied, says Blaise Pascal; you just can't be sated. There is great joy in a glass of cabernet; the whole bottle is another story. Intimate conversation satisfies a different thirst, but how awful to try to arrange for it again the next night and the night after that. The Israelites tried to hoard the manna—and it crawled with maggots. Our soul's insatiable desire becomes the venom Pascal warns of when it demands its fill here and now, through the otherwise beautiful and good gifts of our lives.

God grants us so much of our heart's desire as we delight in him: "You open your hand and satisfy the desires of every living thing" (Ps. 145:16). Not always, not on demand, but certainly more than we deserve. God delights to give good gifts to his beloved. But that old root would have us shift once more from giver to gift, and seek our rest through being full. This is the turn we must be vigilant to see, watching over our hearts with loving care.

(*The Journey of Desire,* 182–83)

We know that the whole creation has been groaning as in the pains of childbirth right up to the present time. Not only so, but we ourselves, who have the firstfruits of the Spirit, groan inwardly as we wait eagerly for our adoption as sons, the redemption of our bodies. For in this hope we were saved. But hope that is seen is no hope at all. Who hopes for what he already has? But if we hope for what we do not yet have, we wait for it patiently. (Rom. 8:22–25)

Amazing. Paul is passing along to us the secret of the sojourning heart. We live in hope, and he says hoping is waiting. And groaning. When was the last time you heard that in a sermon or the title for a new book? *You, Too, Can Groan Inwardly While You Wait Eagerly!* Everything I've seen lately offers a sure-fire way to "get what you want." How to be a success at work. How to be a success at love. How to succeed in work *and* love at the same time.

Here are questions to ask yourself to see if you are a pilgrim or an arranger: *What am I waiting for? Is there anything I ardently desire that I am doing nothing to secure?* The first time I asked myself, I couldn't name a thing. There were many things I was working on, or fretting over, or had given up wanting. Thankfully, this was some time ago. Things are different now. Now I wonder, *What am I still arranging for?* I should like to let it go too.

(*The Journey of Desire*, 184–85)

To wait is to learn the spiritual grace of *detachment*, the freedom of desire. Not the absence of desire, but desire at rest. St. John of the Cross lamented that "the desires weary and fatigue the soul; for they are like restless and discontented children, who are ever demanding this or that from their mother, and are never contented." Detachment is coming to the place where those demanding children are at peace. As King David said, "I have stilled and quieted my soul; like a weaned child with its mother, like a weaned child is my soul within me" (Ps. 131:2). Such a beautiful picture, a young one leaning against her mother's breast. There is no fussing, no insistent tears.

She has learned to wait. The word *detachment* might evoke wrong impressions.

It is not a cold and indifferent attitude; not at all. May writes, "An authentic spiritual understanding of detachment devalues neither desire nor the objects of desire." Instead, it "aims at correcting one's own anxious grasping in order to free oneself for committed relationship to God."

As Thomas à Kempis declared, "Wait a little while, O my soul, wait for the divine promise, and thou shalt have abundance of all good things in heaven." In this posture we discover that, indeed, we are expanded by longing. Something grows in us, a capacity if you will, for life and love and God. I think of Romans 8:24–25: "That is why waiting does not diminish us, any more than waiting diminishes a pregnant mother. We are enlarged in the waiting. We, of course, don't see what is enlarging us. But the longer we wait, the larger we become, and the more joyful our expectancy" (*The Message*). There is actually a sweet pain in longing, if we will let it draw our hearts homeward.

(*The Journey of Desire*, 185–87)

Caring for our own hearts isn't selfishness; it's how we begin to love.

Yes, we care for our hearts for the sake of others. Does that sound like a contradiction? Not at all. What will you bring to others if your heart is empty, dried up, pinned down? Love is the point. And you can't love without your heart, and you can't love well unless your heart is well.

When it comes to the whole subject of loving others, you must know this: how you handle your own heart is how you will handle theirs. This is the wisdom behind Jesus' urging us to love others *as we love ourselves* (Mark 12:31). "A horrible command," as C. S. Lewis points out, "if the self were simply to be hated." If you dismiss your heart, you will end up dismissing theirs. If you expect perfection of your heart, you will raise that same standard for them. If you manage your heart for efficiency and performance, that is what you'll pressure them to be.

"But," you protest, "I have lots of grace for other people. I'm just hard on myself." I tried the same excuse for years. It doesn't work. Even though we may try to be merciful toward others while we neglect or beat up ourselves, they can *see* how we treat our own hearts, and they will always feel the treatment will be the same for them. They are right. Eventually, inevitably, we will treat them poorly too.

(*Waking the Dead*, 211–12)

Caring for your heart is how you protect your relationship with God.

Now there's a new thought. But isn't our heart the new dwelling place of God? It is where we commune with him. It is where we hear his voice. Most of the folks I know who have never heard God speak to them are the same folks who live far from their hearts; they practice the Christianity of principles. Then they wonder why God seems distant. *I guess all that intimacy with God stuff is for others, not me.* It's like a friend who hates the telephone. He neglects to pay the bills, could care less when the phone company disconnects the service. Then he wonders why "nobody ever calls." You cannot cut off your heart and expect to hear from God.

Clairvaux describes Christian maturity as the stage where "we love ourselves for God's sake," meaning that because he considers our hearts the treasures of the kingdom, we do too. We care for ourselves in the same way a woman who knows she is deeply loved cares for herself, while a woman who has been tossed aside tends to "let herself go," as the saying goes. God's friends care for their hearts because they matter to *him.*

(Waking the Dead, 213)

We now are going to war. This is the beginning of the end. The hour is late, and you are needed. We need your heart.

If there were something more I could do to help you see, I wish to God I could have done it. Tears fill my eyes for fear I have not done enough. You must turn, then, back to myth—tomorrow and the next day and the next. Read the battle of Helm's Deep; it's chapter 7 of *The Two Towers*. Watch any of the trilogy of those films. And the opening of *Gladiator*. That is where we are now. Or, if you can bear it, watch the battle of the Ia Drang Valley in *We Were Soldiers*. It is so deeply true to what we must face, will face. Linger over the climax of *The Prince of Egypt*, where God goes to war against Egypt to set his people free. If the images of the Exodus do not move you, I don't know what will.

We are now far into this epic story that every great myth points to. We have reached the moment where we, too, must find our courage and rise up to recover our hearts and fight for the hearts of others. The hour is late, and much time has been wasted. Aslan is on the move; we must rally to him at the stone table. We must find Gepetto lost at sea. We must ride hard, ride to Helm's Deep and join the last great battle for Middle Earth. Grab everything God sends you. You'll need everything that helps you see with the eyes of your heart, including those myths, and the way they illumine for us the words God has given in Scripture, to which "you will do well to pay attention . . . as to a light shining in a dark place, until the day dawns and the morning star rises in your hearts" (2 Peter 1:19).

(*Waking the Dead,* 220–21)

Either (a) we're blowing it, or (b) God is holding out on us. Or some combination of both, which is where most people land. Think about it. Isn't this where *you* land, with all the things that haven't gone the way you'd hoped and wanted? Isn't it some version of "I'm blowing it," in that it's your fault, you could have done better, you could have been braver or wiser or more beautiful or something? Or "God is holding out on me," in that you know he *could* come through, but he hasn't come through—and what are you to make of that?

This is The Big Question, by the way, the one every philosophy and religion and denominational take on Christianity has been trying to nail down since the dawn of time. *What is really going on here?* Good grief—life is brutal. Day after day it hammers us, till we lose sight of what God intends toward us, and we haven't the foggiest idea why the things that are happening to us *are* happening to us. Then you watch lives going down with the Twin Towers, read about children starving in Ethiopia, and wham! If a good God is really in charge . . . and all that.

We need clarity and we need it badly. A simple prayer rises from my heart: *Jesus, take away the fog and the clouds and the veil, and help me to see . . . give me eyes to really see.*

(*Waking the Dead,* 9–10)

A nd now? Now we are living somewhere toward the end of
Act Three. We have a future, but this tale is not over yet—
not by a long shot. We now live between the battle for Helm's
Deep and the Battle of the Pelennor Fields. Between the beaches
of Normandy and the end of the war. Between the fall of the
Republic and the fall of the Empire. Between Paradise lost and
Paradise regained.

We live in a far more dramatic, far more dangerous Story than
we ever imagined. The reason we love The Chronicles of Narnia
or *Star Wars* or *The Matrix* or *The Lord of the Rings* is because they
are telling us something about our lives that we never, ever get on
the evening news. Or from most pulpits. They are reminding us of
the Epic we are created for.

This is the sort of tale you've fallen into. How would you live
differently if you believed it to be true?

The final test of any belief or faith that claims to provide an
answer to our lives is this: Does the one explain the other? Does
the story bring into perspective the pages you were already holding, the days of your life? Does it take everything into account?
Does it explain the longing in your heart for a life you haven't yet
found? Does it explain the evil cast around us? Most of all, does it
give you back your heart, lead you to the Source of life?

Something has been calling to you all the days of your life.
You've heard it on the wind and in the music you love, in laughter
and in tears, and most especially in the stories that have ever captured your heart. There *is* a secret written on your heart. A valiant
Hero-Lover and his Beloved. An Evil One and a great battle to
fight. A Journey and a Quest, more dangerous and more thrilling
than you could imagine. A little Fellowship to see you through.

This is the gospel of Christianity.

(*Epic*, 99–100)

N ow—what is *your* part? What is your role in the Story?
In truth, the only one who can tell you that is the Author.
To find our lives, we must turn to Jesus. We must yield our all to
him and ask him to restore us as his own. We ask his forgiveness
for our betrayal of him. We ask him to make us all he intended us
to be—to tell us who we are and what we are now to do. We ask
him to remove the veil from our eyes and from our hearts.

The Story God is telling—like every great story that echoes it—
reminds us of three eternal truths it would be good to keep in
mind as we take the next step out the door.

First, *things are not what they seem.*

Where would we be if Eve had recognized the serpent for who
he really was? And that carpenter from Nazareth—he's not what
he appears to be, either. There is far more going on around us than
meets the eye. We live in a world with two halves, one part that
we can see and another part that we cannot. We must live as
though the unseen world (the rest of reality) is more weighty and
more real and more dangerous than the part of reality we can see.

Second, *we are at war.*

This is a love Story, set in the midst of a life-and-death battle.
Just look around you. Look at all the casualties strewn across the
field. The lost souls, the broken hearts, the captives. We must take
this battle seriously.

Third, *you have a crucial role to play.*

That is the third eternal truth spoken by every great story, and
it happens to be the one we most desperately need if we are ever
to understand our days. Frodo underestimated who he was. As did
Neo. As did Wallace. As did Peter, James, and John. It is a dangerous thing to underestimate your role in the Story. You will lose
heart, and you will miss your cues.

This is our most desperate hour. You are needed.

(*Epic,* 100)

Jesus of Nazareth was sentenced to death by a vain puppet of the Roman government acting as district governor of Jerusalem. He was nailed to a cross by a handful of Roman soldiers who happened to be on duty, and left there to die. He died sometime around three o'clock in the afternoon on a Friday. Of a broken heart, by the way. And we call it Good Friday, of all strange things, because of what it affected. An innocent man, the Son of God, bleeding for the sins of the world. Standing in for us, as Jack gives his life for Rose in *Titanic*, as Sydney Carton stands in to die for Charles Darnay in *A Tale of Two Cities*, or as Aslan dies on the stone table to ransom the traitor Edmund. We rebelled, and the penalty for our rebellion was death. To lose us was too great a pain for God to bear, and so he took it upon himself to rescue us. The Son of God came "to give his life as a ransom for many" (Matt. 20:28).

You have been ransomed by Christ. Your treachery is forgiven. You are entirely pardoned for every wrong thought and desire and deed. This is what the vast majority of Christians understand as the central work of Christ for us. And make no mistake about it— it is a deep and stunning truth, one that will set you free and bring you joy. For a while.

But the joy for most of us has proved fleeting, because we find that we need to be forgiven again and again and again. Christ has died for us, but we remain (so we believe) deeply marred. It actually ends up producing a great deal of guilt. "After all that Christ has done for you . . . and now you're back here asking forgiveness *again?*" To be destined to a life of repeating the very things that sent our Savior to the cross can hardly be called *salvation*. Think of it.

(*Waking the Dead*, 61–62)

You cannot take your Question to Adam. You cannot look to him for the validation of your soul. But *so* many women do. *If I have a man, then I'm okay. Then I'm loved.* It happens around adolescence for women too. The time for her father to speak into her life begins to wane. A new window opens up—boys. And if her father has not been there for her, she is starving for love, and she'll give herself to boys in the hope of finding it. Remember the old maxim "Girls give sex to get love"? It's true.

What makes this seem so natural, especially for women, is that Eve *was* made for Adam. "It is not good for the man to be alone. I will make a [*ezer kenegdo*] suitable for him" (Gen. 2:18). Eve was literally fashioned from the rib taken out of Adam's side. There is an incompleteness that haunts us, makes us yearn for one another. How many of you sighed at the end of *Jerry Maguire*, when he runs through the airport and races across town to get back to his wife who has separated from him. He says, "You complete me." That is true; it's part of the man-woman design.

And yet.

No man can tell you who you are as a woman. No man is the verdict on your soul. (Dear sister, how many of you have lost yourself in this search?) One woman said to us, "I still feel useless. I am not a woman. I do not have a man. I have failed to captivate someone." The ache is real. But the verdict is false. Only God can tell you who you are. Only God can speak the answer you need to hear. That is why we spoke of the Romance with him first. It comes first. It must. It has to. Adam is a far too unreliable source—amen!

(Captivating, 151–52)

Complicating matters further is the curse upon Eve. "Your desire will be for your husband, and he will rule over you" (Gen. 3:16). There is an ache in Eve now that she tries to get Adam to fill. There is an emptiness given to her to drive her back to God, but she takes it to Adam instead. It makes a mess of many good relationships. You know all about this. No matter how much Adam pours into your aching soul, it's never enough. He cannot fill you. Maybe he's pulled away because he senses you're asking him to fill you. Every woman has to reckon with this—this ache she tries to get her man to fill. In order to learn how to love him, you *must* first stop insisting that he fill you.

We say all this as a sort of prologue, because we cannot talk about loving a man well—whoever he might be in your life—until we see that we cannot look to him for things he cannot give. We cannot love Adam while we are looking to him to validate us. It will usher in too much fear. If he's the verdict on us as a woman, we won't be able to truly and freely offer him our beauty. We'll hold it back in fear. Or, we'll give ourselves over to him in inappropriate ways, in a sort of sexual or emotional promiscuity, desperate for his attention. And we won't be able to confront him and stand up to him when he needs *that* from us as well.

Ask Jesus to show you what you've been doing with your Question and how you've related to Adam. Only then can we talk about loving men.

(*Captivating*, 153)

Let's start with sex.

Not because "it's all men think about" (as many a cynical woman has said), but because it presents the relationship between femininity and masculinity in such a clear way. It is a beautiful and rich metaphor, a very passionate and heightened picture for a much broader reality. The question before us is, "How does a woman best love a man?" The answer is simple: Seduce him.

Think of a woman on her wedding night. She dims the lights and puts on a silky something that accentuates the loveliness of her body, reveals the beauty of her naked form, yet also leaves something yet to be unveiled. She puts on perfume and lipstick and checks her hair. She *allures* her man. She hopes to arouse him and invite him to come to her and enter her. In an act of stunning vulnerability she takes life's greatest risk—offering her unveiled beauty to him, opening herself up to him in every way.

And as for her man, if he does not rise to the occasion, nothing will happen. There will be no consummation of love, no life conceived unless the man is able to offer his strength to his woman. That is how we make love. Femininity is what arouses his masculinity. His strength is what makes a woman yearn to be beautiful.

It's that simple, that beautiful, that mysterious, and incredibly profound.

The beauty of a woman is what arouses the strength of a man. He *wants* to play the man when a woman acts like that. You can't hold him back. He *wants* to come through. And this desire is crucial. Don't you want him to *want* to come through for you? Not to be forced to, not because he "ought to." But because he *wants* to come through. Well, then, arouse his desire. In any facet of life.

(*Captivating*, 154)

We human beings are made up of three interwoven parts. As Paul says, "May God himself . . . sanctify you through and through. May your whole spirit, soul and body be kept blameless at the coming of our Lord Jesus Christ" (1Thess. 5:23). We are body, soul, and spirit. Each part affects the others in a mysterious interplay of life. By seeking healing through counseling, God was addressing my soul. God's provision of the help of antidepressants was a tremendous help to my body. I made real progress. But it was not enough. God wanted me to engage my spirit.

A foul spirit of depression had its bloody claws in my life. It often works like that—the Enemy knows our weaknesses, and he preys upon them. Demons smell human brokenness like sharks smell blood in the water, and they move in to take advantage of the weakened soul. Paul warns about this in Ephesians when, *writing to Christians,* he warns us not to "give the devil a foothold" in our lives through unhealed and mishandled emotions (4:26–27). God had me begin to stand against it.

James and Peter both exhort us to *resist* our Enemy (James 4:7; 1 Peter 5:8–9). Jesus said he has given us his authority to overcome the spiritual attacks against us (Luke 10:18–19). I prayed. John, as my husband, my head, prayed as well. We commanded this foul spirit to leave me by the authority given to believers in Jesus Christ. Deliverance came. Victory. Release. Healing. Restoration. It was the final key. I needed to address all three aspects—my body, soul, and spirit—in order to come more fully into healing. Far too many women will focus only on one or two aspects and not engage in the spiritual warfare that is swirling around us.

But if we would be free, we must.

(Captivating, 192–93)

Life is a journey of the heart that requires the mind—not the other way around. The church sometimes gets this backward and makes knowing the right things the center of life. It's not; the heart is the center of life. Desire is always where the action is. However, staying alive to our desire is not enough; we know that only too well. We must bring the *truth* into our hearts to guard and to guide our desire; this is the other half of our mission. With a recovery of heart and soul taking place in many quarters, my fear now is that we will abandon the pursuit of truth and try to base our journey on our feelings and intuition. "Follow your heart" is becoming a popular message in our culture. Or as Sting sings, "Trust your soul." It will not work. Our spiritual fathers and mothers knew this only too well. In *The Imitation of Christ*, Thomas à Kempis warned, "Our own opinion and our own sense do often deceive us, and they discern but little." We must cling to the truth for dear life. And so our spiritual forebears urged us to bring *both* heart and mind together.

Now, not all truths help us descend with the mind into the heart. There is a way of talking about the truth that can actually deaden our hearts. Most of us were raised in the modern era, the age of reason and science. We came to believe that truth is best discovered in the scientific method.

What is the truth of a kiss? Technically, in a modernistic sense, it is two sets of mandibles pressing together for a certain duration of time. Those of you who have experienced the wonders of a kiss will know that while true, this description is so untrue. It takes away everything beautiful and mysterious and passionate and intimate and leaves you with an icy cold fact. Those who know kissing feel robbed; those who don't are apt to say, "If that's what kissing is all about, I think I'd rather not."

We've done the same thing to theology.

(*The Journey of Desire*, 202–3)

We have dissected God, and man, and the gospel, and we have thousands, if not millions, of facts—all of it quite dead. It's not that these insights aren't true; it's that they no longer speak. I could tell you a few facts about God, for example. He is omniscient, omnipotent, and immutable. There—don't you feel closer to him? All our statements about God forget that he is a person, and as Tozer says, "In the deep of His mighty nature He thinks, wills, enjoys, feels, loves, desires and suffers as any other person may." How do we get to know a person? Through stories. All the wild and sad and courageous tales that we tell—they are what reveal us to others. We must return to the Scriptures for the story that it is and stop approaching it as if it is an encyclopedia, looking for "tips and techniques."

Reminders of the Story are everywhere—in film and novels, in children's fairy tales, in the natural world around us, and in the stories of our own lives. In fact, every story or movie or song or poem that has ever stirred your soul is telling you something you need to know about the Sacred Romance. Even nature is crying out to us of God's great heart and the drama that is unfolding. Sunrise and sunset tell the tale every day, remembering Eden's glory, prophesying Eden's return. These are the trumpet calls from the "hid battlements of eternity." We must capture them like precious treasures, and hold them close to our hearts.

(*The Journey of Desire*, 203–4)

Whatever else it means to be human, we know beyond doubt that it means to be *relational.* Aren't the greatest joys and memories of your life associated with family, friendship, or falling in love? Aren't your deepest wounds somehow connected to some*one* also, to a failure of relationship? That you were loved but are no longer, or that you never have been chosen?

One of the deepest of all human longings is the longing to belong, to be a part of things, to be invited in. We want to be part of the fellowship. Where did *that* come from?

So, too, our greatest sorrows stem from losing the ones we love. Byron lamented,

> What is the worst of woes that wait on age?
> What stamps the wrinkle deeper on the brow?
> To view each loved one blotted from life's page,
> And be alone on earth, as I am now.

Loneliness might be the hardest cross we bear. Why else would we have come up with solitary confinement as a form of punishment? We are relational to the core. We are made, as it says in Genesis, in the image of God or, better, in the image of the Trinity: "Let *us* make man in *our* image" (1:26, emphasis added).

Meister Eckhart had it right when he said that we are born out of the laughter of the Trinity.

From the Heart of the universe come our beating hearts. From this Fellowship spring all of our longings for a friend, a family, a fellowship—for someplace to *belong.*

(*Epic,* 22–24)

Any parent or lover knows this: love is chosen. You cannot, in the end, force anyone to love you.

So if you are writing a story where love is the meaning, where love is the highest and best of all, where love is the *point,* then you have to allow each person a choice. You have to allow freedom. You cannot force love. God gives us the dignity of freedom, to choose for or against him (and friends, to ignore him is to choose against him).

This is the reason for what C.S. Lewis called the Problem of Pain. Why would a kind and loving God create a world where evil is possible? Doesn't he care about our happiness? Isn't he good? Indeed, he does and he is. He cares so much for our happiness that he endows us with the capacity to love and to be loved, which is the greatest happiness of all.

He endows us with a dignity that is almost unimaginable.

For this creator God is no puppeteer.

"Trust me in this one thing," God says to us. "I have given the entire earth to you, for your joy. Explore it; awaken it; take care of it for me. And I have given you one another, for love and romance and friendship. You shall be my intimate allies. But on this one matter, you must trust me. Trust that my heart for you is good, that I am withholding this for a reason. Do not eat of the fruit of the Tree of the Knowledge of Good and Evil . . . or you will die."

And this is where our Story takes its tragic turn.

(*Epic,* 52—54)

We lose the Story every day. It is continually being stolen from us by the Evil One—the ultimate desconstructionist. He twists and spins and pulls apart the truth until the fragments we have left are unrecognizable. Or we lose it ourselves in the marketplace of Vanity Fair. Bombarded by thousands of messages each day, every one of them marked urgent, we leave behind the truly important things, the only refuge for our hearts.

We must be more intentional about holding on to the truth. The spiritual pilgrims who aligned themselves with St. Benedict took this task seriously—far more seriously than we do, I'm afraid. A typical day in the lives of Benedictine monks began in the middle of the night, when they arose for the Night Office. No less than twelve psalms would be said, together with three Scripture readings, several hymns, and prayers. Sunrise brought the Morning Office, followed by six other breaks during the labors of the day for remembering: Prime, Terce, Sext, None, Vespers, and Compline in the evening. Seven times a day set aside for prayer and the recitation of psalms. Together with their night vigil, more than twenty-nine psalms would be said, not to mention numerous lessons, verses, prayers, and hymns.

Now, I'm not suggesting that we all adopt the Rule of Benedict. But think about this: these men left the distractions of the world to focus entirely on God. They lived in an environment *designed* to keep them standing before God, and what did they discover? That they needed reminders every hour of the day and night! Do we, who live in the hostile chaos of the world, think we can do with an occasional visit?

(*The Journey of Desire*, 205–6)

The meadowlark has long been my favorite songbird. I love its song because it evokes so many summer days out in the fields and streams of the West. Its song *means* summer, hay meadows, long lazy days, fly-fishing. More than anything else, it has become for me a symbol of hope. The meadowlark returns to Colorado in the early spring, and as I've mentioned, that typically means it arrives about the same time our major snowstorms hit. What courage; if it were me, I'd wait until June when the weather warms up. But they come in spite of the snow, and take their place on fence posts and the tops of small trees, and begin singing. Hearing a midsummer song almost seems out of place when the flurries are whipping about your face. But that is exactly when we *need* it.

I heard two meadowlarks again this spring, calling and responding to each other on a cold and windy day. God began to speak through them. I heard him urging me to keep my own summer song, even though life's winter tries to throw into my spring cold wind and snow. *Do not throw away your confidence*, he said. *Do not budge from your perch, but sing your song, summer confident, sure of my great goodness toward you. You did not bring this spring, dear child; you do not have to arrange for the summer to follow. They come from thy Father's will, and they will come.*

Brent was buried on a Thursday afternoon. As we gathered by the graveside, Craig read these words: "I am the resurrection and the life. He who believes in me will live, even though he dies; and whoever lives and believes in me will never die" (John 11:25–26). He closed his Bible and we all stood in silence, not really knowing what to say or do; no one wanted to leave; no one really wanted to stay. It seemed so final. At that moment, a meadowlark sang.

This is my song in return.

(*The Journey of Desire*, 210–12)

he spiritual life cannot be made suburban," said Howard Macey. "It is always frontier and we who live in it must accept and even rejoice that it remains untamed." The greatest obstacle to realizing our dreams is the false self's hatred of mystery. That's a problem, you see, because *mystery is essential to adventure.* More than that, mystery is the heart of the universe and the God who made it. The most important aspects of any man's world—his relationship with his God and with the people in his life, his calling, the spiritual battles he'll face—every one of them is fraught with mystery. But that is not a bad thing; it is a joyful, rich part of reality and essential to our soul's thirst for adventure.

There are no formulas with God. Period. So there are no formulas for the man who follows him. God is a Person, not a doctrine. He operates not like a system—not even a theological system—but with all the originality of a truly free and alive person. "The realm of God is dangerous," says Archbishop Anthony Bloom. "You must enter into it and not just seek information about it." Take Joshua and the Battle of Jericho. The Israelites are staged to make their first military strike into the Promised Land and there's a lot hanging on this moment—the morale of the troops, their confidence in Joshua, not to mention their reputation that will precede them to every other enemy that awaits. This is their D-Day, so to speak, and word is going to get around. How does God get the whole thing off to a good start? He has them march around the city blowing trumpets for a week; on the seventh day he has them do it seven times and then give a big holler. It works marvelously, of course. And you know what? It never happens again. Israel never uses that tactic again.

(*Wild at Heart,* 208–9)

John Spillane is a para-rescue jumper sent into the North Atlantic, into the worst storm of the twentieth century, the *perfect storm*, as the book and film called it, to rescue a fisherman lost at sea. When his helicopter goes down, he is forced to jump into pitch blackness from an unknown height, and when he hits the water, he's going so fast it's like hitting the pavement from eighty feet above. He is dazed and confused—just as we are when it comes to the story of our lives. It's the perfect analogy. We have no idea who we really are, why we're here, what's happened to us, or why. Honestly, most days we are alert and oriented times zero. Dazed. Sleepwalking through life.

Has God abandoned us? Did we not pray enough? Is this just something we accept as "part of life," suck it up, even though it breaks our hearts? After a while, the accumulation of event after event that we do not like and do not understand erodes our confidence that we are part of something grand and good, and reduces us to a survivalist mind-set. I know, I know—we've been told that we matter to God. And part of us partly believes it. But life has a way of chipping away at that conviction, undermining our settled belief that he means us well. I mean, if that's true, then why didn't he _____? Fill in the blank. Heal your mom. Save your marriage. Get you married. Help you out more.

Either (a) we're blowing it, or (b) God is holding out on us. Or some combination of both, which is where most people land. Think about it. Isn't this where *you* land, with all the things that haven't gone the way you'd hoped and wanted?

(*Waking the Dead,* 8–9)

The glory of God is man fully alive. (Saint Irenaeus)

When I first stumbled across this quote my initial reaction was . . . *You're kidding me. Really?* I mean, is that what you've been told? That the purpose of God—the very thing he's staked his reputation on—is your coming fully alive? Huh. Well, that's a different take on things. It made me wonder, *What are God's intentions toward me? What is it I've come to believe about that?* Yes, we've been told any number of times that God does care, and there are some pretty glowing promises given to us in Scripture along those lines. But on the other hand, we have the days of our lives, and they have a way of casting a rather long shadow over our hearts when it comes to God's intentions toward *us* in particular. I read the quote again, "The glory of God is man fully alive," and something began to stir in me. *Could it be?*

I turned to the New Testament to have another look, read for myself what Jesus said he offers. "I have come that they may have life, and have it to the full" (John 10:10). Wow. That's different from saying, "I have come to forgive you. Period." Forgiveness is awesome, but Jesus says here he came to give us *life*. Hmmm. Sounds like ol' Irenaeus might be on to something. "I am the bread of life" (John 6:48). "Whoever believes in me, as the Scripture has said, streams of living water will flow from within him" (John 7:38). The more I looked, the more this whole theme of life jumped off the pages. I mean, it's *everywhere.*

"Above all else, guard your heart, for it is the wellspring of life" (Prov. 4:23).

"You have made known to me the path of life" (Ps. 16:11).

"In him was life, and that life was the light of men" (John 1:4).

"Come to me to have life" (John 5:40).

"Tell the people the full message of this new life" (Acts 5:20).

(*Waking the Dead,* 10–11)

Life is not a list of propositions, it is a series of dramatic scenes. As Eugene Peterson said, "We live in narrative, we live in story. Existence has a story shape to it. We have a beginning and an end, we have a plot, we have characters." Story is the language of the heart. Our souls speak not in the naked facts of mathematics or the abstract propositions of systematic theology; they speak the images and emotions of story. Contrast your enthusiasm for studying a textbook with the offer to go to a movie, read a novel, or listen to the stories of someone else's life. Elie Wiesel suggests that "God created man because he loves stories." So if we're going to find the answer to the riddle of the earth—and of our own existence—we'll find it in story.

For hundreds of years, our culture has been losing its story. The Enlightenment dismissed the idea that there is an Author but tried to hang on to the idea that we could still have a Larger Story, life could still make sense, and everything was headed in a good direction. Western culture rejected the mystery and transcendence of the Middle Ages and placed its confidence in pragmatism and progress, the pillars of the Modern Era, the Age of Reason. But once we had rid ourselves of the Author, it didn't take long to lose the Larger Story. In the Postmodern Era, all we have left are our small stories. The central belief of our times is that there is no story, nothing hangs together, all we have are bits and pieces, the random days of our lives. Tragedy still brings us to tears and heroism still lifts our hearts, but there is no context for any of it. Life is just a sequence of images and emotions without rhyme or reason.

So, what are we left to do? Create our own story line to bring some meaning to our experiences. Our heart is made to live in a Larger Story; having lost that we do the best we can by developing our own smaller dramas.

(*The Sacred Romance*, 39–41)

The only fatal error is to pretend that we have found the life we prize. To mistake the water hole for the sea. To settle for the same old thing. Christopher Fry called such a life "the sleep of prisoners." The most tragic day of all is to prefer slavery to freedom, to prefer death to life. We must not stay in this sleep. The time has come for us to wake, to arise from our slumber. As the Scriptures say, "Wake up, O sleeper, rise from the dead" (Eph. 5:14). And so George MacDonald prayed,

> When I can no more stir my soul to move,
> And life is but the ashes of a fire;
> When I can but remember that my heart
> Once used to live and love, long and aspire—
> Oh, be thou then the first, the one thou art;
> Be thou the calling, before all answering love,
> And in me wake hope, fear, boundless desire.
> (*Diary of an Old Soul*)

Bringing our heart along in our life's journey is the most important mission of our lives—and the hardest. It all turns on what we do with our desire. If you will look around, you will see that most people have abandoned the journey. They have lost heart. They are camped in places of resignation or indulgence, or trapped in prisons of despair. I understand; I have frequented all those places before and return to them even still. Life provides any number of reasons and occasions to abandon desire. Certainly, one of the primary reasons is that it creates for us our deepest dilemmas. To desire something and not to have it—is this not the source of nearly all our pain and sorrow?

(*The Journey of Desire,* 14–15)

A sower went out to sow some seed . . .
A man fell into the hands of robbers . . .
Suppose a woman has ten silver coins and loses one . . .
There were ten virgins with ten lamps . . .

Think of it. You are the Son of the living God. You have come to earth to rescue the human race. It is your job to communicate truths without which your precious ones will be lost . . . forever. Would you do it like *this?* Why doesn't he come right out and say it—get to the point? What's with all the stories?

We children of the Internet and the cell phone and the Weather Channel, we think we are the enlightened ones. We aren't fooled by anything—we just want the *facts.* The bottom line. So proposition has become our means of saying what is true and what is not. And proposition is helpful . . . for certain things. Sacramento is the capital of California; water freezes at 32 degrees Fahrenheit. But proposition fails when it comes to the weightier things in life. While it is a fact that the Civil War was fought between the years of 1861 and 1865, and while it is also a fact that hundreds of thousands of men died in that war, those facts hardly describe what happened at Bull Run or Gettysburg. You don't even begin to grasp the reality of the Civil War until you hear the stories, see pictures from the time, visit the battlefields yourself.

How much more so when it comes to the deep truths of the Christian faith. God loves you; you matter to him. That is a fact, stated as a proposition. I'll bet most of you have heard it any number of times. Why, then, aren't we the happiest people on earth? It hasn't reached our hearts. Facts stay lodged in the mind. Proposition speaks to the mind, but when you tell a story, you speak to the heart.

And that's why when Jesus comes to town, he speaks in a way that will get past all our intellectual defenses and disarm our hearts.

(*Waking the Dead,* 23–24)

This is a world at war. We live in a far more dramatic, far more dangerous story than we ever imagined. The reason we love *The Chronicles of Narnia* or *Star Wars* or *The Matrix* or *The Lord of the Rings* is that they are telling us something about our lives that we never, ever get on the evening news. Or from most pulpits. *This is our most desperate hour.* Without this burning in our hearts, we lose the meaning of our days. It all withers down to fast-food and bills and voice mail and who really cares anyway? Do you see what has happened? The essence of our faith has been stripped away. The very thing that was to give our lives meaning and *protect us*—this way of seeing—has been lost. Or stolen from us. Notice that those who have tried to wake us up to this reality were usually killed for it: the prophets, Jesus, Stephen, Paul, most of the disciples, in fact. Has it ever occurred to you that someone was trying to shut them up?

Things are not what they seem. This is a world at war.

(*Waking the Dead*, 32)

Life," as a popular saying goes, "is not a dress rehearsal. Live it to the fullest." What a setup for a loss of heart. No one gets all he desires; no one even comes close. If this is it, we are lost. But what if life *is* a dress rehearsal? What if the real production is about to begin? That is precisely what Jesus says; he tells us that we are being shaped, prepared, groomed for a part in the grand drama that is coming. In *The Call*, Os Guinness writes about a delightful story told by Artie Shaw, a famous clarinetist during the big band era:

> Maybe twice in my life I reached what I wanted to. Once we were playing "These Foolish Things" and at the end the band stops and I play a little cadenza. That cadenza—no one can do it better. Let's say it's five bars. That's a very good thing to have done in a lifetime. An artist should be judged by his best, just as an athlete. Pick out my one or two best things and say, "That's what we did: all the rest was rehearsal."

All the rest was rehearsal—not for just a few shining moments, but for an eternity of joy. Realizing this is immensely freeing. How many of your plans take an unending future into account? "Let's see, I'm going to be alive forevermore, so . . . if I don't get this done now, I'll get to it later." This is so important, for no human life reaches its potential here.

I was talking with a playwright several years ago. His career was not panning out the way he deeply wanted it to, and he was becoming rather depressed. It wasn't a matter of being unqualified; he was, and is, a very gifted writer. But few playwrights achieve anything like success. Life wasn't inviting him to be who he was—yet. He had never once considered that he would be a great writer in the coming kingdom, and that he was merely in training now. His day was yet to come. Understanding that put his life in an entirely new light.

(The Journey of Desire, 158–59)

A judge in his sixties, a real southern gentleman with a pin-striped suit and an elegant manner of speech, pulled me aside during a conference. Quietly, almost apologetically, he spoke of his love for sailing, for the open sea, and how he and a buddy eventually built their own boat. Then came a twinkle in his eye. "We were sailing off the coast of Bermuda a few years ago, when we were hit by a northeaster (a raging storm). Really, it came up out of nowhere. Twenty-foot swells in a thirty-foot homemade boat. I thought we were all going to die." A pause for dramatic effect, and then he confessed, "It was the best time of my life."

Compare your experience watching the latest James Bond or Indiana Jones thriller with, say, going to Bible study. The guaranteed success of each new release makes it clear—adventure is written into the heart of a man. And it's not just about having "fun." Adventure *requires* something of us, puts us to the test. Though we may fear the test, at the same time we yearn to be tested, to discover that we have what it takes. That's why we set off down the Snake River against all sound judgment, why a buddy and I pressed on through grizzly country to find good fishing, why I went off to Washington, D.C., as a young man to see if I could make it in those shark-infested waters. If a man has lost this desire, says he doesn't want it, that's only because he doesn't know he has what it takes, believes that he will fail the test. And so he decides it's better not to try. Most men hate the unknown and, like Cain, want to settle down and build their own city, get on top of their life.

But you can't escape it—there is something wild in the heart of every man.

(*Wild at Heart,* 13–14)

Do we form no friendships because our friends might be taken from us? Do we refuse to love because we may be hurt? Do we forsake our dreams because hope has been deferred? To desire is to open our hearts to the possibility of pain; to shut down our hearts is to die altogether. The full proverb reads this way: "Hope deferred makes the heart sick, *but when dreams come true, there is life and joy.*" The road to life and joy lies through, not around, the heartsickness of hope deferred. A good friend came to this realization recently. As we sat talking over breakfast, he put words to our dilemma:

> I stand at the crossroads, and I am afraid of the desire. For forty-one years I've tried to control my life by killing the desire, but I can't. Now I know it. But to allow it to be, to let it out is frightening because I know I'll have to give up the control of my life. Is there another option?

The option most of us have chosen is to reduce our desire to a more manageable size. We allow it out only in small doses—just what we can arrange for. Dinner out, a new sofa, a vacation to look forward to, a little too much to drink. It's not working. The tremors of the earthquake inside are beginning to break out.

(The Journey of Desire, 23–24)

Eve is God's relational specialist given to the world *to keep relationship a priority.*

Men have a way of letting these things slip. They'll go months without checking in on the health of their relationships. Years, even. And the World simply uses people, then spits them out when they are worn out and no longer "on top of their game." Our Enemy despises relationship, hates love in any form, fears its redemptive power. This is why God sent Eve. Women are *needed* to protect relationships, bring them back to center stage where they belong. You might at times feel like the only one who cares. But as women we must hang on to this—that because of the Trinity, relationship is *the* most important thing in the universe. Let us not give way or yield our intuitive sense of the importance of relationship for anything.

It is here, *starting* with our circles of intimacy, that we are first and foremost women. It is here that we must first turn our gaze to ask, "What does it look like to offer my Beauty, my fierce devotion, my love? How do they need me to be their *ezer?*" You have an irreplaceable role in your relationships. No one can be to the people in your life who you can be to them. No one can offer what you can offer. There are many things God calls us to do, but loving well always comes first. And don't your relationships feel *opposed?* Of course. They must be fought for.

Satan knew that to take out Adam, all he had to do was take out Eve. It worked rather well, and he has not abandoned the basic plan ever since. Your place in the world as God's heart for relationship is vital. All the Enemy has to do to destroy people's lives is to get them isolated, a lamb separated from the flock. He makes a woman feel like, "What do I have to offer, really? They're probably doing fine." Don't you believe it for a moment. You have been sent by the Trinity on behalf of love, of relationships. Fight for them.

(*Captivating,* 209–10)

The life we have is so far from the life we truly want, and it doesn't take us long to find someone to blame. In order for our longings to be filled, we need the cooperation of others. I long for a loving embrace and a kind word when I get home. I long for my boys to listen attentively when I talk about important life lessons. I want my work to be appreciated. I want my friends to be there for me in hard times. "No man is an island," wrote John Donne, and he could have been speaking of desire. We need others—it's part of our design. Very few of our desires are self-fulfilling; *all* our deepest longings require others to come through for us. Inevitably, someone stands in the way.

At its best, the world is indifferent to my desires. The air traffic controllers aren't the least affected when I've been traveling for a week and the flight they've chosen to cancel is my last chance to get home to my family. So long as it doesn't affect them, they couldn't care less. We suffer the violation of indifference on a daily basis, from friends, from family, from complete strangers. We think we've grown to accept it as part of life, but the effect is building inside us. We weren't made to be ignored. And though we try to pretend it doesn't really matter, the collective effect of living in a world apathetic to our existence is doing damage to our souls. Events such as bad traffic or delayed flights are merely the *occasions* for our true desperation to come out. As our desires come into direct conflict with the desires of another person, things get downright hostile.

(*The Journey of Desire,* 25–26)

The reason we don't know what we want is that we're so *unacquainted* with our desire. We try to keep a safe distance between our daily lives and our heart's desire because it causes us so much trouble. We're surprised by our anger and threatened by what feels like a ravenous bear within us. Do we really want to open Pandora's box? If you remember the Greek myth, Pandora was the wife of Epimetheus, given to him by Zeus. The gods provided many gifts to her, including a mysterious box, which she was warned never to open. Eventually, her curiosity got the better of her, and she lifted the lid. Immediately, a host of evils flew out, plagues against the mind and body of mankind. She tried to close the box, but to no avail; the troubles had been loosed.

Dare we awaken our hearts to their true desires? Dare we come alive? Is it better, as the saying goes, to have loved and lost than never to have loved at all? We're not so sure. After his divorce, a friend's father decided to remain single the rest of his life. As he told his son, "It's easier to stay out than to get out." Our dilemma is this: we can't seem to live with desire, and we can't live without it. In the face of this quandary most people decide to bury the whole question and put as much distance as they can between themselves and their desires. It is a logical and tragic act. The tragedy is increased tenfold when this suicide of soul is committed under the conviction that this is precisely what Christianity recommends. We have never been more mistaken.

(The Journey of Desire, 30)

There is nothing so inspiring to a man as a beautiful woman. She'll make you want to charge the castle, slay the giant, leap across the parapets. Or maybe, hit a home run.

A man wants to be the hero to the beauty. Young men going off to war carry a photo of their sweetheart in their wallet. Men who fly combat missions will paint a beauty on the side of their aircraft; the crews of the WWII B-17 bomber gave those flying fortresses names like *Me and My Gal* or the *Memphis Belle.* What would Robin Hood or King Arthur be without the woman they love? Lonely men fighting lonely battles. Indiana Jones and James Bond just wouldn't be the same without a beauty at their side, and inevitably they must fight for her. You see, it's not just that a man needs a battle to fight; he needs someone to fight *for*. Remember Nehemiah's words to the few brave souls defending a wall-less Jerusalem? "Don't be afraid . . . fight for your brothers, your sons and your daughters, your wives and your homes." The battle itself is never enough; a man yearns for romance. It's not enough to be a hero; it's that he is a hero *to someone* in particular, to the woman he loves. Adam was given the wind and the sea, the horse and the hawk, but as God himself said, things were just not right until there was Eve.

Yes, there is something passionate in the heart of every man.

(*Wild at Heart,* 15–16)

There are three desires that I have found essential to a woman's heart, which are not entirely different from a man's and yet they remain distinctly feminine. Not every woman wants a battle to fight, but every woman yearns to be fought *for*. Listen to the longing of a woman's heart: She wants to be more than noticed—she wants to be *wanted*. She wants to be pursued.

Every woman also wants an adventure *to share*. "I want to be Isabo in *Ladyhawk*," confessed a female friend. "To be cherished, pursued, fought for—yes. But also, I want to be strong and a *part* of the adventure." So many men make the mistake of thinking that the woman is the adventure. But that is where the relationship immediately goes downhill. A woman doesn't want to be the adventure; she wants to be caught up into something greater than herself.

And finally, every woman wants to have a beauty to unveil. Not to conjure, but to unveil. Most women feel the pressure to be beautiful from very young, but that is not what I speak of. There is also a deep desire to simply and truly *be* the beauty, and be delighted in.

The world kills a woman's heart when it tells her to be tough, efficient, and independent. Sadly, Christianity has missed her heart as well. Walk into most churches in America, have a look around, and ask yourself this question: What is a Christian woman? Again, don't listen to what is said, look at what you find there. There is no doubt about it. You'd have to admit a Christian woman is . . . tired. All we've offered the feminine soul is pressure to "be a good servant." No one is fighting for her heart; there is no grand adventure to be swept up in; and every woman doubts very much that she has any beauty to unveil.

(*Wild at Heart*, 16–17)

What if? What if those deep desires in our hearts are telling us the truth, revealing to us the life we were *meant* to live? God gave us eyes so that we might see; he gave us ears that we might hear; he gave us wills that we might choose; and he gave us hearts that we might *live*. The way we handle the heart is everything. A man must *know* he is powerful; he must *know* he has what it takes. A woman must *know* she is beautiful; she must *know* she is worth fighting for. "But you don't understand," said one woman to me. "I'm living with a hollow man." No, it's in there. His heart is there. It may have evaded you, like a wounded animal, always out of reach, one step beyond your catching. But it's there. "I don't know when I died," said another man. "But I feel like I'm just using up oxygen." I understand. Your heart may feel dead and gone, but it's there. Something wild and strong and valiant, just waiting to be released.

If you are going to know who you truly are *as a man*, if you are going to find a life worth living, if you are going to love a woman deeply and not pass on your confusion to your children, you simply must get your heart back. You must head up into the high country of the soul, into wild and uncharted regions and track down that elusive prey.

(*Wild at Heart*, 18)

You have your heads in your Bibles constantly because you think you'll find eternal life there. But you miss the forest for the trees. These Scriptures are all about *me!* And here I am, standing right before you, and you aren't willing to receive from me the life you say you want. (John 5:39–40 *The Message*)

The promise of life and the invitation to desire has again been lost beneath a pile of religious teachings that put the focus on knowledge and performance.

History has brought us to the point where the Christian message is thought to be essentially concerned only with how to deal with sin: with wrongdoing or wrong-being and its effects. Life, our actual existence, is not included in what is now presented as the heart of the Christian message, or it is included only marginally. (*The Divine Conspiracy*)

Thus Willard describes the gospels we have today as "gospels of sin management." Sin is the bottom line, and we have the cure. Typically, it is a system of knowledge or performance, or a mixture of both. Those in the knowledge camp put the emphasis on getting our doctrine in line. Right belief is seen as the means to life. Desire is irrelevant; *content* is what matters. But notice this—the Pharisees knew more about the Bible than most of us ever will, and it *hardened* their hearts. Knowledge just isn't all it's cracked up to be. If you are familiar with the biblical narrative, you will remember that there were two special trees in Eden—the Tree of Knowledge of Good and Evil and the Tree of Life. We got the wrong tree. We got knowledge, and it hasn't done us much good.

(*The Journey of Desire*, 38–40)

Christianity is often presented as essentially the transfer of a body of knowledge. We learn about where the Philistines were from, and how much a drachma would be worth today, and all sorts of things about the original Greek. The information presented could not seem more irrelevant to our deepest desires.

Then there are the systems aimed at getting our behavior in line, one way or another. Regardless of where you go to church, there is nearly always an unspoken list of what you shouldn't do (tailored to your denomination and culture, but typically rather long) and a list of what you may do (usually much shorter—mostly religious activity that seems totally unrelated to our deepest desires and leaves us only exhausted). And this, we are told, is the good news. Know the right thing; do the right thing. This is life? When it doesn't strike us as something to get excited about, we feel we must not be spiritual enough. Perhaps once we have kept the list long enough, we will understand.

We don't need more facts, and we certainly don't need more things to do. We need *Life*, and we've been looking for it ever since we lost Paradise. Jesus appeals to our desire because he came to speak to it. When we abandon desire, we no longer hear or understand what he is saying. But we have returned to the message of the synagogue; we are preaching the law. And desire is the enemy. After all, desire is the single major hindrance to the goal—getting us in line. And so we are told to kill desire and call it sanctification. Or as Jesus put it to the Pharisees, "You load people down with rules and regulations, nearly breaking their backs, but never lift even a finger to help" (Luke 11:46 *The Message*).

(The Journey of Desire, 41–42)

Compare the shriveled life held up as a model of Christian maturity with the life revealed in the book of Psalms:

> You have made known to me the path of life;
> > you will fill me with joy in your presence,
> > with eternal pleasures at your right hand. (16:11)

> As the deer pants for streams of water,
> > so my soul pants for you, O God.
> My soul thirsts for God, for the living God.
> > When can I go and meet with God? (42:1–2)

> O God, you are my God,
> > earnestly I seek you;
> My soul thirsts for you,
> > my body longs for you,
> in a dry and weary land,
> > where there is no water. (63:1)

Ask yourself, Could this person be promoted to a position of leadership in my church? Heavens, no. He is far too unstable, to passionate, too desirous. It's all about pleasure and desire and thirst. And David, who wrote most of the psalms, was called by God a "man after his own heart" (1 Sam. 13:14).

Christianity has nothing to say to the person who is completely happy with the way things are. Its message is for those who hunger and thirst—for those who desire life as it was meant to be. Why does Jesus appeal to desire? Because it is essential to his goal: bringing us life. He heals the fellow at the pool of Bethesda, by the way. The two blind men get their sight, and the woman at the well finds the love she has been seeking. Reflecting on these events, the apostle John looked at what Jesus offered and what he delivered and said: "He who has the Son has life" (1 John 5:12).

(*The Journey of Desire,* 42–43)

The reason we enjoy fairy tales—more than enjoy them—the reason we *identify with them* in some deep part of us is because they rest on two great truths: The hero really has a heart of gold and the beloved really possesses hidden beauty. I hope you got a glimpse of God's good heart. But what about the second great truth—could we possess hidden greatness? It seems too good to be true.

Remember, the theme of veiled identity runs through all great stories. As Frederick Buechner reminds us, "Not only does evil come disguised in the world of the fairy tale but often good does too." The heroines and heroes capture our heart because we see long before they ever do their hidden beauty, courage, greatness. Cinderella, Sleeping Beauty, Snow White—they're not simple wenches after all. The beast and the frog—they're actually princes. Aladdin is "the diamond in the rough." If the narrative of the Scriptures teaches us anything, from the serpent in the Garden to the carpenter from Nazareth, it teaches us that things are rarely what they seem, that we shouldn't be fooled by appearances.

Your evaluation of your soul, which is drawn from a world filled with people still terribly confused about the nature of *their* souls, is probably wrong. As C. S. Lewis wrote in *The Weight of Glory*,

> It is a serious thing to live in a society of possible gods and goddesses, to remember that the dullest and most uninteresting person you talk to may one day be a creature which, if you saw it now, you would be strongly tempted to worship, or else a horror and a corruption such as you now meet, if at all, only in a nightmare . . . There are no *ordinary* people. You have never talked to a mere mortal.

(*The Sacred Romance*, 92–93)

When the history of the world is finally told rightly—one of the great joys when we reach the wedding feast of the Lamb—it will be as clear as day that women have been essential to every great move of God upon this earth.

I wanted to say "*nearly* every great move," not wanting to overstate a crucial point and recognizing that there are moments when men have led the way. But Stasi chimed in and said, "Those men had mothers, didn't they?!" I was thinking of Moses, who seemed to lead the Exodus, but it quickly dawned on me that it was his mother who saved his life as a baby (at the risk of her own life and the lives of her entire family). It was his sister who stayed with the babe and suggested a nursemaid when Pharaoh's daughter took him for her own. (That nurse would be, of course, his mother.) Okay. I concede. Women have been essential to every great movement of God.

Certainly there are those amazing moments in the Old Testament like the story of Rahab, who secured the Hebrews' successful military launch into the Promised Land. And Esther, who saved her people from genocide and secured the future of Israel . . . and the world. It's clear that women supported the ministry of Jesus, financially and emotionally, and women were the ones who stayed with him when nearly all the men hightailed it and ran. As we read the story of the spreading gospel and the birth of the church in the New Testament, we encounter women such as Lydia, whose home became the staging point for the evangelism of Thyatira and Philippi; women like Nympha and Apphia, who hosted the emerging church in their homes—again, at great risk to themselves and their loved ones. There is Priscilla, who risked her life to help Paul spread the gospel, and Junias, who was with Paul when he was in prison and whom he calls "outstanding among the apostles" (Rom. 16:7).

And of course, the salvation of mankind rested on the courage of a woman, a teenage girl. What if she had said, "No"? What if any of them had said, "No"?

(Captivating, 203–4)

We are not what we were meant to be, and we know it. If, when passing a stranger on the street, we happen to meet eyes, we quickly avert our glance. Cramped into the awkward community of an elevator, we search for something, anything to look at instead of each other. We sense that our real self is ruined, and we fear to be seen. But think for a moment about the millions of tourists who visit ancient sites like the Parthenon, the Colosseum, and the Pyramids. Though ravaged by time, the elements, and vandals through the ages, mere shadows of their former glory, these ruins still awe and inspire. Though fallen, their glory cannot be fully extinguished. There is something at once sad and grand about them. And such we are. Abused, neglected, vandalized, fallen—we are still fearful and wonderful. We are, as one theologian put it, "glorious ruins." But unlike those grand monuments, we who are Christ's have been redeemed and are being renewed as Paul said, "day by day," restored in the love of God.

Could it be that we, all of us, the homecoming queens and quarterbacks and the passed over and picked on, really possess hidden greatness? Is there something in us worth fighting over? The fact that we don't see our own glory is part of the tragedy of the Fall; a sort of spiritual amnesia has taken all of us. Our souls were made to live in the Larger Story, but as G.K. Chesterton discovered, we have forgotten our part:

> We have all read in scientific books, and indeed, in all romances, the story of the man who has forgotten his name. This man walks about the streets and can see and appreciate everything; only he cannot remember who he is. Well, every man is that man in the story. Every man has forgotten who he is . . . We are all under the same mental calamity; we have all forgotten our names. We have all forgotten what we really are. *(Orthodoxy)*

(The Sacred Romance, 93–95)

The book of Hebrews describes the prayer life of Jesus in the following way: "While Jesus was here on earth, he offered prayers and pleadings, with a loud cry and tears, to the one who could deliver him" (5:7 NLT). That doesn't sound like the way prayers are offered up in most churches on a typical Sunday morning. "Dear Lord, we thank you for this day, and we ask you to be with us in all we say and do. Amen." No pleading here, no loud cries and tears. Our prayers are cordial, modest, even reverent. Eugene Peterson calls them "cut-flower prayers." They are not like Jesus' prayers, or, for that matter, like the psalms. The ranting and raving, the passion and ecstasy, the fury and desolation found in the psalms are so far from our religious expression that it seems hard to believe they were given to us as our *guide* to prayer. They seem so, well, *desperate*. Yet E. M. Bounds reminds us,

> Desire gives fervor to prayer. The soul cannot be listless when some great desire fixes and inflames it . . . Strong desires make strong prayers . . . The neglect of prayer is the fearful token of dead spiritual desires . . . There can be no true praying without desire. *(Man of Prayer)*

(*The Journey of Desire*, 59–60)

A young woman came to see me, as most seeking counseling do, because she was at the end of her rope. What had begun a year earlier as mild depression had sunk deeper and deeper until she found herself contemplating suicide. We met for many weeks, and I came to know a delightful woman with a poet's heart, whose soul was buried beneath years not so much of tragedy but of neglect. This one particular afternoon, we had spoken for more than an hour of how deeply she longed for love, how almost completely ignored and misunderstood she felt her entire life. It was a tender, honest, and deeply moving session. As our time drew to a close, I asked her if she would pray with me. I could hardly believe what came next. She assumed a rather bland, religious tone to her voice and said something to the effect of "God, thank you for being here. Show me what I ought to do." I found myself speechless. *You've got to be kidding me*, I thought. *That's not how you feel at all. I know your heart's true cry. You are far more desperate than that.*

Why are we so embarrassed by our desire? Why do we pretend that we're doing fine, thank you, that we don't need a thing? The persistent widow wasn't too proud to seek help. Neither was the psalmist. Their humility allowed them to express their desire. How little we come to God with what really matters to us. How rare it is that we even admit it to ourselves. We don't pray like Jesus because we don't allow ourselves to be nearly so *alive*. We don't allow ourselves to feel how desperate our situation truly is. We sense that our desire will undo us if we let it rise up in all its fullness. Wouldn't it be better to bury the disappointment and the yearning and just get on with life? As Larry Crabb has pointed out, pretending seems a much more reliable road to Christian maturity. The only price we pay is a loss of soul, of communion with God, a loss of direction, and a loss of hope.

(*The Journey of Desire*, 60–61)

As a teacher, counselor, and author, I love what I do for a living. But it hasn't always been so. I spent a lifetime in Washington, D.C., several years ago. They were two of the most miserable years of my life. I don't like government, and I abhor politics. Harry Truman was right: "If you want a friend in Washington, buy a dog." What in the world was I doing there? I didn't really want to go; my employer talked me into accepting a transfer. But I can't put the blame on them. The truth is, I had come to a point where I didn't really know what I wanted in life. My real passion had been the theater, and for a number of years I pursued that dream with great joy. I had my own theater company and loved it. Through a series of events and what felt like betrayals, I had gotten deeply hurt. I left the theater and just went off to find a job. The Washington offer came up, and even though my heart wasn't in it, I let the opinions of people I admired dictate my course. Without a deep and burning desire of our own, we will be ruled by the desires of others.

I have met many Christians in the same position. I think of Charles, an attorney in his fifties who still doesn't know what he wants to be when he grows up. There is Paul, a young man in his twenties who doesn't know what to do with himself now that college is over. He focused on grades and left his heart behind. Jamie isn't sure if she should get married or stay single. Every one of them has tried to bury their heart under the porch and seek a safer life.

The damage, of course, is a life lost unto itself. Millions of souls drifting through life, without an inner compass to give them direction. They take their cues from others and live out scripts from someone else's life. It's a high price to pay. Too high.

(The Journey of Desire, 62–63)

The reason a woman wants a beauty to unveil, the reason she asks, *Do you delight in me?* is simply that God does as well. God is captivating beauty. As David prays, "One thing I ask of the LORD, this is what I seek: that I may . . . gaze upon the beauty of the LORD" (Ps. 27:4). Can there be any doubt that God wants to be *worshiped?* That he wants to be seen, and for us to be captivated by what we see? As C. S. Lewis wrote, "The beauty of the female is the root of joy to the female as well as to the male . . . to desire the enjoying of her own beauty is the obedience of Eve, and to both it is in the lover that the beloved tastes of her own delightfulness."

This is far too simple an outline, I admit. There is so much more to say, and these are not hard and rigid categories. A man needs to be tender at times, and a woman will sometimes need to be fierce. But if a man is only tender, we know something is deeply wrong, and if a woman is only fierce, we sense she is not what she was meant to be. If you'll look at the essence of little boys and little girls, I think you'll find I am not far from my mark. Strength and beauty. As the psalmist says,

> One thing God has spoken,
> two things have I heard:
> that you, O God, are strong,
> and that you, O Lord, are loving. (Ps. 62:11–12)

(*Wild at Heart,* 37–38)

Our local zoo had for years one of the biggest African lions I've ever seen. A huge male, nearly five hundred pounds, with a wonderful mane and absolutely enormous paws. *Panthera leo.* The King of the Beasts. Sure, he was caged, but I'm telling you the bars offered small comfort when you stood within six feet of something that in any other situation saw you as an easy lunch. Honestly, I felt I ought to shepherd my boys past him at a safe distance, as if he could pounce on us if he really wanted to. Yet he was my favorite, and whenever the others would wander on to the monkey house or the tigers, I'd double back just for a few more minutes in the presence of someone so powerful and noble and deadly. Perhaps it was fear mingled with admiration; perhaps it was simply that my heart broke for the big old cat.

This wonderful, terrible creature should have been out roaming the savanna, ruling his pride, striking fear into the heart of every wildebeest, bringing down zebras and gazelles whenever the urge seized him. Instead, he spent every hour of every day and every night of every year alone, in a cage smaller than your bedroom, his food served to him through a little metal door. Sometimes late at night, after the city had gone to sleep, I would hear his roar come down from the hills. It sounded not so much fierce, but rather mournful. During all of my visits, he never looked me in the eye. I desperately wanted him to, wanted for his sake the chance to stare me down, would have loved it if he took a swipe at me. But he just lay there, weary with that deep weariness that comes from boredom, taking shallow breaths, rolling now and then from side to side.

For after years of living in a cage, a lion no longer even believes it is a lion . . . and a man no longer believes he is a man.

(*Wild at Heart,* 40–41)

Jesus of Nazareth is given many names in Scripture. He is called the Lion of Judah. The Bright and Morning Star. The Wonderful Counselor. The Prince of Peace. The Lamb of God. There are many, many more—each one a window into all that he truly is, all that he has done, all that he will do. But one name seems to have escaped our attention, and that might help explain our misunderstanding of the gospel. Paul refers to Jesus as the Last Adam and the Second Man (1 Cor. 15:45–47). Why is this important? Because of what happened through the *First* Adam.

Our first father, Adam, and our first mother, Eve, were destined to be the root and trunk of humanity. What they were meant to be, we were meant to be: the kings and queens of the earth, the rulers over all creation, the glorious image bearers of a glorious God. They were statues of God walking about in a garden, radiant Man and Woman, as we were to be. Our natures and our destinies were bound up in theirs. Their choices would forever shape our lives, for good or for evil. It is deep mystery, but we see something of a hint of it in the way children so often follow in the steps of their parents. Haven't you heard it said, "He has his father's temper," or "She has her mother's wit"? As the old saying goes, the fruit doesn't fall far from the tree. In fact, we call them family trees, and Adam and Eve are the first names on the list.

Our first parents chose, and it was on the side of evil. They broke the one command, the only command, God gave to them, and what followed you can watch any night on the news. The long lament of human history. Something went wrong in their hearts, something *shifted*, and that shift was passed along to each of us.

(*Waking the Dead,* 59–60)

P arents will often wonder where their toddlers learned to lie or how they came into the world so self-centered. It doesn't need to be taught to them; it is inherent to human nature. Paul makes clear in Romans, "Sin entered the world through one man . . . through the disobedience of the one man the many were made sinners" (5:12, 19). Of course, I am simply restating the doctrine of original sin, a core tenet of Christianity essential to Scripture.

But that is not the end of the Story, thank God. The first Adam was only "a pattern of the one to come" (Rom. 5:14). He would foreshadow another man, the head of a new race, the firstborn of a new creation, whose life would mean transformation to those who would become joined to him: "For just as through the disobedience of the one man [Adam] the many were made sinners, so also through the obedience of the one man [Christ, the Last Adam] the many will be made righteous" (Rom. 5:19).

A man comes down from heaven, slips into our world unnoticed, as Neo does in *The Matrix*, as Maximus does in *Gladiator*, as Wallace does in *Braveheart*. Yet he is no ordinary man, and his mission no ordinary mission. He comes as a substitute, a representative, as the destroyer of one system and the seed of something new. His death and resurrection break the power of the Matrix, release the prisoners, set the captives free. It is a historic fact. It really happened. And it is more than history. It is mythic in the first degree. Lewis said, "By becoming fact, it does not cease to be myth; that is the miracle."

(*Waking the Dead*, 60)

You have been ransomed by Christ. Your treachery is forgiven. You are entirely pardoned for every wrong thought and desire and deed. This is what the vast majority of Christians understand as the central work of Christ for us. And make no mistake about it—it is a deep and stunning truth, one that will set you free and bring you joy. For a while. But the joy for most of us has proved fleeting, because we find that we need to be forgiven again and again and again. Christ has died for us, but we remain (so we believe) deeply marred. It actually ends up producing a great deal of guilt. "After all that Christ has done for you . . . and now you're back here asking forgiveness *again*?" To be destined to a life of repeating the very things that sent our Savior to the cross can hardly be called *salvation*.

Think of it: you are a shadow of the person you were meant to be. You have nothing close to the life you were meant to have. And you have no real chance of becoming that person or finding that life. However, you are forgiven. For the rest of your days, you will fail in your attempts to become what God wants you to be. You should seek forgiveness and try again. Eventually, shame and disappointment will cloud your understanding of yourself and your God. When this ongoing hell on earth is over, you will die, and you will be taken before your God for a full account of how you didn't measure up. But you will be forgiven. After that, you'll be asked to take your place in the choir of heaven. This is what we mean by "salvation."

The good news is . . . that is *not* Christianity. Oh, I know it is what most people now living *think* Christianity is all about, including the majority of Christians. Thank God, they are wrong. There is more. *A lot more.* And that more is what most of us have been longing for most of our lives.

(*Waking the Dead*, 61–62)

> In [Christ] you were also circumcised, in the putting
> off of the sinful nature, not with a circumcision done
> by the hands of men but with the circumcision done
> by Christ. (Col. 2:11)

It's not just that the Cross did something *for* us. Something deep and profound happened *to* us in the death of Christ. Remember—the heart is the problem. God understands this better than anyone, and he goes for the root. God promised in the new covenant to "take away your heart of stone." How? By joining us to the death of Christ. Our nature was nailed to the cross with Christ; we died there, with him, in him. Yes, it is a deep mystery—"deep magic" as Lewis called it—but that does not make it untrue. "The death he died, he died to sin once for all . . . In the same way, count yourselves dead to sin" (Rom. 6:10–11). Jesus was the Last Adam, the end of that terrible story.

You've been far more than forgiven. God has removed your heart of stone. You've been delivered of what held you back from what you were meant to be. You've been rescued from the part of you that sabotages even your best intentions. Your heart has been circumcised to God. Your heart has been set free.

(Waking the Dead, 63)

Most people assume that the Cross *is* the total work of Christ. The two go hand in hand in our minds—Jesus Christ and the Cross; the Cross and Jesus Christ. The Resurrection is impressive, but kind of . . . an afterthought. It was needed, of course, to get him out of the grave. Or the Resurrection is important because it proves Jesus was the Son of God. His death was the *real* work on our behalf. The Resurrection is like an epilogue to the real story; the extra point after the touchdown; the medal ceremony after the Olympic event. You can see which we think is more important. What image do we put on our churches, our Bibles, on jewelry? The cross is the symbol of Christianity worldwide. However . . .

The cross was never meant to be the only or even the central symbol of Christianity.

That you are shocked by what I've just said only proves how far we've strayed from the faith of the New Testament. The cross is not the sole focal point of Christianity. Paul says so himself: "If Christ has not been raised, our preaching is useless and so is your faith . . . If Christ has not been raised, your faith is futile; you are still in your sins" (1 Cor. 15:14, 17).

(*Waking the Dead,* 63–64)

Man's love is of man's life a thing apart
'Tis a woman's whole existence. (Byron)

E ve was created because things were not right without her.
Something was not good. "It is not good for the man to be alone" (Gen. 2:18). This just staggers us. Think of it. The world is young and completely unstained. Adam is yet in his innocence and full of glory. He walks with God. Nothing stands between them. They share something none of us have ever known, only longed for: an unbroken friendship, untouched by sin. Yet something is not good. Something is missing. What could it possibly be? Eve. Woman. Femininity. Wow. Talk about significance.

To be specific, what was "not good" was the fact that the man was "alone." "It is not good for the human to be alone, I shall make him a sustainer beside him" (Gen. 2:18 *Alter*). How true this is. Whatever else we know about women, we know they are relational creatures to their cores. While little boys are killing one another in mock battles on the playground, little girls are negotiating relationships. If you want to know how people are doing, what's going on in our world, don't ask me—ask Stasi. I don't call friends and chat with them on the phone for an hour. I can't tell you who's dating whom, whose feelings have been hurt—ask Stasi.

This is so second nature, so assumed among women it goes unnoticed by them. They care more about relationship than just about anything else. Radio talk-show host Dennis Prager reports that when the topic of the day on his show is a "macro issue" like politics or finance, his callers will be Ed, Jack, Bill, and Dave. But when the topic is a "micro issue" involving human relationships, issues like dating or faithfulness or children, his callers will be Jane, Joanne, Susan, and Karen.

(*Captivating*, 26–27)

Some of the sentences the Enemy accuses each of us with have been there since we were young; others were added in the ensuing years as Satan saw opportunity to strengthen our fear and cynicism through "interpreting" those events in our lives that seem to verify our particular Message of the Arrows. His purpose is to convince us that we need to create a story to live in that is not as dangerous as the Sacred Romance. As long as we do not admit that the deep things of our heart are there—the rejection and hurt, the shame and sorrow, the anger and rage—these rooms of our heart become darkened and the Enemy sets up shop there to accuse us.

I am not just speaking metaphorically or poetically when I refer to the Enemy accusing us. Each of us, Christians included, is oppressed directly and specifically by the Enemy in the way I am describing. This attack happens in the spiritual realm, using the sentences and voices we are familiar with from the past. We feel as if we are simply speaking to ourselves in our heads. And this is the Enemy's first deception: "I am not here. It's just you struggling with all these things." Many of us live our whole lives being defeated by this accusation. And indeed, deep in our hearts, the anxiety, shame, and self-contempt we often feel *are* like the attack of a roaring lion no matter what calmness or other personality device we learn to cover it with on the outside. We hide the lion's roar because he has convinced us that it is just us and we would be roundly scorned if we were to admit these things to others.

(*The Sacred Romance,* 116)

Once we begin thinking of all the deceptions the Enemy is about with regard to our lives, we have a tendency to become obsessed with him, fearful of what he is going to do next. Once we take him seriously, he switches from his tactic of "I'm not here" to one of having us worry about him day and night, which is almost a form of worship.

God's intention, on the other hand, is to use spiritual warfare to draw us into deeper communion with himself. Satan's device is to isolate us and wear us out obsessing about what he has done and what he will do next. And he is very effective in using our particular Message of the Arrows to do it. God desires to use the Enemy's attacks to remove the obstacles between ourselves and him, to reestablish our dependency on him as his sons and daughters in a much deeper way. Once we understand that, the warfare we are in begins to feel totally different. It is not really even about Satan anymore, but about communion with God and abiding in Jesus as the source of life. The whole experience begins to feel more like a devotional.

(*The Sacred Romance*, 119–20)

G. K. Chesterton thought that everybody ought to get drunk once a year because if that didn't do you good, the repentance in the morning would. There's nothing like waking up to what you've done, whether it's too much to drink or eat, or letting your anger fly. The remorse after a flagrant sin often does bring a sense of clarity and resolution. (How many New Year's resolutions are made the morning after?) But if we don't quite overdo it, if we keep our indulgence at a more moderate level, such clarity never comes. We never see it in black and white, for we're always under the influence. No one stops to think about it. Pleasure isn't nearly so much about true enjoyment as it is about anesthetizing ourselves. Think about the relief your idols provide: Is your desire truly and deeply satisfied, or does the relief come more through the temporary *absence* of desire?

I've had a nagging sense I was more pleasure-oriented than might be good, but I didn't see the function of pleasure in my life until I had to face intense grief and loss. I tried every drug I could, and nothing worked. Not food. Not sleep. Not work. Not reading. Not even sex. I could not get away from the pain. And then it occurred to me: If I am trying to use pleasure as a drug in this case, how many of my so-called enjoyments are merely the same thing on a lesser scale?

(*The Journey of Desire,* 79)

U p until the moment that the courier from the Palace arrives at her door, Cinderella's life seems set in stone. She will always be a washerwoman, a cellar girl. Her enemies will forever have the upper hand. She will live a life of enduring disappointments, though she will suffer them nobly. No other life seems possible. This is her fate. Then, word from the Prince arrives—an invitation to a ball. It is at this point that all hell breaks loose. Her longings are awakened. Her enemies become enraged. And her life is never the same.

How gracious that it comes by invitation. As a woman, you don't need to strive or arrange; you don't need to make it happen. You only need to respond. Granted—Cinderella's response took immense courage, courage that came only out of a deep desire to find the life her heart knew it was meant for. She *wanted* to go. But it took steadfastness to press through her fears just to get to the ball. It took courage not to abandon all hope even *after* she danced with the Prince. (She ran back to the cellar, as we all do.) But she became the woman she was born to be, and the kingdom was never the same. It is a beautiful parable.

The invitations of our Prince come to us in all sorts of ways. Your heart itself, as a woman, is an invitation. An invitation delivered in the most intimate and personalized way. Your Lover has written something on your heart. It is a call to find a life of Romance and to protect that love affair as your most precious treasure. A call to cultivate the beauty you hold inside, and to unveil your beauty on behalf of others. And it is a call to adventure, to become the *ezer* the world desperately needs you to be.

(*Captivating,* 203)

The battle of desire is not something that just takes place within us or even between us. It is also taking place *against* us, all the time. Our desire is under nearly constant attack. "We come into the world longing," says Gil Bailie, "for we know not what. We *are* desire. And desire is good, for it's what takes us to God. But our desire is not hard-wired to God." So we look to others to teach us what to desire. We are intensely imitative creatures, as Aristotle pointed out. It is how we learn language; it is how we master just about anything in life. It is also how we come to seize upon the objects of our desire. We all know this, though we don't like to admit it.

One example should suffice. I was at a garage sale, looking for some tools. There was a table saw at a wonderful price. Another fellow was sort of browsing around, standing in front of the saw but not seeming particularly interested. I opened my mouth and made the fatal error: "Wow, that's a great price on that saw." You know what happened next. Immediately, his nonchalance became intense interest, and since he was there before me, he drove off with a table saw that five minutes earlier he couldn't have given two hoots about.

The constant effort to arouse our desire and capture it can be described only as an assault. From the time we get up to the time we go to bed, we are inundated with one underlying message: *it can be done.* The life you are longing for *can* be achieved. Only buy this product, see this movie, drive this car, take this vacation, join this gym, what have you. The only disagreement is over the means, but everyone agrees on the end: we can find life now.

(The Journey of Desire, 82–83)

When I consider all that is at stake in this journey I am on, how vulnerable are my heart and the hearts of those I love, I am moved to fall on my face and cry out to God for the grace to remember. George MacDonald says it better in poetry:

> Were there but some deep, holy spell, whereby
> Always I should remember thee . . .
> Lord, see thou to it, take thou remembrance's load:
> Only when I bethink me can I cry;
> Remember thou, and prick me with love's goad.
> When I can no more stir my soul to move,
> And life is but the ashes of a fire;
> When I can but remember that my heart
> Once used to live and love, long and aspire—
> Oh, be thou then the first, the one thou art;
> Be thou the calling, before all answering love,
> And in me wake hope, fear, boundless desire.
> *(Diary of an Old Soul)*

The final burden of remembrance does not rest on us; if it did, we should all despair. Jesus is called the "author and perfecter of our faith" (Rom. 12:2). He is the One who put the romance in our hearts and the One who first opened our eyes to see that our deepest desire is fulfilled in him. He started us on the journey, even though we may for long seasons forget him, he does not forget us.

> I am always with you;
>   you hold me by my right hand.
> You guide me with your counsel,
>   and afterward you will take me into glory . . .
> My flesh and my heart may fail,
>   but God is the strength of my heart
>   and my portion forever. (Ps. 73:23–24, 26)

(The Sacred Romance, 208–9)

We are now in the late stages of the long and vicious war against the human heart. I know—it sounds overly dramatic. I almost didn't use the term "war" at all, for fear of being dismissed at this point as one more in the group of "Chicken Littles," Christians who run around trying to get everybody worked up over some imaginary fear in order to advance their political or economic or theological cause. But I am not hawking fear at all; I am speaking honestly about the nature of what is unfolding around us . . . *against us*. And until we call the situation what it is, we will not know what to do about it. In fact, this is where many people feel abandoned or betrayed by God. They thought that becoming a Christian would somehow end their troubles, or at least reduce them considerably. No one ever told them they were being moved to the front lines, and they seem genuinely shocked at the fact that they've been shot at.

Hello? That's what happens in war—you get shot at. Have you forgotten? We were born into a world at war. This scene we're living in is no sitcom; it's bloody battle. Haven't you noticed with what deadly accuracy the wound was given? Those blows you've taken—they were not random accidents at all. They hit dead center.

On and on it goes. The wound is too well aimed and far too consistent to be accidental. It was an attempt to take you out; to cripple or destroy your strength and get you out of the action. Do you know why there's been such an assault? The Enemy fears you. You are dangerous big-time. If you ever really got your heart back, lived from it with courage, you would be a huge problem to him. You would do a lot of damage . . . on the side of good. Remember how valiant and effective God has been in the history of the world? You are a stem of that victorious stalk.

(*Wild at Heart*, 85–87)

Certainly, you will admit that God is glorious. Is there anyone more kind? Is there anyone more creative? Is there anyone more valiant? Is there anyone more true? Is there anyone more daring? Is there anyone more beautiful? Is there anyone more wise? Is there anyone more generous? You are his offspring. His child. His reflection. His likeness. You bear *his* image. Do remember that though he made the heavens and the earth in all their glory, the desert and the open sea, the meadow and the Milky Way, and said, "It is good," it was only *after* he made you that he said, "It is *very* good" (Gen. 1:31). Think of it: your original glory was greater than anything that's ever taken your breath away in nature.

> As for the saints who are in the land,
>> they are the glorious ones in whom is all my delight.
>> (Ps. 16:3)

God endowed you with a glory when he created you, a glory so deep and mythic that all creation pales in comparison. A glory unique to you, just as your fingerprints are unique to you, just as the way you laugh is unique to you. Somewhere down deep inside we've been looking for that glory ever since. A man wants to know that he is truly a man, that he could be brave; he longs to know that he is a warrior; and all his life he wonders, "Have I got what it takes?" A woman wants to know that she is truly a woman, that she is beautiful; she longs to know that she is captivating; and all her life she wonders, "Do I have a beauty to offer?"

(*Waking the Dead*, 77–78)

LOOKING FOR A GLORY WE KNOW WE WERE MEANT TO HAVE

The poet Yeats wrote,

> If I make the lashes dark
> And the eyes more bright
> And the lips more scarlet,
> Or ask if all be right
> From mirror after mirror
> No vanity's displayed:
> I'm looking for the face I had
> Before the world was made.
> ("Before the World Was Made" from the poem
> "A Woman Young and Old")

Yes, that's it. When we take a second glance in the mirror, when you pause to look again at a photograph, we are looking for a glory you know you were meant to have, if only because you know you long to have it. You remember faintly that you were once more than what you have become. Your story didn't start with sin, and thank God, it does not end with sin. It ends with glory restored: "Those he justified, he also glorified" (Rom. 8:30). And "in the meantime," you have *been* transformed, and you are *being* transformed. You've been given a new heart. Now God is restoring your glory. He is bringing you fully alive. Because the glory of God is you fully alive.

"Well, then, if this is all true, why don't I see it?" Precisely. Exactly. Now we are reaching my point. The fact that you do not see your good heart and your glory is only proof of how effective the assault has been. We don't see ourselves clearly.

(*Waking the Dead*, 78–79)

One more of my all-time favorite films—Shakespeare's *Henry V*. King Henry's loving courage has captured the hearts of his people, and he has led them into battle against the enemy, just as our Captain has done. Late in the war, the mighty army has been reduced to a small band of warriors. Many are sick and many more are wounded. They come to the field of Agincourt, where they are met by the entire French army. They are outnumbered five to one; the French are rested and fresh, and they have a mounted cavalry. The English have none. Faced with such odds, the men are about to lose heart. But Henry calls them up into a Larger Story:

> This day is call'd the feast of Crispian:
> He that outlives this day, and comes safe home,
> Will stand a tip-toe when this day is nam'd,
> And rouse him at the name of Crispian.
> He that shall live this day, and see old age,
> Will yearly on the vigil feast his neighbors,
> And say, "Tomorrow is Saint Crispian."
> Then will he strip his sleeve and show his scars,
> And say, "These wounds I had on Crispin's day."
> Old men forget; yet all shall be forgot,
> But he'll remember with advantages
> What feats he did that day: then shall our names,
> Familiar in their mouths as household words . . .
> Be in their flowing cups freshly remember'd.
> This story shall the good man teach his son;
> And Crispin Crispian shall ne'er go by,
> From this day to the ending of the world,
> But we in it shall be remembered.
> We few, we happy few, we band of brothers. (Act IV, Scene III)

The English go on to win the battle—a *true* story (!) and one of many we need to keep at hand in our journey.

(The Sacred Romance Workbook & Journal, 198–99)

I s there any doubt that the God John beheld (Rev. 4:3, 6) was beautiful *beyond* description? But of course. God must be even more glorious than this glorious creation, for it "foretells" or "displays" the glory that is God's. John said God was as radiant as gemstones, richly adorned in golds and reds and greens and blues, shimmering as crystal. Why, these are the very things that Cinderella is given—the very things women still prefer to adorn themselves with when they want to look their finest. Hmmm. And isn't that just what a woman longs to hear? "You are radiant this evening. You are absolutely breathtaking."

Saints from ages past would speak of the highest pleasures of heaven as simply beholding the beauty of God, the "beatific vision."

> The reason a woman wants a beauty to unveil, the reason she asks, *Do you delight in me?* is simply that God does as well. God is captivating beauty. As David prays, "One thing I ask of the LORD, this is what I seek: that I may . . . gaze upon the beauty of the LORD" (Ps. 27:4). Can there be any doubt that God wants to be *worshiped*? That he wants to be seen, and for us to be captivated by what we see? *(Wild at Heart)*

But in order to make the matter perfectly clear, God has given us Eve. The crowning touch of creation. Beauty is the essence of a woman. We want to be perfectly clear that we mean *both* a physical beauty and a soulful/spiritual beauty. The one depends upon and flows out of the other. Yes, the world cheapens and prostitutes beauty, making it all about a perfect figure few women can attain. But Christians minimize it too, or over-spiritualize it, making it all about "character." We must recover the prize of Beauty. The church must take it back. Beauty is too vital to lose.

(Captivating, 35–36)

God gave Eve a beautiful form *and* a beautiful spirit. She expresses beauty in both. Better, she expresses beauty simply in who she is. Like God, it is her *essence*.

Stasi and I just spent a weekend together in Santa Fe, New Mexico, where we wandered for hours through art galleries and gardens, looking for those works of art that particularly captured us. Toward the afternoon of our second day Stasi asked me, "Have you seen one painting of a naked man?" The point was startling. After days of looking at maybe a thousand pieces of art, we had not seen one painting devoted to the beauty of the naked masculine form. Not one. (Granted, there are a few examples down through history . . . but only a few.) However, the beauty of Woman was celebrated everywhere, hundreds of times over in paintings and sculptures. There is a reason for this.

For one thing, men look ridiculous laying on a bed buck naked, half covered with a sheet. It doesn't fit the essence of masculinity. Something in you wants to say, "Get up already and get a job. Cut the grass. Get to work." For Adam is captured best in motion, *doing* something. His essence is *strength in action*.

On the other hand, and bear with us a moment, but Eve just doesn't look right in a scene of brutal combat, or chopping a tree down. From time immemorial, when artists have tried to capture the essence of Eve they have painted her (or photographed her, or sculpted her) *at rest*. There is no agenda here, no social stigmatizing or cultural pressure. This is true across all cultures and down through time. What have the artists seen that we have not? Eve speaks something differently to the world than Adam does. Through her beauty.

(Captivating, 36–37)

I n our psychological age, we have come to call our affairs "addictions," but God calls them "adultery." Listen again to his words to the Israelites through Jeremiah:

> You are a swift she-camel
>   running here and there,
> a wild donkey accustomed to the desert,
>   sniffing the wind in [your] craving—
>   in [your] heat [how can I] restrain [you]?
> Any males that pursue [you] need not tire themselves;
>   at mating time they will find [you].
> Do not run until your feet are bare
>   and your throat is dry. (Jer. 2:23–25)

God is saying, "I love you, and yet you betray me at the drop of a hat. I feel so much pain. Can't you see we're made for each other? I want you to come back to me." And Israel's answer, like that of any addict or adulterer, is: "It's no use! I love foreign gods, and I must go after them" (Jer. 2:25).

Perhaps we can empathize with the ache God experienced as Israel's "husband" (and ours when we are living indulgently). Having raised Israel from childhood to a woman of grace and beauty, he astonishingly cannot win her heart from her adulterous lovers. The living God of the universe cannot win the only one he loves, not due to any lack on his part, but because her heart is captured by her addictions, which is to say, her adulterous lovers.

(*The Sacred Romance,* 134–35)

In the years that followed the Fall and our exile from Eden, mankind got worse and worse. Cain killed Abel; Lamech threatened to kill everybody else. The wickedness of the human heart seemed out of control and unstoppable, even by the curses. People were living for seven, eight, even nine *hundred* years. Can you imagine the arranging that one person could accomplish with that sort of time on his hands? Stubbornness seems to come with old age. Haven't you heard your grandmother sigh and say of your grandfather, "He's set in his ways"? Multiply that by a factor of eight or nine, and you get the picture. So God dealt the ultimate blow. "Then the LORD said, 'My Spirit will not contend with man forever, for he is mortal; his days will be a hundred and twenty years'" (Gen. 6:3). He cut our life short; nobody gets to pass 120. However clever we might be in our ability to conjure Paradise, we can never get around death. It is the final thwarting.

You must follow me very carefully now. We can never fully explain the reasons surrounding someone's death. We've come to accept it for the aged, and we try to console ourselves with thoughts like, *He's had a full life*. But death is *never* natural; it was not meant to be. This is why those left behind experience such excruciating pain. The agony is only worsened when the death is what we call "premature," when it takes a life in full bloom, or just as the bud begins to open. Each death can begin to be understood only within the Larger Story God is telling. Much of that story remains for the moment a mystery.

(*The Journey of Desire*, 102–3)

| # WE CAN ONLY HOPE FOR WHAT WE DESIRE

Once we come to accept that we can never find or hang on to the life we have been seeking, what then? As Dallas Willard writes, it matters for all the world to know that life is ahead of us.

> I meet many faithful Christians who, in spite of their faith, are deeply disappointed in how their lives have turned out. Sometimes it is simply a matter of how they experience aging, which they take to mean they no longer have a future. But often, due to circumstances or wrongful decisions and actions by others, what they had hoped to accomplish in life they did not . . . Much of the distress of these good people comes from a failure to realize that their life lies before them . . . the life that lies endlessly before us in the kingdom of God. *(The Divine Conspiracy)*

Blaise Pascal also observed, "We are never living, but hoping to live; and whilst we are always preparing to be happy, it is certain, we never shall be so, if we aspire to no other happiness than what can be enjoyed in this life."

Desire cannot live without hope. Yet, we can only hope for what we desire. There simply must be something more, something out there on the road ahead of us, that offers the life we prize. To sustain the life of the heart, the life of deep desire, we desperately need to possess a clearer picture of the life that lies before us.

(The Journey of Desire, 104–5)

"I have much more to say to you, more than you can now bear. But when he, the Spirit of truth, comes, he will guide you into all truth." (John 16:12–13)

There's more that Jesus wants to say to you, much more, and now that his Spirit resides in your heart, the conversation can continue. Many good people never hear God speak to them personally for the simple fact that they've never been told that he *does*. But he does—generously, intimately. "He who belongs to God hears what God says" (John 8:47).

> The man who enters by the gate is the shepherd of his sheep. The watchman opens the gate for him, and the sheep listen to his voice. He calls his own sheep by name and leads them out. When he has brought out all his own, he goes on ahead of them, and his sheep follow him because they know his voice . . . I am the good shepherd. (John 10:2–4, 11)

You don't just leave sheep to find their way in the world. They are famous for getting lost, being attacked by wild animals, falling into some pit, and that is why they must stay close to the shepherd, follow his voice. And no shepherd could be called good unless he personally guided his flock through danger. But that is precisely what he promises to do. He *wants* to speak to you; he wants to lead you to good pasture. Now, it doesn't happen in an instant. Walking with God is a way of life. It's something to be learned; our ability to hear God's voice and discern his word to us grows over time. As Brother Lawrence said it, we "practice the presence of God."

(*Waking the Dead*, 102–3)

When we set out to hear God's voice, we do not listen as though it will come from somewhere above us or in the room around us. It comes to us from *within*, from the heart, the dwelling place of God. Now, most of us haven't been trained in this, and it's going to take a little practice "tuning in" to all that's going on in there. And there's a lot going on in there, by the way. Many things are trying to play upon the beautiful instrument of the heart. Advertisers are constantly trying to pull on your heartstrings. So is your boss. The devil is a master at manipulating the heart. So are many people—though they would never admit that is what they are doing. How will you know what is compelling you? "Who can map out the various forces at play in one soul?" asked Augustine, a man who was the first to write out the story of listening to his heart. "Man is a great depth, O Lord . . . but the hairs of his head are easier by far to count than . . . the movements of his heart."

This can be distressing at times. All sorts of awful things can seem to issue from your heart—anger, lust, fear, petty jealousies. If you think it's you, a reflection of what's really going on in your heart, it will disable you. It could stop your journey dead in its tracks. What you've encountered is either the voice of your flesh or an attempt of the Enemy to distress you by throwing all sorts of thoughts your way and blaming you for it. You must proceed on this assumption: your heart is good.

(*Waking the Dead,* 105–6)

This stream of Counseling doesn't just flow to us directly from Christ, *only* from him; it flows through his people as well. We need others—and need them deeply. Yes, the Spirit was sent to be our Counselor. Yes, Jesus speaks to us personally. But often he works through another human being. The fact is, we are usually too close to our lives to see what's going on. Because it's *our* story we're trying to understand, we sometimes don't know what's true or false, what's real or imagined. We can't see the forest for the trees. It often takes the eyes of someone to whom we can tell our story, bare our soul. The more dire our straits, the more difficult it can be to hear directly from God.

In every great story the hero or heroine must turn to someone older or wiser for the answer to some riddle. Dorothy seeks the Wizard; Frodo turns to Gandalf; Neo has Morpheus; and Curdie is helped by the Lady of the Silver Moon.

Having a doctrine pass before the mind is not what the Bible means by knowing the truth. It's only when it reaches down deep into the heart that the truth begins to set us free, just as a key must penetrate a lock to turn it, or as rainfall must saturate the earth down to the roots in order for your garden to grow.

"Behold, you desire truth in the innermost being" (Ps. 51:6 NASB). Getting it there is the work of the stream we'll call Counseling.

(Waking the Dead, 124—27)

Several years ago I went through one of the most painful trials of my professional life. The story involves a colleague whom I will call Dave, a man I hired and with whom I had labored several years in ministry. We spent many hours on the road together, speaking to churches about the Christian life. A point came when I needed to confront Dave about some issues in his life that were hurting his own ministry and the larger purposes of our team. In all fairness, I think I handled it poorly, but I was totally unprepared for what happened next. Dave turned on me with the ferocity of a cornered animal. He fabricated lies and spread rumors in an attempt to destroy my career. His actions were so out of proportion it was hard to believe we were reacting to the same events. He went to the head pastor in an attempt to have me dismissed. The attempt failed, but our friendship was lost, and several others were hurt in the process.

In the midst of the crisis, I spoke with Brent one afternoon about the turn of events and the awful pain of betrayal. He said, "I wonder what God is up to in all this?"

"God?" I said. "What's *he* got to do with it?" My practical agnosticism was revealed. I was caught up in the sociodrama, the smaller story, completely blind to the true story at that point in my life. Brent's question arrested my attention and brought it to a higher level. In fact, the process of our sanctification, our journey, rests entirely on our ability to see life from the basis of that question. As the poet William Blake warned long ago, "Life's dim window of the soul distorts the heavens from pole to pole, and leads you to believe a lie, when you see with, not through, the eye."

(*The Sacred Romance,* 146–47)

Allow me, then, to review what we have encountered. First, our lives are not a random series of events; they tell a Story that has meaning. We aren't in a movie we've arrived at twenty minutes late; we are in a Sacred Romance. There really is something wonderful that draws our heart; we are being wooed. But there is also something fearful. We face an enemy with vile intentions. Is anyone in charge? Someone strong and kind who notices us? At some point we have all answered that question "no" and gone on to live in a smaller story. But the answer is "*yes*"—there is someone strong and kind who notices us. Our Story is written by God, who is more than author, he is the romantic lead in our personal dramas. He created us for himself, and now he is moving heaven and earth to restore us to his side. His wooing seems wild because he seeks to free our heart from the attachments and addictions we've chosen, thanks to the Arrows we've known.

And we—who are we, really? We are not pond scum, nor are we the lead in the story. We are the Beloved; our hearts are the most important thing about us, and our desire is wild because it is made for a wild God. We are the Beloved, and we are addicted. We've either given our heart to other lovers and can't get out of the relationships, or we've tried our best to kill desire (often with the help of others) and live lives of safe, orderly control. Either way, we play into the hands of the one who hates us. Satan is the mortal enemy of God and therefore ours as well, who comes with offers of less-wild lovers, hoping to deceive us in order to destroy our heart and thus prevent our salvation or cripple our sanctification. These are the stage, the characters, and the plot in the broadest possible terms. Where do we go from here?

(*The Sacred Romance,* 147–48)

Our search for the Golden Moment is not a search in vain; not at all. We've only had the timing wrong. We do not know exactly how God will do it, but we do know this: the kingdom of God brings restoration. The only things destroyed are the things that are outside God's realm—sin, disease, death. But we who are God's children, the heavens and the earth he has made, will go on. "The wolf will live with the lamb, the leopard will lie down with the goat, the calf and the lion and the yearling together" (Isa. 11:6). "And Jerusalem will be known as the Desirable Place," the place of the fulfillment of all our desires (Isa. 62:12 NLT). This is significant because it touches upon the question: What will we *do* in eternity? If all we've got are halos and harps, our options are pretty limited. But to have the whole cosmos before us—wow. Thus George MacDonald writes to his daughter, whom he will soon lose to tuberculosis,

> I do live expecting great things in the life that is ripening for me and all mine—when we shall have all the universe for our own, and be good merry helpful children in the great house of our father. Then, darling, you and I and all will have the grand liberty wherewith Christ makes free—opening his hand to send us out like white doves to range the universe. (*The Heart of George MacDonald*)

(*The Journey of Desire,* 123)

After creating this stunning portrait of a total union, the man and woman becoming one, God turns the universe on its head when he tells us that this is what *he* is seeking with *us*. In fact, Paul says it is *why* God created gender and sexuality and marriage—to serve as a living metaphor. He quotes Genesis, then takes it to the nth degree:

> "For this reason a man will leave his father and mother and be united to his wife, and the two will become one flesh." This is a profound mystery—but I am talking about Christ and the church. (Eph. 5:31–32)

A profound mystery indeed. All the breathtaking things in life are. The Cross is a great mystery, but we are helped in understanding it by looking back into the Old Testament and finding there the pattern of the sacrificial lamb. Those early believers did not understand the full meaning of what they were doing, but once Christ came, the whole period of ritual sacrifice was seen in a new light, and in turn gave a richer depth to our understanding of the Cross.

We must do the same with this stunning passage; we must look back and see the Bible for what it is—the greatest romance ever written. God creates mankind for intimacy with himself, as his beloved. We see it right at the start, when he gives us the highest freedom of all—the freedom to reject him. The reason is obvious: love is possible only when it is freely chosen. True love is never constrained; our hearts cannot be taken by force. So God sets out to woo his beloved and make her his queen.

(The Journey of Desire, 130)

I have in my files a copy of a letter written by Major Sullivan Ballou, a Union officer in the 2nd Rhode Island. He writes to his wife on the eve of the Battle of Bull Run, a battle he senses will be his last. He speaks tenderly to her of his undying love, of "the memories of blissful moments I have spent with you." Ballou mourns the thought that he must give up "the hope of future years, when, God willing, we might still have lived and loved together, and seen our sons grown up to honorable manhood around us." Yet in spite of his love the battle calls and he cannot turn from it. "I have no misgivings about, or lack of confidence in the cause in which I am engaged, and my courage does not halt or falter . . . how great a debt we owe to those who went before us through the blood and sufferings of the Revolution . . . Sarah, my love for you is deathless, it seems to bind me with mighty cables that nothing but Omnipotence could break" and yet a greater cause "comes over me like a strong wind and bears me unresistably on with all these chains to the battle field."

A man must have a battle to fight, a great mission to his life that involves and yet transcends even home and family. He must have a cause to which he is devoted even unto death, for this is written into the fabric of his being. Listen carefully now: *You do*. That is why God created you—to be his intimate *ally*, to join him in the Great Battle. You have a specific place in the line, a mission God made you for.

(*Wild at Heart,* 141)

However strong a castle may be, if a treacherous party resides inside (ready to betray at the first opportunity possible), the castle cannot be kept safe from the enemy. Traitors occupy our own hearts, ready to side with every temptation and to surrender to them all. (John Owen, *Sin and Temptation*)

Ever since that fateful day when Adam gave away the essence of his strength, men have struggled with a part of themselves that is ready at the drop of a hat to do the same. We don't want to speak up unless we know it will go well, and we don't want to move unless we're guaranteed success. What the Scriptures call the flesh, the old man, or the sinful nature, is that part of fallen Adam in every man that always wants the easiest way out. It's much easier to go down to the driving range and attack a bucket of balls than it is to face the people at work who are angry at you. It's much easier to clean the garage, organize your files, or cut the grass than it is to talk to your teenage daughter.

To put it bluntly, your flesh is a poser. And your flesh is *not you*. Did you know that? Your flesh is not the real you. When Paul gives us his famous passage on what it's like to struggle with sin (Rom. 7), he tells a story we are all too familiar with:

"I decide to do good, but I don't *really* do it; I decide not to do bad, but then I do it anyway. My decisions, such as they are, don't result in actions. Something has gone wrong deep within me and gets the better of me every time. It happens so regularly that it's predictable. The moment I decide to do good, sin is there to trip me up. I truly delight in God's commands, but it's pretty obvious that not all of me joins in that delight. Parts of me covertly rebel, and just when I least expect it, they take charge." (vv. 19–21, *The Message*)

Paul says, "Hey, I know I struggle with sin. But I also know that *my sin is not me*—this is not my true heart."

(*Wild at Heart*, 143–44)

Y ou are not your sin; sin is no longer the truest thing about the man who has come into union with Jesus. Your heart is good. "I will give you a new heart and put a new spirit in you" (Ezek. 36:26). The Big Lie in the church today is that you are nothing more than "a sinner saved by grace." You are a lot more than that. You are a new creation in Christ. The New Testament calls you a saint, a holy one, a son of God. In the core of your being you are a good man. Yes, there is a war within us, but it is a *civil* war. The battle is not between us and God; no, there is a traitor within us who wars against our true heart fighting alongside the Spirit of God in us:

> A new power is in operation. The Spirit of life in Christ, like a strong wind, has magnificently cleared the air, freeing you from a fated lifetime of brutal tyranny at the hands of sin and death . . . Anyone, of course, who has not welcomed this invisible but clearly present God, the Spirit of Christ, won't know what we're talking about. But for you who welcome him, in whom he dwells . . . if the alive-and-present God who raised Jesus from the dead moves into your life, he'll do the same thing in you that he did in Jesus . . . When God lives and breathes in you (and he does, as surely as he did in Jesus), you are delivered from that dead life. (Rom. 8:2, 9–11 *The Message*)

The *real* you is on the side of God against the false self. Knowing this makes all the difference in the world. The man who wants to live valiantly will lose heart quickly if he believes that his heart is nothing but sin. Why fight?

(*Wild at Heart*, 144–45)

W alking with God leads to receiving his intimate counsel, and counseling leads to deep restoration. As we learn to walk with God and hear his voice, he is able to bring up issues in our hearts that need speaking to. Some of those wounds were enough to break our hearts, create a rift in the soul, and so we need his healing as well. This is something Jesus walks us into—sometimes through the help of another person who can listen and pray with us, sometimes with God alone. As David said in Psalm 23, He leads us away, to a quiet place, to restore the soul. Our first choice is to go with him there—to slow down, unplug, accept the invitation to come aside. You won't find healing in the midst of the Matrix. We need time in the presence of God. This often comes on the heels of God's raising some issue in our hearts or after we've just relived an event that takes us straight to that broken place, or waking as I did to a raw emotion.

> Teach me your way, O LORD,
>   and I will walk in your truth;
> give me an undivided heart,
>   that I may fear your name.
> I will praise you, O Lord my God, with all my heart;
>   I will glorify your name forever. (Ps. 86:11–12)

When we are in the presence of God, removed from distractions, we are able to hear him more clearly, and a secure environment has been established for the young and broken places in our hearts to surface.

(*Waking the Dead*, 140–41)

The assault on femininity—its long history, its utter vicious-ness—cannot be understood apart from the spiritual forces of evil we are warned against in the Scriptures. This is not to say that men (and women, for they, too, assault women) have no accountability in their treatment of women. Not at all. It is simply to say that no explanation for the assault upon Eve and her daughters is sufficient unless it opens our eyes to the Prince of Darkness and his special hatred of femininity.

Turn your attention again to the events that took place in the Garden of Eden. Notice—who does the Evil One go after? Who does Satan single out for his move against the human race? He could have chosen Adam . . . but he didn't. Satan went after Eve. He set his sights on *her*. Have you ever wondered why? It might have been that he, like any predator, chose what he believed to be the weaker of the two. There is some truth to that. He is utterly ruthless. But we believe there is more. Why does Satan make Eve the focus of his assault on humanity?

Because she is captivating, uniquely glorious, and he cannot be. She is the incarnation of the Beauty of God. More than anything else in all creation, she embodies the glory of God. She allures the world to God. He hates it with a jealousy we can only imagine.

And there is more. The Evil One also hates Eve because she gives life. Women give birth, not men. Women nourish life. And they also bring life into the world soulfully, relationally, spiritually—in everything they touch. Satan is a murderer from the beginning (John 8:44). He brings death. His is a kingdom of death. And thus Eve is his greatest human threat, for she brings life. She is a lifesaver and a lifegiver. *Eve* means "life" or "life-producer."

Put those two things together—that Eve incarnates the Beauty of God *and* she gives life to the world. His bitter heart cannot bear it. He assaults her with a special hatred. Do you begin to see it?

(*Captivating*, 82–85)

et me say this again: the story of your life is the story of the long and brutal assault on your heart by the one who knows what you could be and fears it. I hope you are beginning to see that more clearly now. Otherwise, much of the Bible will not make sense to you. Much of your *life* will not make sense to you.

> I will go before you
> > and will level the mountains;
> I will break down gates of bronze
> > and cut through bars of iron.
> I will give you the treasures of darkness,
> > riches stored in secret places,
> so that you may know I am the LORD,
> > the God of Israel, who summons you by name. (Isa. 45:2–3)

Doesn't the language of the Bible sometimes sound . . . overblown? Really now—God is going to level mountains for us? We'd be happy if he just helped us get through the week. What's all that about breaking down gates of bronze and cutting through bars of iron? I mean, it sounds heroic, but, well, who's really in need of that? This isn't ancient Samaria. We'd settle for a parking place at the mall.

If we *are* in an epic battle, then the language of the Bible fits perfectly. Things are not what they seem. We are at war. That war is against your heart, your glory. Once more, look at Isaiah 61:1:

> He has sent me to bind up the brokenhearted,
> to proclaim freedom for the captives
> and release from darkness for the prisoners.

(*Waking the Dead*, 149–50)

Over the years we've come to see that the only thing *more* tragic than the things that have happened to us is what we have done with them.

Words were said, painful words. Things were done, awful things. And they shaped us. Something inside us *shifted*. We embraced the messages of our wounds. We accepted a twisted view of ourselves. And from that we chose a way of relating to our world. We made a vow never to be in that place again. We adopted strategies to protect ourselves from being hurt again. A woman that is living out of a broken, wounded heart is a woman who is living a self-protective life. She may not be aware of it, but it is true. It's our way of trying to "save ourselves."

We also developed ways of trying to get something of the love our hearts cried out for. The ache is there. Our desperate need for love and affirmation, our thirst for some taste of romance and adventure and beauty is there. So we turned to boys or to food or to romance novels; we lost ourselves in our work or at church or in some sort of service. All this adds up to the woman we are today. Much of what we call our "personalities" is actually the mosaic of our choices for self-protection plus our plan to get something of the love we were created for.

The problem is, our plan has nothing to do with God.

The wounds we received and the messages they brought formed a sort of unholy alliance with our fallen nature as women. From Eve we received a deep mistrust in the heart of God toward us. Clearly, he's holding out on us. We'll just have to arrange for the life we want. We will control our world. But there is also an ache deep within, an ache for intimacy and for life. We'll have to find a way to fill it. A way that does not require us to trust anyone, especially God. A way that will not require vulnerability.

(*Captivating,* 74–75)

I t's the great company at the party in *Titanic* that brings such happy tears. It's the boys making it safely home in *Apollo 13*. It's Maximus reunited with his family. So the fellowship finds Gandalf alive—no longer Gandalf the Grey, fallen beyond recovery in the mines of Moria, but Gandalf the White, whom death can never touch again. So Frodo and Sam are rescued from the slopes of Mount Doom, and when they wake, it is to a bright new morn. This is our future.

After he laid down his life for us, Jesus was laid in a tomb. He was buried just like any other dead person. Family and friends mourned. Enemies rejoiced. And most of the world went on with business as usual, clueless to the Epic around them. Then, after three days, also at dawn, his story took a sudden and dramatic turn.

> Very early on the first day of the week, just after sunrise, they were on their way to the tomb and they asked each other, "Who will roll the stone away from the entrance of the tomb?" But when they looked up, they saw that the stone, which was very large, had been rolled away. As they entered the tomb, they saw a young man dressed in a white robe sitting on the right side, and they were alarmed. "Don't be alarmed," he said. "You are looking for Jesus the Nazarene, who was crucified. He has risen! He is not here. See the place where they laid him. But go, tell his disciples . . . 'He is going ahead of you into Galilee. There you will see him, just as he told you.'" (Mark 16:2–7)

Jesus came back. He showed up again. He was restored to them. He walked into the house where they had gathered to comfort one another in their grief and asked if they had anything to eat. It was the most stunning, unbelievable, happiest ending to a story you could possibly imagine. And it is also ours.

(*Epic*, 85–87)

Prayers

ere are three different daily prayers I've used over the years to enter more deeply into Christ and his work for me each day, and to gain victory over the Enemy. The first is simple and straightforward. The second is a bit longer. The third looks long, but after you've been battling a while you'll find it easy to pray 'cause it's really, really powerful. Use what's helpful for you.

◈

The Daily Prayer
(From *Victory of the Darkness* by Neil Anderson)

Dear Heavenly Father, I honor you as my sovereign Lord. I acknowledge that you are always present with me. You are the only all-powerful and all-wise God. You are kind and loving in all your ways. I love you, and I thank you that I am united with Christ and spiritually alive in him. I choose not to love the world, and I crucify my flesh and all its passions. I thank you for the life that I now have in Christ, and I ask you to fill me with your Holy Spirit that I may live my life free from sin. I declare my dependence upon you, and I take my stand against Satan and all his lying ways. I choose to believe the truth, and I refuse to be discouraged. You are the God of all hope, and I am confident that you will meet my needs as I seek to live according to your Word. I express with confidence that I can live a responsible life through Christ who strengthens me. I now take my stand against Satan and command him and all his evil spirits to depart from me. I put on the whole armor of God. I submit my body as a living sacrifice and renew my mind by the living Word of God in order that I may prove that the will of God is good, acceptable, and perfect. I ask these things in the precious name of my Lord and Savior, Jesus Christ. Amen.

SAINT PATRICK'S BREASTPLATE
(As presented in Thomas Cahill's *How the Irish Saved Civilization*)

I arise today
Through a mighty strength, the invocation of the Trinity,
Through belief in the threeness,
Through confession of the oneness
Of the Creator of creation.

I arise today
Through the strength of Christ's birth with his baptism,
Through the strength of his crucifixion with his burial,
Through the strength of his resurrection with his ascension,
Through the strength of his descent for the judgment of Doom.

I arise today
Through the strength of the love of cherubim,
In obedience of angels,
In the service of archangels,
In hope of resurrection to meet with reward,
In prayers of patriarchs,
In predictions of prophets,
In preaching of apostles,
In faith of confessors,
In innocence of holy virgins,
In deeds of righteous men.

I arise today
Through the strength of heaven:
Light of sun,
Radiance of moon,
Splendor of fire,
Speed of lightning,
Swiftness of wind,
Depth of sea,

Stability of earth,
Firmness of rock.

I arise today
Through God's strength to pilot me:
God's might to uphold me,
God's wisdom to guide me,
God's eye to look before me,
God's ear to hear me,
God's word to speak for me,
God's hand to guard me,
God's way to lie before me,
God's shield to protect me,
God's host to save me
From snares of devils,
From temptations of vices,
From everyone who shall wish me ill,
Afar and anear,
Alone and in multitude.

I summon today all these powers between me and those evils,
Against every cruel, merciless power that may oppose my body
    and soul,
Against incantations of false prophets,
Against black laws of pagandom,
Against false laws of heretics,
Against craft of idolatry,
Against spells of witches and smiths and wizards,
Against every knowledge that corrupts man's body and soul.

Christ to shield me today
Against poison, against burning,
Against drowning, against wounding,
So that there may come to me abundance of reward.
Christ with me, Christ before me, Christ behind me,

Christ in me, Christ beneath me, Christ above me,
Christ on my right, Christ on my left,
Christ when I lie down, Christ when I sit down, Christ when
     I arise,
Christ in the heart of every man who thinks of me,
Christ in the mouth of everyone who speaks of me,
Christ in every eye that sees me,
Christ in every ear that hears me.

I arise today
Through a mighty strength, the invocation of the Trinity,
Through belief in the threeness,
Through confession of the oneness,
Of the Creator of creation.

A DAILY PRAYER FOR FREEDOM

My dear Lord Jesus, I come to you now to be restored in you—to renew my place in you, my allegiance to you, and to receive from you all the grace and mercy I so desperately need this day. I honor you as my sovereign Lord, and I surrender every aspect of my life totally and completely to you. I give you my body as a living sacrifice; I give you my heart, soul, mind, and strength; and I give you my spirit as well. I cover myself with your blood—my spirit, my soul, and my body. And I ask your Holy Spirit to restore my union with you, seal me in you, and guide me in this time of prayer.

Dear God, holy and victorious Trinity, you alone are worthy of all my worship, my heart's devotion, all my praise and all my trust and all the glory of my life. I worship you, bow to you, and give myself over to you in my heart's search for life. You alone are Life, and you have become my life. I renounce all other gods, all idols, and I give you the place in my heart and in my life that you truly deserve. I confess here and now that it is all about you, God, and not about me. You are the Hero of this story, and I belong to you.

Forgive me for my every sin. Search me and know me and reveal to me any aspect of my life that is not pleasing to you, expose any agreements I have made with my Enemy, and grant me the grace of a deep and true repentance.

Heavenly Father, thank you for loving me and choosing me before you made the world. You are my true Father—my Creator, my Redeemer, my Sustainer, and the true end of all things, including my life. I love you; I trust you; I worship you. Thank you for proving your love for me by sending your only Son, Jesus, to be my sacrifice and my new life. I receive him and all his life and all his work, which you ordained for me. Thank you for including me in Christ, for forgiving me my sins, for granting me his righteousness, for making me complete in him. Thank you for making me alive with Christ, raising me with him, seating me with him at your right hand, granting me his authority, and anointing me with your Holy Spirit. I receive it all with thanks and give it total claim to my life.

Jesus, thank you for coming for me, for ransoming me with your own life. I honor you as my Lord; I love you, worship you, trust you. I sincerely receive you as my redemption, and I receive all the work and triumph of your crucifixion, whereby I am cleansed from all my sin through your shed blood, my old nature is removed, my heart is circumcised unto God, and every claim being made against me is disarmed. I take my place in your cross and death, whereby I have died with you to sin and to my flesh, to the world, and to the Evil One. I am crucified with Christ. I now take up my cross and crucify my flesh with all its pride, unbelief, and idolatry. I put off the old man. I now bring the cross of Christ between me and all people, all spirits, all things. Holy Spirit, apply to me the fullness of the work of the crucifixion of Jesus Christ for me. I receive it with thanks and give it total claim to my life.

Jesus, I also sincerely receive you as my new life, my holiness and sanctification, and I receive all the work and triumph of your resurrection, whereby I have been raised with you to a new life, to walk in newness of life, dead to sin and alive to God. I am crucified with Christ, and it is no longer I who live but Christ who lives in me. I now take my place in your resurrection, whereby I have been made alive with you, I reign in life through you. I put on the new person in all holiness and humility, in all righteousness and purity and truth. Christ is now my life, the one who strengthens me. Holy Spirit, apply to me the fullness of the resurrection of Jesus Christ for me. I receive it with thanks and give it total claim to my life.

Jesus, I also sincerely receive you as my authority and rule, my everlasting victory over Satan and his kingdom, and I receive all the work and triumph of your ascension, whereby Satan has been judged and cast down, his rulers and authorities disarmed, all authority in heaven and on earth given to you, Jesus, and I have been given fullness in you, the Head over all. I take my place in your ascension, whereby I have been raised with you to the right hand of the Father and established with you in all authority.

I bring your authority and your kingdom rule over my life, my family, my household, and my domain. And now I bring the fullness of your work—your cross, resurrection, and ascension—against Satan, against his kingdom, and against all his emissaries and all their work warring against me and my domain. Greater is he who is in me than he who is in the world. Christ has given me authority to overcome all the power of the Evil One, and I claim that authority now over and against every enemy, and I banish them in the name of Jesus Christ. Holy Spirit, apply to me the fullness of the work of the ascension of Jesus Christ for me. I receive it with thanks and give it total claim to my life.

Holy Spirit, I sincerely receive you as my Counselor, my Comforter, my Strength, and my Guide. Thank you for sealing me in Christ. I honor you as my Lord, and I ask you to lead me into all truth, to anoint me for all of my life and walk and calling, and to lead me deeper into Jesus today. I fully open my life to you in every dimension and aspect—my body, my soul, and my spirit—choosing to be filled with you, to walk in step with you in all things. Apply to me, blessed Holy Spirit, all of the work and all of the gifts in pentecost. Fill me afresh, blessed Holy Spirit. I receive you with thanks and give you total claim to my life.

Heavenly Father, thank you for granting to me every spiritual blessing in the heavenlies in Christ Jesus. I receive those blessings into my life today, and I ask the Holy Spirit to bring all those blessings into my life this day. Thank you for the blood of Jesus. Wash me once more with his blood from every sin and stain and evil device. I put on your armor—the belt of truth, the breastplate of righteousness, the shoes of the readiness of the gospel of peace, the helmet of salvation. I take up the shield of faith and the sword of the Spirit, the Word of God, and I wield these weapons against the Evil One in the power of God. I choose to pray at all times in the Spirit, to be strong in you, Lord, and in your might.

Father, thank you for your angels. I summon them in the authority of Jesus Christ and release them to war for me and my household. May they guard me at all times this day. Thank you for those who pray for me; I confess I need their prayers, and I ask you to send forth your Spirit and rouse them, unite them, raising up the full canopy of prayer and intercession for me. I call forth the kingdom of the Lord Jesus Christ this day throughout my home, my family, my life, and my domain. I pray all of this in the name of Jesus Christ, with all glory and honor and thanks to him.

ABOUT THE AUTHOR

JOHN ELDREDGE is the founder and director of Ransomed Heart™ Ministries in Colorado Springs, Colorado, a fellowship devoted to helping people recover and live from their heart. John is the author of numerous books, including *Epic, Waking the Dead, Wild at Heart, The Journey of Desire,* and coauthor of *Captivating* (with his wife) and *The Sacred Romance* (with Brent Curtis). John lives in Colorado with his wife, Stasi, and their three sons, Samuel, Blaine, and Luke. He loves living in the Rocky Mountains so he can pursue his other passions, including fly-fishing, mountain climbing, and exploring the waters of the West in his canoe.

ACKNOWLEDGMENTS

A special thanks to my friend Craig McConnell, who selected these readings from my various writings and offered much encouragement along the way. And to my allies at Thomas Nelson Publishers and Yates & Yates, with whom all these works have been both formed and fought for.